CRAZY for ITALIAN FOOD

"JOE FAMULARO takes us back to the sights, sounds, and mostly the delicious smells of life in an Italian-American household on New York's far west side during the middle of the twentieth century. And best of all, not only does he describe the remarkable food, at the end of each chapter he gives beautifully-worked-out and irresistible recipes for it. In the best of all worlds a person could sit at the table eating one of his glorious meals and reading about his family."

Nancy Nicholas,

Author and Editor

Other Books by Joe Famularo

Viva La Cucina Italiana: Long Live the Italian Cooking★ (Amazon)
A Cook's Tour of Italy (Berkley)
The Italian Soup Cookbook (Workman)
The Joy of Pasta★★ (Barrons)
The Joy of Grilling (Barrons)
Celebrations (Barrons)
Vegetables★★ (Barrons)
Healthy Pasta (Barrons)
Healthy Grilling (Barrons)
The Festive Famularo Kitchen★★ (Atheneum)

★ with Cristopher Laus
★★ with Louise Imperiale

PERDUTAMENTE

CRAZY for ITALIAN FOOD

A MEMOIR of FAMILY, FOOD,
and PLACE with RECIPES

JOE FAMULARO

Library of Congress Control Number: 2013902384
ISBN: Hardcover 978-1-4797-9071-5
Softcover 978-1-4797-9070-8
Ebook 978-1-4797-9072-2

This book was printed in the United States of America.

Rev. date: 06/12/2013

To order additional copies of this book, contact:
Xlibris Corporation
1-888-795-4274
www.Xlibris.com
Orders@Xlibris.com
77778

TABLE OF CONTENTS

ACKNOWLEDGMENTS

Most of the people in this memoir have left me; their spirit and memory have not. They all knew they came to America to become Americans; they could leave Italy but not their customs, traditions, family style of living, and, especially, their food traditions. That I remember them so clearly, so lovingly, is proof of their meaningful lifelong impressions on me. I live their legacies for them. This book is dedicated to them.

At a dinner party in Key West four years or so ago, I recounted some of these stories to a group of friends. You must write a book and call it *Perdutamente,* said Micky Wolfson. A larger-than-life creator of the Wolfsonian Museum in South Beach, Florida, Micky is the consummate Italophile, once the owner of a palazzo outside Genoa. The idea of *Perdutamente* gave me no peace until I started writing it—always encouraged by my dear friend Phyllis Rose, an excellent cook by the way, who gave me the encouragement to move ahead. David Schorr designed the cover, as he did my *Viva La Cucina Italiana.* David's heart is in Italy, for who else would fly New York to Milan and back after a singular performance at La Scala?

David Wolkowsky, entrepreneur and benefactor, supporter of the arts and education, generous to a fault, tracked the progress of this book as earnestly as a parent keeps his child's weight and height measurements.

I could not have completed this work without Mary Goodbody, who loved these stories from the moment she first read a draft—her loyalty to *Perdu*, as we called the manuscript from the beginning, was constant. Nancy Nicholas fully edited the work and was fully devoted to it. She found my voice and kept it.

Susan Schulman, literary agent, nurtured the book, paragraph by paragraph with the patience of a saint. The time and loving care she gave the memoir was extraordinary. My assistant, Cristopher Laus, was there every moment I needed him, as was his daughter Keeshia.

At age two, his youngest daughter, Chiara, now seven years old, wanted to know all about cappuccino; at age three, she started eating *Parmigiano* and wants some at every meal; and before going to bed every night, she whispers, "Te voglio bene assaie." And so continues the new *perdutamente* generation. To all of you, I say thanks.

Joe Famularo
Key West, Florida

joefamularocookbooks.com

INTRODUCTION

The era between World Wars I and II has become romanticized for many. The two decades were a crazy juxtaposition of excess and parsimony, of good times and despair. The European immigrants living in the United States heard the drumbeat of war far more loudly than other Americans; and, coupled with the adjustment to their new country, this inspired them to cleave tightly to their heritages even as it aroused strong feelings of patriotism for their new homeland.

I grew up during this time and entered young adulthood as the Second World War broke out. In these pages, I recount time spent as part of a boisterous and loving family who lived on the West Side of Manhattan in a small flat with a hand-painted tile on the kitchen wall that read, "Il padrone sono io, ma mia moglia commanda" (I am the boss, but my wife is in charge).

Mine is a story of an America now gone. Yet a very similar story is still experienced by every new immigrant group that folds into an urban landscape. Then there is the food. Readers will share my Italian American family's unhurried suppers, when we feasted on slow-cooked soups and stews, handmade pasta, and homemade sauces. We sat down *pronto!* at 7:00 p.m. and remained in our seats until dismissed. On Sunday, dinner began at 1:00 p.m., and we often were still at the table at 4:00 or 5:00 p.m. When we ate at our grandparents' nearby apartment, meals lasted even longer. A lot of our lives revolved too around visits to relatives—picnics with baskets filled with Italian salads, cold meats, and cheese and vacations with aunts, uncles, cousins, and *paisanos.* Every event was, above all else, about food.

My family lived in a railroad flat in a tenement on New York's West Forty-Sixth Street. Our apartment was exactly like the one above us, the one below us, and those across the hall. In the 1930s and '40s, everyone knew, to the tiny village, where in Italy their neighbors had immigrated from. Everyone's mother watched all the kids living on the street, which meant you couldn't get away with much. Neighbors got together to make large batches of tomato sauce and sausages to store in the tenements' basements for the long winters. Fresh vegetables were sold in small local Italian groceries, and also from a push cart, which visited the street every day.

The legal name for our neighborhood is Clinton, after a former governor of New York State. It is incorrectly called Hell's Kitchen. I think shop owners use the latter name, as it seems sexier and draws more customers. As far as I know, Hell's Kitchen was originally on Tenth Avenue, between Thirty-Sixth and Thirty-Ninth Streets. There are a number of famous people who came from Clinton, notably Alice Faye, Mario Puzo, Sylvester Stallone, Judge Fanelli, the corporate CEO Robert Miano, and Senator Patrick Moynihan.

It wasn't especially rough-and-tumble, nor was it desperately poor or particularly rich. It was a family neighborhood, and its inhabitants were hardworking immigrants—primarily Italians but also Greeks, Irish, and Jews—all of whom were striving for better lives for their children.

There was a sense of *perdutamente* in the air. *Perdutamente* means "desperately" or "hopelessly." *Essere perdutamente innamorati* means "to be madly in love," in this case with food. We were *all* "crazy in love" with Italian food, and no one considered our passion for it out of the ordinary or special. It simply "was."

In our household, it was mostly my mother who supplied the food. She rarely followed a recipe, and because we children learned to cook at her side, we didn't either. Later, when our interest in cooking developed and sharpened, we asked Mama to write down some of her recipes. One of the first she shared with us was missing ingredients. "What about the olive oil, garlic, and tomatoes?" we asked. "You should have known about them" was her deadpan answer. And she meant it. For her, knowing how to use those basic ingredients was as instinctive as breathing.

Today, there is so much emphasis on restaurants and new cooking styles, I feel we forget about the food that grounds us. Of course, cutting-edge cooking is exciting, but there is no reason to create a new fusion recipe every day of the week. Andy Warhol once said he couldn't have painted as he did without a deep understanding of the classics. Experimental writers and musicians say the same. It's believed by many that the person with the best future is the one with the longest memory, which is another way of saying that if our food is not somehow related to the food of the past, it probably will not have much of a future. The food discussed here, and the recipes, relies greatly on the past and yet are all fresh and new, ready to satisfy a contemporary generation of cooks and eaters.

The stories are about my family and Italian American life in a New York City tenement when I was growing up. In most of the stories, I use "we," and that means my brothers and sisters. I'm not saying it was without stress. We all climbed those three flights of stairs innumerable times every day. My mother washed heaps of clothes and cooked meal after meal for her six children. Both she and Papa had full-time jobs too, but this was how everyone lived, all trying to get ahead, all devoted to their families and our neighborhood.

Mama and Papa, my grandparents, and my aunts and uncles understood they were bringing forth more than food from their pasta boards, stoves, and ovens. At our table were also traditions, family history, humor, anger, and everything in between. Every day Mama helped us cope with the exigencies of life and tried to ensure that we were happy. Nothing mattered more to her.

The portrait I've drawn here is of life in a loving Italian American family who, through food, found great happiness and the meaning of life—and whatever comes with it.

Joe Famularo
Key West, FL

1

HOME SWEET HOME

Except for the youngest of us, seven of my eight brothers and sisters and I were born at home in our tenement on West Forty-Sixth Street. Most of these buildings on New York's West Side were pre–World War I, each composed of eight units, two on a floor. The apartments were called "railroad flats" because each room followed the other in a straight line. As second-generation Italians, we complained bitterly about our living conditions; but Papa quickly reminded that it was in this railroad flat that we were provided for and our bellies were filled with the best *minestre*, macaroni and meat, money could buy. You entered at the back of the flat through the kitchen, which led into three bedrooms, one after the other. The last room was the parlor or living room, almost always called the front room. It had its own door to the corridor, but it usually was kept locked, except for funerals or during the summer months for ventilation. Most doors were kept closed during cold weather, but each family had lots of kids; and there was a lot of traffic in the hallways, so doors were ajar much of the time. In summer, they were always ajar to create a cross current breeze.

In the summer, as the heat from the pavements worked its way through the building, the indoor atmosphere was stifling. Older people on their way to the higher flats would pause at each landing, sometimes in between landings, to catch their breath. I would often hear old men grumbling, "Che catza di calda"—loosely translated as "What f——g heat!" Older women would sigh, "Madonna, non posso fare un'altra"

(God, I can't take another [step]!) In the winter, the doors were kept shut to conserve heat. In those days, most landlords lived in the buildings they owned, and they controlled the furnace valves.

Both the kitchen and front room had two large windows. The middle rooms had none. There was no direct light in the bedrooms, but in our flat, the kitchen was filled with morning sun that gave light to the first and middle bedrooms. The front room received the brilliant afternoon sunlight, which illuminated the third and middle bedrooms. When the weather cooled in autumn, front-room doors were shut tight, but kitchen doors were kept slightly ajar. While each family maintained surprisingly high levels of privacy, everyone seemed to want to know what their neighbors were preparing to eat, especially at supper, the main culinary event of the day. The smell wafting from the kitchen doors of garlic simmering in olive oil was ubiquitous in the building, as were those of roasting pork, cooked cabbage, and baking bread. The dados (the lower portion of the walls) in the halls of the tenement were wooden and painted dark brown, and the upper part of the wall was sponged to simulate grain. The only lighting was a single bulb so that the overall effect was dark and sinister. This was during the Depression, and landlords did not spend much money on electricity or heating bills in those buildings; it was downright scary to walk through the hallways, especially at night.

On the third floor our next-door neighbors were the LoPicholo family, Sicilians. The landlord, Damiano, and his wife Graziella, also Sicilian, lived above us. The Sicilian Lofortes were the landlord's neighbors. Below us were the DeNicolas, my mother's sister's family, and the Scarangellis (from Bari) were next door to them. The Galganos, from Naples, lived on the first floor, and the flat next to them kept changing tenants, so they were hard to pin down and difficult to get to know. Everyone in the tenement was friendly, and the women were especially conversant. As immigrants and mothers, they had much in common; not the least being they were competitive cooks. Everyone was *perdutamente*, crazy in love, with the Italian food they made in New York as much as they had been taught to make it when they lived in Italy—and always from scratch because at that time, there weren't many other options.

All the front rooms in our building and others like it faced the street; all the kitchens were in the back. When these tenements were built, toilets, or "backhouses," were outside on the ground floor in the rear. In the 1920s, the plumbing was modernized so that each floor was provided with one toilet meant to serve two families. Each kitchen had a door into a miniscule foyer with an inner door to the toilet chamber. It was necessary to knock on the inner door to be sure the toilet was not occupied. My brother and sisters and I wished for better living quarters or at least ones where we didn't have to share the toilet with the LoPicholos, or any other family? Sister Mary hated the time she was on the potty, and Mr. LoPicholo inadvertently opened the door. She screamed—we all heard it—what an embarrassment for Mr. LoPicholo too. The incident became a *cause célèbre,* and for weeks, if any one was heading toward the toilet, the rest of us would say, "Don't forget to latch the door!"

We dreamed of a house with large rooms and many baths. New living quarters were discussed around our kitchen table all the time. We had faith in the future. We knew that Mama and Papa worked hard and understood what really mattered. They were mostly concerned about our health and safety, about getting us good food, and good schooling. We were well dressed, well fed, had good teeth, and an abundance of energy. Mama and Papa never questioned our love for each other, and they wanted all of us to celebrate life every day.

Mama's mind was active—we knew when she was thinking, and she once confessed that she always thought in Italian, never in English. That did not surprise us. Sometimes we would catch an expression on her face that would say to us, "She's thinking hard and fast"—just as she did adding a long column of figures—she was so good at that, so fast. Every time she rushed through a set of additions, she'd say, "With all you kids and not much money, I've got to know they charged the right amount."

Mama and Papa would say, "Finche c'e vita, c'e speranza" (Where there's life, there's hope). So we settled for the shared toilet, only because we shared each other. Still, Papa's words became true.

In the 1930s, the building was renovated, and the foyer space was used to create two toilet chambers so that each flat had its own. Bathtubs were in the kitchen. Most of the time, ours was covered with an enameled top and used like any other counter. We had a schedule for baths and the kitchen during which the room was off limits to anyone not bathing. It was not a simple schedule, but for some reason, it worked. When we were tots, Mama bathed two of us at the same time.

My mother's sister, our aunt Mary, lived in the apartment just below ours. When someone in our family used a broom handle to pound the floor, it meant, "Send someone up" (usually to sample some food). A tap on the exposed steam pipe in the corner of the kitchen meant, "Someone from our family is coming down with food." We were happy my aunt's family lived below; one reason being it was easier for us to know what was happening in their flat than it was for them to know what we were up to over their heads. Since we were above them, we always went past their apartment to get to ours. They rarely went past ours because they didn't have to. You'd be surprised what one could hear and see just by passing their flat.

We called Aunt Mary's neighbors, the Scarangellis, the "Scratch-Your-Bellies." Angelina and her husband, Gaetano, were from Bari, on the Adriatic Coast of Italy, were good Catholics who baked special braided bread on March 19, St. Joseph's Saint Day (more about the day and the bread later.) They always gave us a loaf, a gesture we appreciated for its neighborliness; but the bread, made without eggs, was not like the richer bread Mama usually baked. We were forced to eat some to be polite. As far as I was concerned, it tasted as dry as a communion host.

I can't forget Angelina Scarangelli. One day, she fell through an opening in the fire escape, and the entire block sounded the verbal alarm. I was out playing, and when I heard "Angelina fell from the fire escape," I thought it meant my mother, also named Angelina. I ran home as fast as I could and was greatly relieved to discover the truth. Thankfully, she was not seriously hurt.

Our tenement had an extra added attraction. It was one of several on the street with a ground-floor commercial store—in our case, Manuel's Grocery, a lively, busy place redolent with all the heavenly smells of Italian foods. The fresh produce overflowed onto the sidewalk, at times making it difficult to get to the front door of the building. This probably violated city ordinances, but Manuel's meat-filled sandwiches, studded with vinegar peppers, prosciutto, salamis, and cheeses, and held between fresh slices of Italian bread, paid off many policemen and inspectors. Manuel's wife, Lucy, and their plump daughters sat out front pretty much all year long and knew everything that happened in the neighborhood. They were always eager to share their news with others, whether you were interested or not. Lucy was short and rotund, always dressed in black with her graying hair pulled into a bun, and eyes that shifted left to right, right to left, to catch all the activity on the block.

The grocery store was filled with bushels of *cipollini* (bitter small onions), fresh zucchini, stands of broccoli and broccoli rabe and *veze* (Savoy cabbage), arugula, small artichokes with long stems, and *carduni* (cardoons). A pathway through the middle of the fresh-food displays made an entrance to the store. Inside, dried macaroni, scooped into bags, was sold from bins for a few cents cheaper than the packaged variety. Mama always bought the packaged type. She was partial to La Rosa pasta because of the clip-off rose coupon. After time and about two thousand coupons, we were rewarded with a china service for eight. Before the celebratory day of redemption, we kids had to count and then rubber band the clipped roses into packets of one hundred each. This chore made order out of the kitchen drawer into which the roses were tossed whenever one or two pounds of pasta were cooked. Since our large family could easily consume three or four pounds of pasta a week, with a little determination and a lot of patience, the china set was ours in about two years. The dishes' pattern of small red roses strewn over a cream background brought a smile of contentment to Mama's face.

Manuel stocked Italian imports of olive oil, olives, cheeses, salamis, and other cold cuts. Upon entering this oasis of Italian foods, the smell of almond biscotti competed with the aroma of hanging cheeses, dried sausages, salted anchovies sold from extralarge cans, and plum tomatoes. Bright white waxed paper from a large roll was cut to wrap generous slices of cheese and sliced salamis well studded with pea-size black peppercorns. A large glass cabinet was filled with both round and long loaves of fresh Italian bread Manuel got from a bakery. When we ran out of Mama's home-baked bread, one of us would run down three flights of stairs to buy a loaf from Manuel. If Mama forgot fresh Italian parsley in her major shopping trip on Ninth Avenue at Paddy's Market, down we'd fly for the parsley.

I always felt that Lucy watched me as I entered the building with full shopping bags from Paddy's. The prices at the Ninth Avenue market were far better than at Manuel's, but that didn't stop us from feeling a little guilty for shopping there. Everyone in the building learned to walk past Lucy, whose eyes were fixed on the shopping bags, with a "Buona sera Signora, com'e sta?" (Good evening, how are you?)

Mr. Galgano, who lived on the first floor, was old, had lots of hair and a full mustache. He was a quiet man who died when I was eight years old. His wake was held in the front room of his flat, and, as was the custom, the door was kept wide open. There was no way to avoid this macabre scene on the way to our third-floor flat. The "funeral door" was open all day and all night for three long, frightening days. When I left for school in the morning, I walked backward to avoid the open doorway. However, I turned around often enough to make sure he was still in the casket—not out of it and following me! Later when the room was filled with mourners, Mr. Galgano's profile, particularly his mustache, was clearly in view as I wrapped myself around the banister, holding on tightly for fear he would suddenly reach out and pull me into his coffin. My fright didn't let up as I ran errands or returned home after playing with other kids. Passing Mr. Galgano and his coffin after nine in the evening was awful—by then, all the visitors had left, the family members had retired to the kitchen, and there was only the corpse in the coffin, lined with tufted white satin, framed by the open doorway. A frantic moment for an eight-year-old with a vivid imagination! The stifling aroma of lilies, carnations, and gladioli added to my anguish and fright; I could barely get up the stairs fast enough.

At the end of each day, we could hear the Galgano family members in their kitchen after grueling hours of tending the corpse, obviously in need of food and rest. Although we didn't know what they were eating, we suspected they were getting sustenance from Italian cold cuts, pickled vegetables, or a pasta with a quick sauce such as aglio olio or a puttanesca. Most of the food came from neighbors like us, and when one of us arrived at their flat with a covered dish, the Galganos enthusiastically described what others had brought. These gifts were offered in a studied yet offhand way: "See what I made today? Please have a taste. I hope you like it." If Mama or Papa didn't have time to deliver the food, one of the younger children was asked to do it.

All the women were good cooks—they, too, learned from their mothers, fathers, and grandparents. They truly enjoyed sharing their food and had *molto confidenza* in their abilities. In those days, almost all women could cook, regardless of her age or marital status. In fact, there was a healthy sense of competition among these generous women. If someone brought some food to another family, regardless of the reason, the recipient soon followed up with an offer of her own. This was a way to say thank-you, but clearly it also was a way to say, "Look what I can do."

In each flat, a woman was in charge of cleaning, laundering, and fulfilling their kids' needs for breakfast, lunch, and dinner—a full plate of activity for sure. Despite these taxing schedules, there was always time to share food with other families in and outside the building.

When Mama talked about one of her favorite foods, *caponata*, she called it "the spice of life." The many dreary chores and the routine of working in and outside the house made her feel a need for spice, and her hands turned to making caponata. She loved selecting the ingredients, always seeking freshness and the best quality—the oil, garlic, homemade tomato sauce, olives, capers, basil, vinegar, and sugar spiced the eggplant, onions, and celery just the way she liked.

She smiled as she cooked and thought, "It makes me happier." She remembered it as one of the first dishes she had made with her mother in Italy. There were many things she knew how to prepare even as a little girl, attached to her mother's apron, shadowing her from cabinet to table, to sink, and around again. She thought making tomato paste was like the meaning of life—like the essence of life—because you start with God's gift of ripe, firm, bright red plum tomatoes. She was charmed by the simplicity of tomato paste and its value as a flavoring agent in other foods, such as soups, sauces, or a simple pasta topping.

She had wondered the whole year before leaving Italy at age eight for America how her life would change. It wouldn't, she assured herself, and asked her mother repeatedly what would happen to them when they left Italy. Together they agreed life would become bigger, busier, and better. To begin with, they would join Papa and be a family once more.

When they were aboard the overcrowded filthy ship bringing them across the ocean, they ate little because it was not their kind of food. Mama spent hours imagining making tomato paste with her mother. They would start with a bushel of the best, largest, ripest, freshest plum tomatoes—enough that after coring, peeling, and removing the seeds, they would be able to measure out eight quarts. They added little else in the way of ingredients, a teaspoon of kosher salt, one or two large, peeled garlic cloves, and finely chopped eight or ten fresh basil leaves cut into strips. Mama always wanted the task of slicing the basil leaves. She stacked them and, with a sharp knife, cut to very thin slices. She said you wouldn't believe the lovely, refreshing smell from cutting the basil. It was as if the kitchen turned into a large hotel suite facing the bay in Naples. She loved removing the tomato skins—so easy, she said. The trick is to add a few tomatoes at a time to a pot of boiling water, count to fifteen, remove them to cold water, and the skins will slide off easily. But be sure to core them before putting them into the boiling water. She and her mother worked together. Her mother would core and put them carefully into the boiling water—they counted together, and her mother would remove them to cold water in a large basin. As soon as Mama touched the tomato, the peel came off quickly. She would cut them in halves crosswise, not lengthwise, squeeze them to get rid of the seeds and some of the watery juice, and put them in a large bowl. They took turns putting the peeled tomato pieces through the food mill that was set atop a large soup pot. Mama adored working the food mill—it was as simple as a tool can be—no electricity needed, no batteries, just a clean mill, easy to turn, and it did a good job. There was no need to rinse the mill, as it would receive another batch of peeled tomatoes as soon as they were skinned and seeded. Mama liked the looks and feel of the processed tomatoes—a rich red color like red velvet fabric. The processed tomatoes were put in a colander that was lined with cheesecloth and set over another large bowl or pot to drain more liquid. That juice was good enough to drink or could be saved and used in soups and sauces. When all the tomatoes were processed and drained, my mother and grandmother would add the chopped garlic with the salt, sugar, and basil leaves. Then it was divided between two soup pots and simmered for as long as it took to render it into a thick paste, maybe two to three hours before the paste would be thick enough to mound on a spoon. Stirring was necessary to keep the inside bottom of the pot from burning and blackening. Then came the fun—the fun of spreading the paste onto low-rimmed baking sheets (or pizza pans) and drying the paste in the sun. This could take two or three days depending on the warmth of the sun. The result would fill eight half-pint jars. Before closing, a thin layer of olive and one or two whole basil leaves were added to each. The canning jars had to be the kind that have lids and rubber rings and could be processed in a water bath canner.

A scant teaspoon of the paste will work magic especially on tomato-based recipes, or it could be used in quick pasta sauces where a bit of water and/or oil can be added to the paste with garlic, hot pepper flakes, more chopped basil or parsley to make a quick sauce for spaghetti or other pasta.

On that nine-day trip across the Atlantic, in cramped and smelly quarters, clinging to her mother's side, Mama realized she would be cooking all of her life. She would love and enjoy it. She would cook with her mama until she was grown and then spend a lifetime cooking for her husband and children. Yes, it seemed like a dream, but it was not. She said again and again—this is what I want to do.

Graziella, the landlord's wife, Lucy from the grocery store, and Mama formed a triumvirate of cooks. They were busier than most others but, nonetheless, engaged in an intratenement competition. Mama knew darn well that *caponata* originated in Sicily, but she also knew how to make a very good one. Each Sicilian family made a version of this dish. Its fragrance is pungent and exciting to the appetite because of its sweet/sour component. With kitchen doors opened in the summer when there was a true bounty of fresh vegetables, everyone enjoyed its aroma and ate it with homemade bread. She wanted the Sicilians in and out of the building to know this. The truth was that every Sicilian in the neighborhood who tasted Mama's caponata thought it was special. She did not share her "secret." Mama's caponata was light and fresh and a genuine treat. Her "secret" was to sauté the eggplant cubes first and then set them aside. She then sautéed the other ingredients and did not mix them with the eggplant until all the cooking was done. The caponata can be an appetizer, spooned onto small slices of toasted homemade Italian bread. It also can be a condiment to eat alongside chicken, pork, beef, lamb—or scrambled eggs.

Graziella, our landlord's wife, was exceptionally proud of her tuna dish. A quiet and soft spoken Sicilian, she competed with the other Sicilians on our block where food was involved. If you were non-Sicilian, she was always ready to instruct you how to prepare a food from her island home, such as her tuna. Her sauce is tasty and flavorful, and there will be more than you need. The leftovers may be used as a delicious topping for small crostini or mixed with cooked pasta, such as penne or small rigatoni. The sauce keeps in the refrigerator for about a week.

Lucy, the grocer's wife, was proud of her Sicilian cake. The two primary Sicilian desserts are *cannoli* and *cassata,* and Lucy was a champion in the preparation of both. She did not sell the *cassata,* or cream cake, from her family's grocery store; but if she liked you, you might receive one on your birthday. There are many versions of *cassata*, but regardless of the small differences, all include candied fruit.

Mama claimed tuna was too expensive for our family and that the landlord's family obviously had more money to spend on food than we did. Plus, Graziella only had two mouths to feed in her flat. Her comment about Lucy's cake was "It's too sweet for us. It's better we eat fresh fruit."

Sweet and Sour Vegetables

Caponata

Serves up to 12

2 ½ pounds eggplant, peeled and cut into 1-inch squares
¾ cup vegetable oil mixed with ¼ cup olive oil
1 large onion, peeled and chopped
6 ribs celery (do not use outer stalks), cut into 1-inch pieces, steamed to precook them
3 cloves garlic, minced
2 cups homemade tomato sauce
1 ⅓ cups green olives, pitted and halved
½ cup capers, rinsed and drained
½ cup finely sliced basil leaves
Kosher salt and freshly ground black pepper
1 ¼ cups red wine vinegar
3 tablespoons sugar

1. Put the eggplant pieces in a large colander and sprinkle with salt. Allow to drain a minimum of thirty minutes. Dry them using paper or cloth kitchen toweling.
2. Pour half of the mixed oils into a heavy skillet and heat. Add half of the dried eggplant and cook, stirring frequently over moderate heat, ten to fifteen minutes, or until browned on all sides. Drain on paper towels and set aside. Repeat with the remaining eggplant.
3. In the same skillet, without the eggplant, add the onion and celery and sauté over medium heat, about ten minutes, stirring frequently. Add more oil if needed. After eight minutes of cooking, add the garlic, stir, and continue cooking until the garlic is soft.
4. Stir in the tomato sauce, olives, capers, and basil. Add some salt and freshly ground pepper. Bring to boil and add the vinegar and sugar. Simmer over low heat, about fifteen minutes. The vegetables

should be cooked through but not be mushy. Drain off as much liquid as you can. Stir in the eggplant, adjust seasoning, and allow to stand at room temperature until ready to serve. Refrigerate if not to be served right away. Before serving, leave dish at room temperature, thirty minutes, and sprinkle a little more finely chopped fresh basil over the top.

Aromatic Tuna Steak

Bistecca di tonno aromatico
Serves 4

1 or more thick tuna steaks, to weigh about 1 to 1 ½ pounds
1 cup dry white wine
4 tablespoons extra-virgin olive oil
2 tablespoons chopped parsley
2 tablespoons chopped basil
2 tablespoons chopped mint
Freshly ground black pepper
2 tablespoons unsalted butter
1 small onion, peeled and minced
1 large clove garlic, peeled and minced
1 carrot, trimmed, scrubbed and finely diced
2 large tomatoes, peeled, seeded and diced
1 tablespoon tomato paste
Kosher salt

1. Rinse the fish and pat dry with paper towels. Put the steak(s) in one layer in a glass or nonmetal container and pour in one-half cup of the wine. Sprinkle all over with two tablespoons of the oil, pinches of the parsley, basil, and mint, and a liberal grind of freshly ground black pepper. Turn the steaks over and let marinate for at least one hour in the refrigerator. Remove from the refrigerator ten to fifteen minutes before sautéing.
2. Heat the remaining olive oil with the butter in a skillet and sauté the onion, about three minutes. Add the garlic and sauté one

minute longer. Then add the carrot, remaining parsley, basil, mint, the tomatoes, tomato paste, remaining half cup of wine, and some salt and freshly ground pepper. Cook over low heat until the sauce combines and thickens, about twelve minutes.

3. Drain the tuna steak and, in another skillet, sauté on both sides over very high heat, two minutes per side. Then pour the sauce over the fish and cook to marry the two, three to six minutes, depending on how rare or well done you like tuna. Remove from the heat, let stand a couple of minutes, slice, and serve with some of the vegetable mixture.

Sicilian Cream Cake

Torta di crema siciliana

Serves 12

Sponge cake:

4 large eggs
⅔ cup sugar
1 cup sifted all-purpose flour
½ cup (8 tablespoons) unsalted butter, melted and cooled

Filling:

1 ½ pounds fresh ricotta or cottage cheese
2 cups sugar
1 teaspoon vanilla
2 tablespoons tangerine or orange liqueur
5 ounces (5 squares) bitter chocolate, chopped into small bits
½ cup candied fruit, finely diced
¼ cup whole pistachio nuts
Confectioners' sugar, for dusting
Buttered 9-inch cake pan

To make the sponge cake:

1. Preheat the oven to 350°F.

2. Put the eggs and sugar in a bowl and beat with an electric mixer. Put the bowl over but not touching the simmering water and continue to beat until the mixture is warmed and doubled in volume, about five minutes. Remove from above the simmering water and beat until the mixture has cooled.
3. Fold in the flour and butter with a rubber spatula. Do not overwork the mixture; the goal is simply to incorporate the flour and butter. Transfer, with the help of a spatula, to the well-buttered cake pan and bake until the center feels firm, about forty minutes. Invert onto a flat dish.

To make the filling:

1. Put the ricotta, sugar, vanilla, and liqueur in a food processor and process until smooth, about fifteen seconds. Transfer to a bowl and fold in the chocolate, fruit, and pistachios. Mix well.
2. Cut the sponge cake into one-half-inch pieces and use some of the slices to line a ten-inch rounded glass bowl. Spoon the creamed ricotta mixtures over the sponge cake pieces and pat down with a rubber spatula. Cover the top with the remaining slices of sponge cake. Cut a piece of cardboard the same size as the top of the cake inside the bowl. Cover with plastic wrap and press the plastic side of the cutout onto the top of the cake. Weight it with one or two full cans and place in the refrigerator for a minimum of four hours or overnight.
3. When ready to serve, remove the cake from the refrigerator, take off the can weights, and place a large platter or plate over the top of the bowl. Turn the bowl over, holding the cardboard and bowl steady and securely. Remove the bowl, dust it with confectioners' sugar, and serve. I like to be able to see the pattern of the turned-over cake slices through the confectioners' sugar.

2

BACCALA ON THE CLOTHESLINE

Mama and Papa had the first of the three bedrooms in the flat next to the kitchen. The three girls were in the middle room, and three boys in the third. When my older brother Jerry left for college, we reveled in the extra space.

With that many children, there was a lot of laundry. Mama much preferred cooking to laundry, but every week, she rose to the challenge of the mounds of dirty clothes, sheets, towels, and tablecloths. The bathtub/laundry tub in the kitchen had a large and sturdy washboard. Luckily, Mama was the right height to fit snugly over the board when it was in the tub. She scrubbed and scrubbed, moving the clothing and other items up and down in the soapy water until she was exhausted. Our stomachs turned as we witnessed her knuckles redden so that they seemed to bleed, and we agreed that when we grew up, we would buy her the best washing machine ever made.

She beat us to the punch and was the first on the block to buy a Maytag washing machine, the old-fashioned kind with a large rolling wringer on top of the tub. No one had dryers in those days, and Mama hung our wet clothes on two lines that stretched from each of the kitchen windows to a pole in the small backyard. The pole and others just like behind most tenements were there for this express purpose and served all the flats. To hang the laundry, you had to clamber onto the fire escape's landing through one of the windows or lean far out on the second window with no fire escape outside it. At this second window, Papa built a strong wooden sill that extended beyond the stone sill. Mama could balance "sidesaddle" on this sturdy sill and pin clothes to the line.

It was important to Mama that her laundry be whiter than white while on display on the laden lines. She even spent an extra twenty-five cents for a jug of Javelle, a popular whitening agent. We kids had a game of choosing the most tattletale gray clothes on our neighbors' lines and ranked them according to degrees of dinginess. Our games were the most fun in the wintertime, when the laundry froze on the line.

Even in the winter, Mama's coordination and dexterity meant the laundry made it to the line no matter what. Clearly it was far more difficult in January and February (when we called the frozen sheets and towels "baccala" because they resembled dried codfish) than in June and July.

In case you have not seen *stoccafisso* (dried cod) baccala, it's stiff and whitish. There are three kinds of baccala or cod: *merluzzo* (fresh); salt cod, which is preserved in salt; and *stoccafisso* (stockfish or dried), which is sold whole. Salted or dried, the cod must be soaked in freshwater for at least twenty-four hours, with changes of water every four or five hours to rid the fish of its extreme saltiness. As kids, we couldn't stand the strong fishy smell of baccala but loved to eat it. Both Mama and Papa loved this dish. The recipe requires real salt cod, as you find in Italian and other ethnic markets. Many supermarkets carry "salted cod," but it is not the same as the "real thing" from an Italian market. Beware of salt cod covered in plastic; it is apt to be soft and not very salty. Buy the thick, white slices of salt cod, which might cost a little more than the plastic covered type, but it will be skinned and boned and therefore easy to cook.

In our home, baccala was soaked in freshwater for up to two days, even getting up at night to change the water every four or five hours . We can still hear the request, "Cambia l'acqua" (Change the water), when we think about baccala. The pan holding the soaking fish was covered, but nonetheless, the odor was strong, especially in the beginning of the process. Thinking of the end product made the task easier.

Later in life, we discovered a fabulous preparation for it at Chez Panisse, Alice Water's restaurant in Berkeley, California. There, they sauté the soaked and dried cod in olive oil and serve it with chopped capers and oil—very similar to Mama's way of cooking it.

When the laundry reminded us of baccala, we would gleefully hold up brother Charlie's and Mama's underpants as they came off the line and compare sizes. Mama's fingers were raw with cold by this point, and she had little patience for our earthy humor. The frozen laundry just meant extra work, as it had to be rehung on temporary lines strung across the kitchen. Her patience was tested further when we decided to play hide-and-seek, in, out, and around the chilly, rigid clothes draped in the kitchen.

We spent many hot summer afternoons perched on the large, wooden sill, contemplating the clotheslines stretching from the many windows to the single pole. We reached no earthshaking conclusions, but when the lines were full of billowing sheets and shirts, they reminded us of the pictures we had seen of the rows of bright white houses balanced high on mountain cliffs in Italy. On windy days, the clothes danced on the lines, flapping so wildly; we were astonished the ropes did not snap. If the weather changed suddenly and a summer downpour was imminent, Mama's face turned as white as the laundry, and we hurried to haul the clothes inside. Once, the line did break, and we scurried down the stairs to the yard to retrieve the soiled clothing and the fallen line.

In our home, a long wooden pole draped with cut pasta was as enduring as any piece of furniture, and it was no coincidence that our daily lives revolved around the large, round kitchen table. It was here that Mama worked on a homemade pasta board, thick and heavy and never washed, but instead scraped clean after every use and stored against the wall behind the bathtub. Like our cleavers and knives, the pasta board received special care and protection.

An Italian carpenter had made the board, which was nearly four feet square. My mother rolled out sheet after sheet of pasta on that board, each one gently folded over and cut into strips or shapes large enough to fold around delicious fillings. From a very early age, I remember neighbors and relatives comparing pasta boards with as much concern and care as they did children. "Pazze? E cosa certa!" (Madness? It's a sure thing!)

The kitchen was kept cozy and warm by our black iron, wood-burning stove. Two openings on one side, one behind the other, held the wood that heated the stovetop for cooking and the oven for baking. Like similar stoves, ours was built with back guards to hold large containers of salt, pepper, and so on. The design included six legs and broad decorative rims, all made of highly polished steel alloy. One of our favorite pastimes was to smile or scowl into those brilliant borders, which served as mirrors for all of us—Mama even used these bright surfaces to adjust a hairpin now and then. Most of our food was cooked on the stove, and in the winter when the landlord was being stingy with the heat, it heated the kitchen and first bedroom.

Mama often let minestrone soup or zucchini stew sit on the stove overnight or longer to develop their flavors. She liked to put a piece of clean, scraped rind from Parmesan or Pecorino cheese in the soup as it simmered. Because she used Italian cheese in much of her cooking, there were always several crusts stored in the refrigerator waiting for the minestrone. She added bread balls to the minestrone an hour or so before serving and put eggs on top of the stew at the last minute. Mama could make this zucchini stew blindfolded. These days, we serve it in fancier bowls and with a variety of breads. It makes a lovely Sunday lunch in the country when it is starting to get cool, but there are some flowers still blooming. If you want a vegetarian version, eliminate the sausage and use vegetable broth instead of the beef and chicken broth.

Both dishes were easy to make, healthful, thrifty, and, like all of Mama's cooking, totally delicious.

Eventually, we were able to buy a small country house in upstate New York, where we spent most weekends in the warm weather. In the summer months and through the first half of the fall, we carried bushels of zucchini and other vegetables from the country to the city. We gave about half of it away, but not before Mama decided what she would need. No matter how long the day had been or how tired she might be, she always arranged the vegetables into piles, deciding which were for the "Scratch-Your-Bellies" and which for Teresa or Mary or Rose.

Sunday was the day for the big meal when we were growing up, and so it was much anticipated and enjoyed. Preparation began early in the morning when enticing aromas began to fill the air. The forty-minute church break fit neatly into the morning's culinary events and did not interfere with the creation of the meal, which was served at three o'clock in the afternoon. This soup often was the first course, and the chicken the second, or main course. Everyone loved the stuffing. Mama usually had to make extra and bake it separately in a big white oven dish. All that was needed to finish the meal was a crisp, fresh green salad. Mama showed her ingenuity about food when she cooked the stuffed chicken. She was cooking the chicken, but she also was making more broth to use later in the week.

Homemade Minestrone with Bread Balls

Minestrone casalingo con palline di pane

Serves 6

2 tablespoons extra-virgin olive oil
2 tablespoons unsalted butter
1 onion, cut into ½-inch dice
2 cloves garlic, minced
2 carrots, thinly sliced
1 large celery rib with leaves, thinly sliced
2 potatoes, peeled and cut into ½ inch cubes
1 ½ cups frozen lima beans
2 zucchini, 1 x 6 inches, scrubbed, ends removed (leave on the skin), cut into ½-inch dice
1 cup fresh or canned peeled, seeded, tomatoes with juice
6 cups broth, either homemade mixed, or 1 ½ cups each chicken and beef broth with 3 cups water
1 cheese crust from a 1 pound piece of Parmesan or Pecorino cheese, scraped clean
Salt and freshly ground black pepper
20 Bread Balls, see below

1. Heat the oil and butter in a large soup pot and sauté the onions and garlic until they begin to turn golden, about five minutes.
2. Add the carrots, celery, and the potatoes and cook, partially covered, until the vegetables are lightly sautéed, about ten minutes.
3. Add the lima beans, zucchini, tomatoes, the broth, and the cheese crust.
4. Bring to a boil, lower the heat to get a slow, steady simmer, and cook, covered, until the soup is thick, about two and a half hours. Stir occasionally. Ten minutes before the cooking is completed, add the bread balls and be sure the pot is covered. Salt and pepper to taste.

Bread Balls for Minestrone

Palline di pane

Makes about 20 balls

1 cup fresh bread crumbs
6 tablespoons freshly grated Parmesan or Pecorino cheese
1 tablespoon finely chopped fresh flat-leaf parsley
2 teaspoons finely chopped fresh oregano or 1 teaspoon dried
1 egg, lightly beaten
¼ cup milk
Salt and freshly ground black pepper

1. Combine all the ingredients in a bowl and mix well but lightly. Divide into four pieces, and from each quarter, make five small bread balls, about one inch diameter, twenty in all. Set aside or, if you are not ready to use, refrigerate. If balls have been refrigerated, bring to room temperature before adding to the soup.
2. To serve, spoon the warm minestrone with several bread balls into warm bowls. Be careful not to add the cheese crust, which should be discarded.

Zucchini Stew with Poached Eggs

Zuppa di zucchini con uova in camicia
Serves 6

3 tablespoons extra-virgin olive oil
3 Italian sausage links, sweet or hot
1 clove garlic, halved
3 medium potatoes, peeled and cut into ½-inch cubes
1 onion, thinly sliced
2 celery ribs with leaves, thinly sliced
2 tablespoons finely chopped fresh flat-leaf parsley
1 tablespoon finely chopped fresh oregano or ½ teaspoon dried
6 cups broth, either homemade or mixed or 1 ½ cups each beef and chicken broths plus 3 cups water
1 large tomato, peeled and seeded, chopped or ½ cup canned, seeded
1 pound small zucchini (1 x 6 inches) rinsed, ends removed, thinly sliced unpeeled
Salt and freshly ground black pepper
½ cup freshly grated Pecorino cheese
6 eggs, room temperature

1. Heat oil in a large soup pot and brown sausage links over medium heat. Oil will splatter, so be careful. When sausage is browned, about ten minutes, remove and set aside to cool.
2. Brown the garlic halves in the remaining oil in which sausage cooked. Remove and discard them. Add the potatoes, stir to coat with oil, and cook over medium heat for five minutes.
3. Add the onion, celery, parsley, and the oregano and cook, uncovered, until the onions soften and begin to turn golden, about five minutes.
4. Add the broth, tomatoes, and zucchini with a dash of salt. Also return sausage pieces to the pot. Bring to a boil, lower the heat to get a slow, steady simmer, and cook, covered, until the zucchini are fork-tender, about twenty minutes.

5. Carefully break the eggs over the hot stew. Cover, as quickly as you can, and cook until the eggs are poached, three to five minutes. Add the pepper.
6. Carefully spoon an egg with some of the zucchini soup into six warm bowls then add more zucchini liquid into each bowl. Add some cheese. Crisp Italian bread should be served with this to mop up the sauce.

Sunday Chicken Soup with Whole Stuffed Chicken

Zuppa con pollo intero farcito

Serves 6

For the stuffing:

2 tablespoons unsalted butter
1 gizzard, liver, and heart (from the chicken below), finely chopped
½ medium onion, chopped into ½-inch dice
1 cup fresh bread crumbs
¼ cup finely chopped cured ham or prosciutto or pork sausage, removed from casing
1 egg, lightly beaten
½ cup freshly grated Parmesan cheese
¼ cup golden raisins
¼ teaspoon dried fennel seeds
Salt and freshly ground black pepper

For the broth:

One 3-pound broiler chicken, excess fat removed, rinsed inside and out, dried with paper toweling
2 quarts water
3 carrots, thinly sliced
2 celery ribs with leaves, thinly sliced
1 large onion, cut into ½-inch dice
½ cup finely chopped fresh flat-leaf parsley
1 tablespoon finely chopped fresh thyme or 1 teaspoon dried
Salt and freshly ground black pepper

½ cup rice
1 cup grated Parmesan cheese

1. Heat the butter in a large skillet over medium heat and sauté the gizzard, liver, heart, and the onion—if using the pork sausage instead of ham or prosciutto, add it now—until lightly browned, about eight minutes. Transfer to a large mixing bowl, scraping the skillet with a rubber spatula. Add all other stuffing ingredients and mix thoroughly.
2. Put the stuffing in the chicken's cavity and truss both openings. Use kitchen string to tie the legs together and the wings to the body. Place the stuffed chicken in a large soup pot.
3. Add the water, the vegetables, herbs, and the salt and pepper. Bring to a boil over medium high-heat, lower the heat, and cook four or five minutes, skimming off any foam rising to the top. Cover and simmer until the chicken is cooked through, about one and a half hours. Carefully remove the chicken and keep warm by covering with a clean kitchen towel or aluminum foil.
4. Add the rice to the soup pot and cook, covered, for fifteen minutes until the rice is al dente. Serve the broth hot with Parmesan cheese. Then cut up the chicken, slice the stuffing, and serve as a main course with salad. On holidays or special days, we served a pasta dish in between, and the chicken was accompanied by a salad.

Slow-Cooked Salted Cod with Green Olives and Peppers

Baccala cotto lentamente con olive verdi e peperoni

Serves 4 to 6

2 pounds salted cod
¼ cup olive oil
6 cubanelle or Italian peppers, cored, seeds removed, and sliced lengthwise into ½-inch strips
⅔ cup flour
2 medium onions, chopped finely

2 tablespoons tomato paste
1 cup water
1 tablespoon capers
½ cup green Italian olives, pitted and sliced lengthwise
A good pinch of red pepper flakes
2 tablespoons finely chopped Italian parsley

1. Put the salt cod in a deep pan with a cover and cover with cold water. Let the fish soak for at least twenty-four hours and up to forty-eight hours. Change the water every four or five hours. Drain the fish.
2. Heat oil in a large skillet, and when hot, add sliced peppers and sauté until tender and somewhat charred, about six to eight minutes. Stir peppers frequently. Remove pan from heat and, with a slotted spoon, remove peppers and set aside.
3. If necessary, skin the fish and remove any visible bones. Cut into three-inch square pieces. Replace skillet with oil on heat. Dry fish squares and flour them. Brown well on both sides. Remove to dish with peppers.
4. Add onions to skillet and brown them. Add tomato paste and water and cook for several minutes, stirring. Add capers and olives. Return peppers and fish to skillet and simmer twenty minutes.
5. During this cooking time, spoon pepper sauce over fish every five minutes or so.
6. Add red pepper flakes five minutes before fish is cooked. Add parsley and serve.

3

ANGELINA, TERESA, AND MORNING GLORIES

There were many Angelinas on the block and in our building and in our lives. When someone mentioned Angelina, we didn't exactly know whom they were talking about. In our building, there was an Angelina in every flat.

The conversation went: "Angelina!" "Angelina who?" "On the third floor." "You mean LoPicholos?" "Yes." "The mother or the daughter?" "The mother, of course!"

If the Angelina in question was from another neighborhood, the conversation might sound like this: "I ran into Angelina on Ninth Avenue in the market." "Angelina who?" "I can't remember her last name." "Where is she from?" "The last I knew she lived in Queens." "Queens?" "There are over a thousand Angelinas there!" "Her husband drank a lot. I think his name was Angelo." "Oh you mean Comara, Angelina's daughter on Ditmars Boulevard—the Andraccis." "That's the one. Now you know who I mean."

Angelina, Angelina, Angelina. If you talked about an Angelina, you had to say Angelina Scarangelli, the mother. We wasted a lot of time figuring out which Angelina was the subject of discussion.

To set our mother apart, we started to call her Angela instead of Angelina, which was the name on her Italian certificate of birth. Papa had always called Mama Angela, not Angelina, the way some people say "calama" for "calamari." We children called her Mama, but we also sometimes called her Angela—and when we did, she seemed more like a sister than our mother.

Mrs. Teresa Lo Forte, who became one of Mama's lifelong friends, came from Agrigento in the south of Sicily. She was deeply proud of this heritage, and when we first knew her, she spent hours talking about the customs, arts, and food of Sicily. These conversations never took place on the fly but instead in her kitchen or front room. She would begin by saying that Sicily had been part of a unified Italy since 1860, but before that, it was as much a part of Africa and the Middle East, as it was of Europe. During its long history, Teresa explained, Sicilians had been conquered and ruled by many outsiders. First came the Greeks, then the Romans, Byzantines, Arabs, Normans, and the Spaniards—and all left their mark on the local cuisine, which later was copied by the Romans and then by the Europeans. Because the island bridged two continents and was the link between East and West for more than a thousand years, Sicilians spoke Arabic and Greek before they spoke Latin. She would insist with considerable conviction that, with few exceptions, these conquests added little to the well-being of the island, except to benefit the cuisine. In particular, she mentioned spices, almonds, and pine nuts and noted that the food of Sicily never disappoints. "There is profuse color, flavor, and character in the food," Teresa said. "Most of the pasta eaten there," she explained, "are of the tubular variety served with strong flavored sauces." Spring, she said, comes early in Sicily, and the island's gardens produced a cornucopia of vegetables: eggplant, (my favorite), artichokes, asparagus, broccoli, fennel, mushrooms, pimentos, pumpkins, and tomatoes. All over the island are groves of olives, fruit, and grapes. Sicilians rarely cooked with smoked meats, hams, and sausages, except in very small amounts and just for flavoring. Being island people, they like tuna, swordfish, sardines, mussels, clams, and gray mullet," she concluded.

Teresa, who was ninety-seven years old at her death, spent most of her life working in the textile district on New York's West Side. Her husband died young, leaving his widow with two daughters to raise. As children, we heard many descriptions of what her life was like after her husband died. (His wake was in her flat on the top floor—which meant, thankfully, that I did not have to walk past the flat's open door on my way in and out of the building.) Mama was a patient listener and wanted to show support because of all Teresa had lived through. Every now and then, Teresa paused in her conversation and looked into space, seeming to search for the courage to keep on talking. She would wipe tears from her eyes and take Mama's hand.

My sister Bea and I thought Therese actually enjoyed telling these stories, some of which we found hard to believe. As a young widow, she said everyone in her life watched her too closely for her comfort, as if to remind her she had lost her husband and couldn't possibly get close to another man. "And what about *le figle*?" (What about your daughters?) she said they would ask, implying her widowhood was to be a permanent state whether she liked it or not. She spent years in mourning and always wore black—we heard via the women's network that even her underwear was black. She was always part of any group of Sicilian widows who gathered, usually at a wake, to cry together. They held each other, screaming and yelling in a Sicilian dialect. If they were interrupted, they resumed their keening as soon as they could, chanting as if nothing had happened.

Teresa said the first year of mourning was the worst. She stayed home and wasn't even supposed to cook. Friends and neighbors supplied food for her and her daughters, but as the months passed, she could not resist cooking. She found, for instance, that making *stracciatelle* (similar to Roman stracciatella and often called "Sciuscieddu") was not only easy and quick but also healthful and tasty.

She also broke the routine and made another family favorite, rigatoni with eggplant in a creamy curry sauce. She justified this by saying she worried about the girls eating "other people's food" all the time and insisted they sometimes didn't like the dishes that were delivered to the flat. Teresa called this dish *rigatoni del Curato* (rigatoni in the style of the rustic priest). Rigatoni are made from durum wheat and are sold dried on just about every supermarket shelf in America. Teresa added a hint of curry, which found its way into Italy through early spice routes that crisscrossed Southern Italy and Sicily.

Teresa and Mama found ways to help each other. They cooked and shared special foods, compared notes on just about any subject, and, in their later years, helped each other thread needles. Teresa, her eyesight failing, squinted as she clenched her teeth. She fixed her right elbow on crossed legs and darted the thread toward the eye of the needle, held high in her left hand. After several tries, she usually was able to ease the thread through.

Although Teresa moved from our tenement shortly after her husband died, she visited Mama several times a week. On one of those occasions, we asked her what the secret of her long, healthy life was. We assumed she would talk about a lifetime of climbing up and down stairs or credit the good Sicilian olive oil she always used. Maybe she would talk about working hard, six days a week for many years. Instead, she looked at me and simply said, "Lecithin, Joey, Lecithin. I take two pills of it every day."

The tenants in our building were always ready to find fault with how our landlord Damiano and his wife Graziella ran things: The heat was not high enough; the door to the roof was locked when we could use some more air in the summertime; the front door was left unlocked to benefit anyone who forgot his or her keys; and, perhaps most common, the backyard was an eyesore. Everyone's rear kitchen windows overlooked the small backyard and so its rundown appearance affected everyone. Damiano made several attempts to beautify the space by planting morning glories along the wooden fences. This inspired tenants to put flower boxes planted with morning glories as well on the fire escape. They climbed up the metal framing for the fire escapes, which was a fire hazard, but no one seemed to care. The morning glory display along the fences and on the fire escape lifted everyone's spirits.

Mama found a way to reach through the tangle of plants to hang her laundry from the fire escape. We were fascinated by this feat. She held two clothespins between her teeth, hefted a bunched wet sheet or tablecloth over the line, and secured it with the pins. Wet sheets, bath towels, and tablecloths were heavy and, draped over her arm, were opened a little at a time as they went on the line, two clothespins at a time.

Windows were important to us for more than reaching the clothesline. We used the air and light wafting through them for drying tomato paste and ripening fresh tomatoes. We planted pots and window boxes with basil, thyme, and rosemary, which we set in the windows. Our kitchen windows, facing north onto the tenement's backyard, resembled the balconies you see all over Italy: profusions of colorful blooms with lots of greenery ready to be pinched and added to a sauce simmering on the stove. As a rule, Papa and Grandpa made the window boxes. They customized them for Mama, even making triangular-shaped ones to fit in the corners of the fire escape.

For my family, windows represented tragedy as much as they symbolized life. Before I was born, Mama and Papa's third child, a little girl named Beatrice, had fallen from a front room window and died in the street below. The window was fitted with a guard, and it's always been a mystery how Beatrice managed to climb out the window. We can only imagine Mama racing down the stairs to lift up the lifeless body of her little girl.

Mama had eight children and two miscarriages before she was twenty-eight years old. We could never mention the miscarriages while she was alive. She had married young and, when we were kids, was full of energy. When her oldest son, Jerry, was ready for college, her youngest daughter was still a toddler. It never occurred to Mama that we would not go to college, and to ensure we could, she worked in the textile district during the Depression. Her job on Thirty-Sixth Street, between Eighth and Ninth Avenues, was a quick, ten-block walk from our flat. She worked long hours doing piecework and usually brought home a paycheck exceeding $100, twice the amount Papa earned.

Her days were demanding. She left the flat by seven in the morning to go to work, and then about seven in the evening, I was assigned to meet her at the corner of Forty-Second Street and Ninth Avenue. She would fill two or three bags with groceries from Paddy's and the other markets along the avenue, bags that I helped carry and eventually toted home so that she could cook supper.

Cooking for us was something she obviously loved to do, and she never seemed tired or bored when she was in the kitchen. My older sister usually prepped the meals before Mama got home, but Mama did the cooking. Her face lit up in the kitchen, and we covered a far-reaching litany of subjects during the time before supper. When she quietly interrupted one of us to say she was putting the zucchini or whatever in the pot, she would always reassure us by saying, "Keep talking. I can hear you . . ." Even as she questioned us about our days, the minor decisions we had made, and the people we had encountered, she would also interject utterances such as "I think I need a little more oil . . . Joey, cut the bread . . . Mary, set the table . . . Louise, put the water glasses on the table—you know how finicky your papa is about his water."

Cooking and talking were our favorite pastimes in those days. Papa knew this was Mama's special time with us, although he could not resist tossing in a comment here and there about a stew that might scorch or pasta that might overcook without his diligence. He never raised his voice and was very much part of the group, even if this was Mama's moment.

Mama had a dish for every night. It might be her breaded asparagus. Another of the best was escarole soup with a chicken broth base and enhanced with small bread or beef balls. She sometimes mixed the beef with pork or veal. We nearly always had homemade bread on the table, warmed in the oven, and slathered with sweet butter. In those days, dipping bread in olive oil was not the common practice that it is now. Although that delicious habit might not have been in fashion yet, it didn't stop us from dipping our bread in salad dressings and pasta sauces. In other words, the bread was how we cleaned our plates—and we pretty much cleaned them every night!

Mama was always asked about her special Sunday sauce for macaroni. When this happened, whether the question came from a close relative or casual friend, she would describe how to make it leaving out the olive oil, garlic, and tomatoes. This wasn't done to be spiteful; Mama just thought anyone who didn't realize you had to use these three iconic ingredients didn't know much about food or cooking. Our other name for this Sunday treat was "happiness sauce." We all loved it, and although our feeling was it is the best sauce to serve with heavier pastas, such as ziti, rigatoni, or large penne, it works with spaghetti and most other string pastas. I don't think Mama would have thought it the best sauce for the very light pastas such as vermicelli and angel hair. Mama said what made it so good was that it had sausages, pork, spareribs, and meatballs in it. "How can you miss?" she asked. Mama was a piece of work.

Sicilian Stracciatella

Stracciatella alla siciliana

Serves 6

6 eggs
2 ½ cups grated Parmesan cheese
1 ¼ cups plain bread crumbs (from Italian bread)
2 garlic cloves, minced
2 tablespoons minced Italian parsley
6 cups mixed broth, homemade meat and poultry broth, or 1 ½ cups each of canned beef and chicken broths plus 3 cups of water
Salt, if needed
Freshly ground pepper

1. Beat eggs with Parmesan cheese and bread crumbs. Add minced garlic and parsley.
2. Heat broth to a simmer in a medium soup pot and add the mixture by large spoonfuls, stirring all the time. Add freshly ground pepper and salt to taste, cook one to two minutes, and serve. This is a much thicker soup than the Roman one.

Rigatoni with Eggplant in a Creamy Curry Sauce

Rigatoni con melanzane in salsa cremosa al curry

Serves 6 to 8

One 1-pound eggplant, unpeeled, trimmed, and diced
Salt
½ cup extra-virgin olive oil
¾ pound zucchini, peeled in stripes and diced

- 1 medium onion, diced
- 2 cups pureed tomatoes
- 1 ½ cups heavy cream or half and half
- 1-pound rigatoni
- 1 cup fresh basil, finely chopped
- 1-tablespoon curry
- ½ cup freshly grated Parmesan cheese

1. Sprinkle salt over the eggplant (in a colander) and drain for about one hour. Dry eggplant with kitchen toweling and sauté in one-fourth cup of oil using a large skillet. Drain on paper towels and set aside.
2. Sauté zucchini in remaining oil, drain on paper towels, and set aside.
3. Sauté the onions in the same skillet until they become transparent, six to eight minutes. 4. Add the tomatoes, some salt, and freshly ground pepper. Cover and cook, eight minutes, over medium heat. Remove from the heat and stir in the cream and the curry.
4. Boil the rigatoni until al dente, drain, and add it to the skillet. Add the eggplant, zucchini, and the basil. Mix well over high heat for several minutes to bring the sauce and pasta together. Serve right away with Parmesan on the side.

Special Sunday Sauce for Macaroni

Ragu casalinga con carne

Serves 8 to 10

For the meatballs

- 4 slices enriched white bread covered with milk, squeezed and set aside
- ½ pound each ground beef and ground pork
- 1 cup chopped onion
- 2 cloves garlic, minced
- 2 tablespoons finely chopped Italian parsley

⅔ cup grated Pecorino cheese
2 eggs, lightly beaten
Salt and freshly ground pepper to taste
Vegetable oil for frying the meatballs

For the sauce:

⅓ cup extra-virgin olive oil
3 to 3 ½ pounds pork spareribs (one rack cut into individual ribs)
3 large pork chops, about 1 pound, without bones, each cut in half
8 links (about 1 pound) Italian sausage, made with fennel seeds
2 cups chopped onions, preferably red
2 tablespoons minced fresh garlic
3 cans, each 28 ounces, peeled Italian plum tomatoes, chopped into small pieces plus liquid in cans
½ cup finely chopped fresh basil
½ teaspoon each of the following: dried oregano, dried basil, red pepper flakes
Salt and freshly ground black pepper to taste
1 to 1 ½ pounds macaroni, such as ziti, rigatoni, or large penne
1 cup freshly grated Parmesan or Pecorino cheese

1. To make the meatballs, combine all the ingredients above, except for the oil, in a large mixing bowl. Mix lightly with splayed fingers, enough so that the ingredients are well distributed. Turn out onto a clean counter and divide the mixture into ten to twelve sections.
2. Moisten your hands with cool water and form each into meatballs.
3. Heat about one-eighth-inch vegetable oil in a large skillet and carefully add the meatballs, one at a time. Watch out for splattering. Cook until browned on the bottom, four to five minutes, turn each over, and cook the other side for four or five minutes. Remove them onto paper toweling and set aside until ready to add to the sauce.
4. To make the sauce: Put one-half of the oil in a large cooking pan and sauté the meats in batches, adding more oil as needed. When

the meat gets brown, remove it piece by piece to paper toweling. Don't crowd the meat.

5. Add the onions to the same pot and brown for four or five minutes, turning frequently. Add the garlic and cook a minute longer.
6. Add the tomatoes, one-fourth cup of the fresh basil, the dried oregano and dried basil, red pepper flakes, salt and pepper. Stir well and add all the meat except the meatballs. Bring the sauce to a boil, partially cover, and reduce heat to a simmer. Cook for one hour.
7. Add the meatballs, stir carefully, and simmer for one hour more. When the sauce has cooked for two hours, remove the meats onto a large platter.
8. Cook the pasta according to package directions. Drain well and return pasta to the pot in which it cooked. Add some sauce, enough to lightly coat the pasta. Serve either in individual plates or on a large platter. Add more sauce and garnish with a sprinkle of the remaining fresh basil.
9. Serve the cooked meat on the side, allowing each diner to choose some. Also pass the cup of grated cheese.

Note: The meatballs can be made one day ahead, covered, and refrigerated until ready to be added to the tomato sauce. The sauce with meats can be made a day ahead too and reheated before serving.

Mama's breaded asparagus is easy to prepare if you set up for it properly. Here's Mama's routine. One, keep the scraped asparagus stalks in iced water until you are ready to use them. Two, dry the stalks and have three plates lined up in a row: one for flour, one for eggs, and one for bread crumbs. Follow an assembly-line routine: while the first stalk is cooking in the oil, prepare the next one and add it to the oil, and so on. Three, they cook quickly and are at their best if eaten just as soon as they are done. (However, they will keep in warm oven for up to one hour. Place them on a baking tray, making sure that the stalks are not touching).

Breaded Asparagus

Asparagi impanati

Serves 4

1 cup vegetable oil (or peanut or corn oil)
20 medium-size asparagus stalks
1 cup all-purpose flour
2 eggs, well beaten with salt and freshly ground pepper added to taste
1 to 1 ½ cups fresh bread crumbs

1. Heat the oil in a large, heavy skillet.
2. While the oil is heating, roll each asparagus stalk in flour, and shake off excess. Dip the stalk in the beaten egg. Next, roll the stalk in the bread crumbs. Put the stalk in the hot oil and cook it until lightly browned (about five minutes) on all sides. (Do not overcook the stalks; they should be al dente.)

4

TOMATOES ON THE WINDOWSILL, SAUSAGE MAKING, AND CARLO BUTTI'S TONIC

Mama put food on a high pedestal. My friends today think I'm joking, or surely exaggerating, when I say I never tasted canned food until I went to college, but the truth is that even our tomato paste was homemade. In this book, I call for canned tomato paste because very few people make their own anymore. Every August, when tomatoes were red, ripe, and juicy, Mama spent hours boiling them to a pulp, straining out the seeds, and cooking the pulp to a paste. She spread the paste onto oversized cookie sheets or huge aluminum trays and placed them on the windowsills to dry in the sun. The trays were set first on the kitchen windowsills, for they faced east and caught the morning sun. Later, the trays were moved to the front room for the afternoon sun, which bathed the west-facing windows. You can't imagine the experience of sitting in our front room next to an open window, reading a novel, and inhaling the smell of fresh basil and homemade tomato paste.

When the mixture was dry and darkened enough to Mama's satisfaction, she spooned it into Ball jars and topped it off with olive oil and more basil before processing the jars in boiling water for storage in our city cellar. I grew to detest requests, such as "Joey, go down for a jar of tomato paste . . . sausage . . . tomatoes," especially after dark. The basement was damp and breathlessly quiet, except for the occasional rodent scurrying by, and spooky with cobwebs pressed in the corners of the old, gray stone walls. The basement space allotted each tenant was considerable, about the size of one of our bedrooms; and ours contained a wine press, several barrels of homemade wine, and shelves on all sides to hold the too-numerous-to-count jars of tomatoes, tomato paste, and dried sausage.

Tomato paste was an important ingredient in many dishes. Of course it was added to pasta sauces—called macaroni gravy in those days—as well as stews and was especially important to a preparation we called a quick sauce: garlic lightly browned in good olive oil, homemade tomato paste added to the skillet and thinned with some water, flavored with a sprinkle of red pepper flakes, and then tossed with al dente spaghetti. This dish took only ten to fifteen minutes to pull together and was a family favorite just about any time. It nearly always was served to relatives who came to visit without warning from Connecticut, New Jersey, and Pennsylvania; sometimes from Chicago or California. Mama would say to anyone and everyone, "This is a very old family recipe."

In our home, this sausage was made several hundred pounds at a time. It was an annual family event in which everyone participated. Some of the sausage was eaten fresh as soon as we finished making it; the rest was kept for weeks in the refrigerator or icebox to be used as needed. The aroma of sautéing sausage seemed to be with us always. It was always added to tomato and other sauces for spaghetti, macaroni, ravioli, manicotti, cavatelli, lasagne, and all the other pastas.

It was cooked with vegetables and therefore added bounce to escarole, broccoli, brussels sprouts, and cabbage. It was used to stuff chickens, capons, turkeys, and other birds, bringing forth the comment, "Why doesn't my stuffing taste like this?" It pocketed chops, flank steaks, and rollatini and added special flavor to meats that were roasted, stewed, and braised. It was fried with peppers and roasted with potatoes (liberally sprinkled with oregano). It was eternally on hand because it was put up in tens of jars, the sausage first dried then packed into the jars filled with homemade lard (fat rendering from the sausage). We went to great lengths to explain, sometimes in an apologetic tone, the family sausage-making ritual to non-Italian friends (who, when they visited, would see sausage links hanging from poles competing for space with the drying pasta), but we knew that both the men and the women of the family took pride in the amount and the quality of the riches stored away in the family's *salsiccia* bank. Our friends came back for more.

Mama used a link or two of sausage to her advantage, especially when she made soups and stews. Her "bean, basil, and escarole soup with sausage" is a basic, beautiful Angela soup—simply delicious, healthy, and easy to make. Italians like escarole and prepare it in many ways. It is used in soups with beans and sausage as it is here, or with chickpeas, or with carrots, celery, and many other vegetables. A "penicillin" type of soup for us was homemade chicken broth with escarole cooked in it. If Mama decided to make this a main course, she added some sausage to make it "bigger," as she does with this soup.

Mama was a good organizer. When it was time to make sausage for the year, she recruited several other women to join her in our kitchen. It's difficult to imagine the quantity of pork butts on the kitchen table, all of which first were stripped of excess fat and then cut by hand into tiny pieces. Removing the fat was important, in part because it was needed for the sausage making and also any extra could be used to flavor other dishes. Mama melted it in a large frying pan and then used it to cover the dried sausage in Ball jars before they were sealed. We also used this rendered lard by teaspoonfuls as a flavor enhancer for soups and stews. We were especially fond of it rubbed on potato pieces before they were baked. Mama always used it instead of olive oil to sauté carrots, onions, and celery for her main dishes of spaghetti sauces, soups, and stews.

As children, we took turns "pricking" the sausage during sausage-making days. With a long needle, we pierced the sausages every inch or so as the meat was forced by hand into the expandable pork casings. This exercise was to rid the sausages of air bubbles. My sister Bea and I tried desperately not to laugh as the women squeezed the meat into the casing, firming it in the thin skins. Some women were clearly more adept than others, and while as children, we were not supposed to speculate where they acquired their prowess; not doing so was just about impossible as we witnessed various neighbors tie the filled casings with string to make links. Bea and I wondered why the links were not all of the same size . . .

Yes, it was a chore for my sister and me during these sausage-making sessions; and at first, we felt like "people who just got off the boat (although we were born here) as friends came to see us at home. Almost always, someone would ask, "Tell us about that," pointing to the sausages. They asked more questions and showed interest by asking, "Can we come see how your mother makes it?" At first, we were embarrassed; but in time, we felt proud of our customs and culture and began "showing off" the jars and jars of homemade sausage. When the sausage-making party ended, Mama hung yards of tied links over poles suspended in most corners of the kitchen and front room. She wanted the sausage to be hit by cold air, and so she opened windows. We put on wool sweaters to enter the front room, perhaps a small price to pay for the homemade sausage. Several weeks went by before Mama thought the sausage was dry enough for preserving. By this time, the preserved lard had jelled; and so Mama reheated it to liquefy it before pouring it over the sausages filling Ball jars, which then went to the cellar.

We wanted Mama to open a restaurant in which she would be the main cook. In our thoughts, hers would be better than Mama Leone's, the Italian trattoria that reigned over the theater district for many decades. Mama, the immigrant child and exceptionally young bride, thought differently. She wanted "my son the lawyer, my son the doctor." She didn't care about the accomplishments of Armando Orsini, Tony May, and Sirio Maccioni, all successful restaurateurs. It wasn't for her.

Yet as a family, we were familiar with Barbetta's, the longtime Italian restaurant on the block of West Forty-Sixth Street known as Restaurant Row. We all grew up walking past the restaurant, filled as it was with red-checkered tablecloth-covered tables. In those days, if you owned an Italian restaurant, you employed only Italian waiters, and Mama and Papa knew many of those at Barbetta's. Some were haughty Northern Italians who looked down their noses at Southern

Italians, the "Mezzogiorno scums." Mama was able to speak Florentine Italian, so they treated her kindly. These waiters viewed their jobs as careers and spent lifetimes waiting tables. They were knowledgeable enough about food to dispense recipes, Italian style—meaning the recipe might be undependable. There was no question about Mama's respect for these waiters, and perhaps she viewed herself in their role rather than as an owner. Whatever the reason, operating a restaurant held little interest for her.

Even Mama, as great a cook as she was, had difficulty with recipes. She never wrote anything in recipe format and cooked by instinct. She rarely measured flour, oil, water, or anything. Nonetheless, we talked about the possibility of a restaurant for years—Mama in the kitchen, Papa out front. As we ate at home, we'd vote on whether the dish was worthy of being included on Mama's restaurant menu.

Over the years, we became addicted to Mama's food. She could cook anything Italian. She was brilliant when she combined beans, basil, and escarole in a soup or stew. Her stuffed artichokes and fettuccini preparations became classics for anyone who ate them, all enhanced by her omnipresent homemade sausage—every dish, maddeningly tasty. Our favorite way to cook fettuccini when we were kids was to cook it with mascarpone, sage, and sausage. We still cook it Mama's way. It makes a great one-dish meal and needs only a green salad topped with a tomato slice. Mama always said, "Be sure the mascarpone cheese is at room temperature and that the bread crumbs are made fresh."

We ate Italian fare nearly every day, but Saturday was an exception. The flat received its major cleaning that morning, and Mama put each of us to work doing one thing or another. One of my responsibilities was to go to Marquardt's Deli on Forty-Seventh Street and Tenth Avenue and buy lunch. I loved the German-style store. Hundreds of sausages hung on big steel hooks above and behind whichever Marquardt was working the counter. The refrigerated cases were filled with all sorts of cold cuts, and just the smell of homemade German potato salad, vinegary enough to excite and power the senses, brought the juices to my stomach. Huge dill pickles, bathed in unlidded, large white ceramic containers, added to the culinary sensations. On top of the counters were stacks of loaves of sliced American white bread, but as tempting as they were to a kid, I was not allowed to buy them. When I got home, we made our sandwiches on Mama's homemade Italian bread. Still the essence of the meal was "German delicatessen," and we loved it.

Mama liked to see us eat, and where matters of health were concerned, she couldn't have cared less about what others thought of her instructions or our own feelings about what was good for us. When I was in grade school and junior high, I was so thin every one called me Bones. Hearing her son Joey referred to as Bones irritated Mama, who did not appreciate nicknames, and so she determined to fatten me up. She ordered a "tonic" advertised on the New York City Italian radio station, one she listened to as often as time allowed. Carlo Butti, a popular Italian singer, was a favorite of hers, and his sponsors manufactured the tonic. She ordered a large bottle and daily filled smaller bottles with it for me to carry to school. I was so embarrassed by this routine that I hid the bottle in a pocket, sneaked off to the boys' room, and, when no one was looking, I'd swallow it so that I could bring the bottle home for a refill. The tonic did not work. Mama kept listening to the melodic tunes of Carlo Butti, and I stayed skinny, not gaining weight until I hit my forties. (Speaking of nicknames, we had some cousins across the street whose buttocks hung low on their backsides. We nicknamed them "lead asses." Mama, not especially fond of these cousins, nonetheless reprimanded us each time we referred to them this way. I suspect she was not too upset.)

As practical and straightforward as she was, Mama had a sentimental side too. What is it about mothers and photographs of their offspring? Mama was no different from anyone else on this front, and we always had family photographs, notably of children, to remind us of ourselves and other family members. There are three of me that may be worth mentioning. The first, my baby picture, taken when I was about nine months old: I am lying on my belly, full face forward, arms and elbows holding me up to project my face, and buttocks unclothed—in fact, the only piece of clothing is a wide bow wrapped around my waist, made of some sort of netting material similar to that used to make wedding dresses and veils. Everyone still laughs at it at my expense, but Mama loved the photo and had copies made and passed around to her friends and distant relatives. The second photo is when I am five or six, in full dress with top hat, taken at the time I was asked to sing "Bye, Bye, Blackbird" at a wedding. The third photo, perhaps my favorite, was taken on the roof of our tenement, a favorite location for family pictures. My older brother has me to his right, and my middle brother to his left. It was taken during the first summer after my brother's freshman year at college. At ten years old, I am still in knickers. Mama liked this photo—her boys were young, thin, rather good looking, and at this point in time, our lives still revolved around home and family. Mama also loved a shot of her son Charlie posed on a horse at the entrance to the tenement. Little Lord Fauntleroy couldn't be more appropriately dressed, and anyone viewing this photo would inevitably ooh! and aah!

When it came to her three daughters, Mama prized their Holy Communion pictures. She also was fond of a picture of her eldest daughter at sixteen, and another one of the two younger daughters, ages eight and six, dressed in her own homemade dresses with high yolks and matching broad, flouncing summery hats. Each of my sisters wore short white socks and black patent leather Mary Janes.

Mama and Papa's wedding photo is wonderful. He wore a shirt with a high-rounded collar and a tie stuck with a diamond pin. I have the photo, but the pin went to son number one when Papa died. The photo was displayed on a table in the front room next to one of Papa before he married Mama.

We were a photogenic family and were sought after as ushers, bridesmaids, and ring bearers at family and neighborhood weddings. Mama kept all the wedding pictures, and as the years went by, a favorite pastime was to view them, with the expected observations such as "Oh, look at how young Jerry and Mary were" or "I just can't believe that's Jerry!" Mama loved hearing others exclaim over her children, and if we were not the most handsome, Mama thought we were.

Homemade Pork Sausage

Salsiccia di maiale fatte in casa
Makes 2 to 3 pounds

3 pound pork butt, as lean as possible
1 ½ tablespoons kosher salt
1 teaspoon fennel seeds
1 ½ tablespoons paprika
½ teaspoon freshly ground black pepper
2 yards sausage casing, soaked in ½ cup orange juice for several hours or overnight

1. Cut the meat into thin strips, then cut these strips by hand into the smallest pieces possible. Put the cut meat into a large bowl, and keep it cold for ease in handling. Add the salt, fennel seeds, paprika, and pepper, and mix well.
2. Thoroughly wash the casing in lukewarm water and fit it over a sausage funnel. (About one yard of the casing should fit over the cone of the funnel, leaving one or two inches of casing overhanging from the funnel cone.) Tie off the end of the casing (with strong string) and feed the sausage meat into the funnel with your thumb. As the casing fills, puncture it with a needle to release air. (Rotate and puncture the casing every few inches.) The casing should be firmly packed; if it is too loose, use your hand to squeeze the casing to pack it more fully.
3. Tie the end of the casing with string then tie it off each five inches or so to form the individual sausage links. If the casing breaks, stop funneling, tie the casing at the break, and start again.

Note: This sausage may be kept in the refrigerator uncovered for three weeks; it may be kept frozen for one month.

Bean, Basil, and Escarole Soup with Sausage

Zuppa di scarola e basilica di fagioli con salsiccia

Serves 6 to 8

1 pound Italian sausage, sweet or hot, pricked in various places with a small sharp knife to allow some fat to escape while sautéing
½ pound dried white kidney beans
2 quarts, plus 3 cups, water
3 tablespoons extra-virgin olive oil
2 cloves garlic, minced
2 cups chopped, seeded, peeled, fresh ripe tomatoes or 2 cups canned, seeded
1 tablespoon finely chopped fresh basil
1 tablespoon kosher salt
4 celery ribs with leaves, thinly sliced
1 carrot, thinly sliced
1 ½ pounds escarole, trimmed, rinsed well, and coarsely chopped
Freshly ground black pepper
½ cup freshly grated Parmesan cheese

1. Soak the beans overnight in water to cover. The next day, drain the beans and put them in a large soup pot with two quarts of water. Cook, covered, over low heat for about one and a half hours, until tender. Set aside.
2. While beans are cooking, put one tablespoon oil in a soup pot and sauté the sausage, turning links as they brown. It will take about ten minutes to brown all sides (they will cook longer in the soup). Remove from pot, cool, then slice as thinly as you can, and set aside.
3. Heat the remaining oil in a medium to large soup pot and cook the garlic for one minute. Add the tomatoes, three cups of water, basil, and salt. Cook over medium heat, partially covered, for ten minutes. Add celery and carrot and cook for fifteen minutes. Transfer this mixture to the bean pot. Add the browned sausage slices.

4. Add the escarole, mixing it in well. Cook over medium-high heat to bring to a boil. Lower the heat to get a slow, steady simmer. Cover and cook for thirty minutes. Add pepper to taste.
5. Serve in warm bowls sprinkled with cheese.

Stuffed Artichokes

Carciofi ripieni

Serves 6

⅓ pound sausage links, or pepperoni, ham, or prosciutto
1 teaspoon olive oil
1 ½ cups fresh bread crumbs
2 tablespoons fresh parsley, chopped (or 1 teaspoon dried)
2 cloves garlic, minced fine
3 eggs
¼ cup milk
6 tablespoons olive oil
Salt and freshly ground pepper
6 large artichokes
½ cup fresh tomatoes, peeled, drained, and crushed
(or canned plum tomatoes, drained and chopped coarse)
4 cups water
2 cloves garlic, whole

1. Cut the meat into small pieces. In a small skillet, heat one teaspoon oil and cook the meat, five minutes, shaking the skillet and stirring. Drain the meat and transfer it to a mixing bowl. Add the bread crumbs, parsley, and minced garlic, and toss well.
2. Beat the eggs with the milk and two tablespoons olive oil. Add this to the meat and bread crumb mixture. Add salt and pepper to taste, and stir to blend.
3. Using a sharp knife, cut the stem off each artichoke to make a flat base. Pull off the tough outer leaves. Cut off about one-half inch of the top of each artichoke and open the leaves with your fingers. Invert the artichokes on a flat surface, pressing down on each one to open its leaves.

4. Divide the filling into six equal parts. Stand each artichoke on its base and stuff the center first, then add some filling between the leaves more or less at random. Be sure to push the stuffing down as you add it.
5. Select a casserole with a cover large enough to hold the artichokes snugly in one layer. (If they do not fit close together in the casserole, tie each one around the center with string to help retain the shape.) Arrange the artichokes in the casserole and spoon the same amount of the tomatoes on top of each. Pour the water around them and add the whole garlic cloves to the water. Sprinkle the artichokes with the remaining four tablespoons olive oil. Cover the casserole tightly and bring water to a boil. Reduce the heat and simmer until the artichoke bottoms are tender, forty-five minutes to one hour. (To test for doneness, pull off an outside leave; if it comes off easily, the artichokes are done.)
6. Remove the artichokes from the casserole with a slotted spoon. Do not serve any of the cooking liquid. Serve one artichoke per person.

Fettuccini with Mascarpone, Sage, Sausage, and Toasted Bread Crumbs

Fettuccine con mascarpone, salvia, salsicca e briciole di pane tostato
Serves 4 to 6

2 tablespoons butter
½ cup fresh bread crumbs
1 tablespoon finely chopped fresh sage leaves
Salt and freshly ground pepper
1 pound Italian sausage, sweet or hot
1 tablespoon olive oil
8 ounces mascarpone cheese at room temperature
1 cup freshly grated Parmesan cheese
9 ounces fresh fettuccini

1. In a large skillet, heat butter and sauté bread crumbs, sage, with salt and pepper until lightly browned, about three minutes. Set aside.
2. Sauté sausage links in a tablespoon oil and cook until browned on all sides. Remove from pan, allow to cool just enough to handle, then slice sausages as thinly as possible. Keep them warm.
3. In a large bowl, combine softened mascarpone and Parmesan cheeses.
4. Cook pasta and drain, reserving about one cup of boiling pasta water. Add pasta to bowl with cheeses. Toss lightly and well. Check for salt seasoning and add black pepper. If sauce is too thick, thin with some of the reserved hot water.
5. To serve, divide the pasta among individual plates and sprinkle each with a full tablespoon or more of bread crumbs or put the pasta in a large platter and sprinkle bread crumbs on it. Add cooked sausage slices around pasta.

5

WHITE AS A PILLOWCASE

As soon as I began working and earning money, I put some aside to buy a house in the country for the family. Long island, our dream location, was growing more and more expensive, so I started looking elsewhere. Eventually, I found a dilapidated old building in Pawling, New York, seventy miles north of New York City in Dutchess County.

One of the first things we did when we took possession was put in a large vegetable garden. Once Mama passed on, it became difficult to keep the vegetable garden going, and it has been replaced over the years with easy-to-care-for trees, bushes, and some perennials, such as peonies and mint. There is also still some room for annuals. The house, originally built in 1840, has been greatly improved and is now a good-looking home.

Back when we all used the house, whenever we got there, Mama would immediately exchange her city clothes for country clothes, tie a scarf around her head, and white sneakers on her feet, grab a sharp paring knife, and head for the large field next to the house, as if she were a character in a De Sica film.

Her objective was to fill a large brown paper sack with wild greens, including chicory, dandelions, mustard, endive, funny-looking lettuce, and one I'll never forget—something she called *piedi rossi*, meaning red feet, a weed whose bottom stem was a bright red, almost purple. Because she was born in Italy, we always considered this trek of hers to be a fundamental connection to the old country. Truly it was an essential part of her life: she lived to the age of ninety-one and collected these wild greens every year until she turned ninety.

Back in the kitchen, she soaked them without sorting in a large basin, changing the water at least twice and frequently more often, depending on the dirt in the rinse water. If she wanted the greens dried for a salad, she clutched a big bunch in her hand and shook them wildly before rolling them in dry kitchen towels. If the greens were for soup, pasta, or frittatas, she let them drain in a large colander. For these preparations, the leaves could have water clinging to them. Whatever their fate, the greens were delicious.

When she made the wild greens soup (and most others), she didn't use bouillon cubes because she always had homemade stock on hand. This is not always the case with today's home cooks, and so if you use canned broth, add a bouillon cube to punch up the flavor, but don't add any more salt to the soup; the bouillon cube is very salty. Mama may have picked these greens, but these days, supermarkets carry most of them, so look for a good variety.

To this day, we see women in the fields in Italy searching for similar harvests and our mouths water imagining what wonders those cooks will create.

One of Mama's favorite dishes was the wild greens soup. Yes, it kept a connection to the old country, but there was more to it. If someone asked her why she liked it so much, her answer was because it's something direct and simple. It concentrates on the meaning of life and not on fancy things—it's getting things from the earth, life's simple bounty—that is making the wild greens soup. Just compare that with the complexity of making money and the aggravation, the competition, and the disappointments that often go with it. Making the wild greens soup always works for you. You get the satisfaction, the simplicity, the happiness, and the comfort from making and eating it. It doesn't cost much, and that's important when you have a family and are trying to raise six children. And it's healthy for them, me, and Papa.

The world is changing and sometimes too rapidly—each of us needs to return to some earthly projects. Any wonder why so many Italians in this country and overseas have vegetable gardens—some are very small and sit by the side of their houses. Some use fire escapes—almost everyone I know has one or more pots of herbs out there. Gardening is to keep in touch with the simple and satisfying ways of living to uncomplicate our lives. To look at a tomato on the vine, deep, lush, red, waiting to be eaten, is one of the most satisfying things one can do. The same for cherries, figs, lettuce, asparagus—anything that grows in the ground and ripens to be eaten and enjoyed. That is what my wild greens soup means to me and to my family. Every single child of mine, when in his or her own home, has or had a vegetable garden. So you see, as it is said in Italian, "La mela non cade lontana dall'albero" (An apple never falls far from the tree).

Mama went to great lengths to cook something special for company. She would coax us to invite our friends for a meal and often invited them directly, perhaps as a way to keep us home and off the city's wild streets. For these meals, she prepared "show-off dishes" (our term and not appreciated by her), and two of our favorites were duck lasagna (with homemade lasagna pasta) and veal shanks limone. She always said that veal was more elegant than lamb, and she was sure to make that point when "Aunt" Margaret was around. Margaret was a close friend who had been born in the town of Stigliano, right next door to Accettura, Mama's home village. Stigliano was known as a "lamb town." Accettura was best known for its pork, despite Mama's appreciation of veal, and she seemed to like veal as much as pork and preferred both to lamb. Her duck lasagna is an unusual and spectacular lasagna dish with a delicate flavor. "Cut the lasagna as thinly as possible," she always advised. It's a good idea to have a few extra pasta pieces on hand in case some break during cooking and draining. Sometimes she served in small portions, for this makes an excellent and unusual first pasta course, but mostly it was and is a glorious main course.

Veal shanks cooked Mama's way, *limone*, is a typical Italian classic called *osso buco*. It may be served with a sprinkling of anchovy fillets, but she omitted them because she thought the cooked-down wine and broth was salty enough. The dish is combined with lots of parsley and other vegetables. The resulting bouquet of flavor, Mama said, "E fantastico"—even more so if combined with a risotto. And she never failed to say, "Sprinkle it liberally with grated Parmesan cheese!"

Tony, her butcher for seventy-five years, knew how to prepare meat to Mama's liking, and she ordered it on her way to work so that it was ready for her on the way home. His shop was in the middle of Forty-Sixth Street, between Ninth and Tenth Avenues, until he moved up the street to the northwest corner of Ninth. Mama always said it was important to be "kind to your butcher," and she became very attached to Tony's family. When Tony's daughter got married, she received from us an envelope filled with a generous amount of cash. Mama sent small gifts to Tony's wife and saw to it that Papa dropped by the shop with an occasional bottle of wine or box of pastries from downtown.

Mama didn't talk a lot, although when she spoke, it was always with a certain clarity. Her softly uttered requests were never ambiguous, which made her easy to obey. On the other hand, she used a number of malapropisms—and was extremely sensitive to criticism from her children or anyone else. It was difficult to keep a straight face when she said, "My face got as white as a pillowcase." When I suggested the expression was "white as a sheet," she countered with "What is the difference? Sheet or pillowcase, you know what I mean." Of course she was right. When she said, "You have gone too further," instead of "too far," I didn't say a word.

Our language at home was filled with oddities that did not come from Mama. For years, we kids thought *baa-cow-za* was a legitimate Italian word rather than the immigrants' word for backhouse or outhouse (the toilets for many tenements were outdoors behind the buildings). Pocketbook was *pockabooka,* and to this day, it's still possible to hear a few old-timers from those days say "earl" for oil.

Mama insisted on clean language, always, although she broke her own rule one Christmas Eve. We were helping her trim the tree. Mama was on a ladder attempting to put a fragile silver and red star on the top of the tree. The ladder was wobbly, and while we should have been concerned for her safety, we were giggling instead. Fully frustrated and annoyed, Mama yelled down at us, "Oh fuck!" As far as I know, this was the one and only time she uttered the word, and it rapidly became a favorite family story—"Remember the time Mama used the F word?"—although she never admitted to saying it.

She was strict in other ways, as well. Before television, we depended on the radio for entertainment, and she permitted us to gather in the front room after supper for an hour or so to listen to *Just Plain Bill* and *Myrt and Marge*. Two more innocuous programs never existed, and I am hard pressed to explain their attraction. Perhaps it postponed our homework time before going to bed.

Mama took a real interest in our musical training. Jerry played the violin for years before he left for college, and Mary played the piano. Our piano had a normal keyboard but also played perforated rolls of music with renditions of *Ramona, Sonny Boy,* and *Bye, Bye, Blackbird.* My brothers, sisters, and I grew up humming those tunes and carried them into adulthood.

The day the piano was delivered, it was hoisted by pulley and a heavy rope attached to the roof up to the third floor before being eased inside through the window, which had been completely removed. You would have thought the circus had come to town; neighbors and friends excitedly filled the block to watch the event, and when the piano successfully entered the building, the crowd let out a roar of approval. Mama had duck lasagna in the oven, in anticipation of a celebratory meal in honor of the piano. We also believed she made the heady dish so neighbors would comment on the tantalizing aroma. When that happened, Mama smiled sheepishly and said, "Oh, that's the duck lasagna the kids wanted me to make so we can have a party with the new piano."

But she also said making lasagna was like raising kids. You needed a lot of patience for both. Mama would explain to her friends that each of her kids was different. "I love them all, but each one is different. I have to think all the time how to handle each kid. They are good children, but their needs are not the same. I used to feel that in my pregnancies and each time, I wondered what kind of child I would deliver. If each acted differently inside me, how would they act after they were born. I talked to the midwife, Mrs. Colangelo, about this many times, and all she could offer was 'Well, Angela, we'll have to wait and see.'

"I waited, and now I can see what she meant. I make many different kinds of lasagnas, like most Italian women—we like to try different combinations. Of course there are the classics such as lasagna alla Bolognese, or alla Napolitano, or the *vincisgrassi le Marchigiani*, but each cook ends up making her own version; and to tell the truth, you never know what it tastes like until it comes out of the oven and you taste it. And you need the patience. The best lasagna is made with lasagna pasta made at home. That takes time, but it is worth it. It will make a big difference in the quality of the finished dish. I believe every Italian cook will agree to that. Everyone I know precooks the lasagna pasta, even when it is homemade. The fillings have to be carefully made and the layering of pasta and filling takes time and care. Oh, how we love our lasagna. So you can see why I say that raising children is like making lasagna."

As the years went by, we realized that if one of us was not up to Mama's standards at any time, it was not for her lack of trying. When we looked back, we realized that we could not come up with many instances when one of us needed severe discipline. We recalled the time Charlie erased the date of his birth on his birth certificate to make himself four years older in order to get a driver's license (despite the fact we had no car). Mama was livid. Another time, Sister Bea skipped school to see Frank Sinatra at the Paramount Theatre in New York City. "You knew you were going to the Paramount. Why did you take the school lunch money?" Mama demanded when she found out. She was so upset over this transgression, she even cried. (At the time, Bea was a freshman at Julia Richmond High School on East Sixty-Eighth Street, where her classmate was Betty Persky, later known as Lauren Bacall.)

Mama was always receptive to any friend we brought into our home. There never was a question about why we might be hanging out with Andy, Charlie, Dan, Sophie, or Doris. Looking back now, Mama liked some of our friends more than others, but she never shared her reservations with us. Because our parents trusted our judgment about our friends, we worked hard to find companions who met their expectations. This raised our standards for friendship. There was always food for our friends and always a cookie, often those made in Sienna. These are delicious cookies. Mama didn't make them too often because they were always available in the downtown New York pastry shops. Since Papa worked in that area, he frequently stopped and returned home with a white bakery box tied with red and white string and filled with cookies. Mama liked having these cookies around for us kids and our friends. Later in life, when she had more time, she made them more often herself.

When my sister Mary was to be married, I was almost thirteen and wanted a suit with long pants for the wedding. Mama agreed it was time to leave the knickers behind, and so some weeks before the wedding, we marched into Orbachs department store on West Fourteenth Street. Standing in front of several racks of young men's suits, my mother asked me to choose one. I saw a gray plaid—something I really wanted—but when I glanced at the ticket price, I knew I could never ask my mother to spend the money. I put my hand on one and then another suit, all considerably lower in price than the gray plaid. Finally, Mama looked at me and said, "Joey, I have faith in your judgment. I want *you* to pick out the suit you think is best for you." We left with the gray plaid and a shopping experience I have recalled fondly all my life. Yes, I liked the suit, but more importantly, my mother's confidence in me has lasted a lifetime.

I was to get another surprise that day. After we bought the suit, we took a cab to Twenty-Eighth Street and Third Avenue to a restaurant called Lombari's. I was stunned because Mama rarely ate in restaurants—Why spend all that money, and for what? was her reasoning. As it turned out, the restaurant's owner's wife worked with Mama at the dress factory, and when we walked through the door, she met us with enthusiasm. "Angela! What a wonderful surprise. Joey, sit down. I like your mother so much, and it's so good to see her away from the shop." This greeting was followed by antipasti, two bowls of soup, and then pasta with meat sauce, and loaves of crispy Italian bread. Always polite, Mama tasted everything and encouraged me to fill up, and I was more than happy to oblige. Mama tried to pay for the meal, but her friend insisted it was "Impossible . . . you're in my home now, Angela." Mama scored again.

When we got home, she was mum about the restaurant meal, and I took my cue from her. Some moments remain between mother and son.

Angela's Wild Greens Soup with Potatoes

Zuppa di verdure selvatiche con patate all' Angela

Serves 6

1 ½ pounds fresh wild greens, such as chicory, dandelion, radish greens, mustard, or sorrel
½ cup extra-virgin olive oil
2 pounds white potatoes, peeled and cut into ½-inch dice and dried with kitchen toweling
2 large cloves garlic, minced
6 cups homemade chicken or mixed broth, or 3 cups canned with 3 cups water
Salt and freshly ground black pepper
½ cup freshly grated Parmesan cheese
¼ cup finely chopped fresh flat-leaf parsley mixed with 1 teaspoon lemon juice

1. Pick over the greens, removing any dead leaves, tough stems, etc., and rinse thoroughly (a salad spinner basket is a good way to do this). Cut the greens in one-inch pieces and set aside. You may use one kind of greens, such as dandelions, or a combination of any of those mentioned above.
2. Heat the oil in a large soup pot, add the potatoes, and cook, uncovered, over medium heat until the potatoes take on a little color but do not stick to the pot, about ten minutes. Stir frequently. Add the garlic, stir well, and cook, one minute.
3. Add the broth (and the chicken or beef cube, if you wish), raise the heat, and bring to a boil. Lower the heat to get a slow, steady simmer and cook covered until the potatoes are al dente, about twenty minutes. Add the greens, stir well, and cook, covered, until the greens are tender, about five minutes. Do not overcook the greens.
4. To serve, spoon the soup into warm bowls. Add some Parmesan and dot with the parsley mixture. Serves 6.

Duck Lasagna with Porcini and Truffles

Lasagne di anitra con porcini e tartufo

Serves 12 as first course; 6 as main course

1 cup finely chopped porcini (dried Italian mushrooms)
½ cup dry sherry
24 lasagna noodles
6 cups rich duck stock
2 cups chopped duck meat
1 black truffle (1-inch thick), cut into julienne strips, ½ inch by 1⁄16 inch or several drops of truffle olive oil
¾ cup grated Parmesan cheese
4 tablespoons butter, in ½-inch pieces

1. Soak the mushrooms in sherry for one hour, or until they swell to original size.
2. Cook six strips of lasagne pasta, four minutes. Drain in colander, which *sits in another pan in order to catch the water for reuse.* Carefully transfer each strip to cotton kitchen toweling and pat dry. Boil the same cooking water again and cook six more strips. Drain and pat dry and cook until all pasta is cooked.
3. Preheat oven to 350°F. To assemble and bake, use a baking dish nine by eleven inches or twelve inches oblong, two inches deep. Put a little stock in the bottom of the baking dish and lay three strips of pasta at a time slightly overlapping lengths. There will be about seven or eight layers of pasta. Over each layer, pour some broth then add some duck meat, Parmesan cheese, and mushrooms. After four layers, add some truffles or truffle oil. Add remaining truffles or oil to the top layer. Dot with butter every other layer.
4. Cover with foil and bake, thirty to forty minutes. Let stand ten minutes before serving.

Note: To make duck stock, use a three- to four-pound duck, cut into quarters. Allow to cool just to a point where you can handle it, then remove enough breast, thigh, and leg meat and dice. If truffles are not available, use a few drops of truffle oil instead.

Veal Shanks Limone

Osso buco al limone

Serves 4

4 veal shanks, cut into 1 ¾- to 2-inch-thick slices
4 tablespoons peanut oil
4 tablespoons butter
Flour for dredging veal
2 large cloves garlic, chopped fine
3 celery stalks, including leaves sliced fine
2 medium-size onions, sliced fine
3 carrots, scraped and sliced fine
1 ½ cups dry white wine
2 cups beef broth
2 teaspoons fresh thyme (or 1 teaspoon dried)
4 tablespoons lemon zest, diced very fine
Salt and freshly ground pepper
2 tablespoons fresh parsley, preferably flat Italian type, chopped

1. Be sure your butcher saws through the bones.
2. In a heavy covered saucepan large enough to hold the shanks in one layer (or a large Dutch oven or enameled iron saucepan), heat the oil and butter. Flour the shanks and add them to brown well on all sides (fifteen to twenty minutes); they should be a deep, rich brown. This is an important step, so don't skimp. The shanks won't brown once you add the rest of the ingredients.
3. Add the garlic, celery, onions, and carrots. Move the shanks to the side of the pan, stacking them, or remove them from the pan. Stir the vegetables to brown them partially, about ten minutes. Rearrange the shanks in one layer, cover them with the vegetables, and add the wine, broth, thyme, and two tablespoons lemon zest. Salt and pepper to taste. Cover and cook at a low simmer for one

and a half to two hours. (Veal shanks are served well cooked and tender to the point that the meat can be separated from the bone with a fork.) After about forty-five minutes, turn the shank over, stir the vegetables, and baste, if necessary. When they are done, transfer the shanks to a serving platter and keep them warm.

4. Turn the heat to high and boil sauce until it is reduced and is the thickness you prefer. Pour this sauce over the cooked shanks. Sprinkle the remaining two tablespoons lemon zest and the chopped parsley overall and serve the dish with risotto.

Note: An important part of this dish is the marrow inside the bones. If you can, supply marrow forks so that your guests can dig out the marrow. If you don't have these forks, you will figure out a way to improvise; the marrow is that good.

Famous Cookies from Siena

Biscotti da Siena

Makes 16 to 20 cookies

2 large egg whites, room temperature, beaten until foamy
7 ounces pure almond paste, such as Odense or Betty Crocker
1 cup confectioners' sugar
1 teaspoon almond extract
2 teaspoons minced orange zest
Confectioners' sugar for dusting

1. Preheat oven to 275°F. Line two baking sheets with parchment.
2. It is easiest to whip the egg whites in a mixer with a balloon whisk. Be sure the bowl is absolutely clean. These egg whites are not to be beaten to the soft stage, or to peaks—they are simply beaten to become foamy, but they should triple to quadruple in volume. Set aside. They will not be pure white as in meringue—if they get to that stage, they have been whipped too much.

3. If the almond paste is in a block or formed like a sausage, it should be cut into one-half-inch cubes and put in the bowl of a processor and pulsed until softened. It should look like a smooth paste.
4. Add the cup of confectioners' sugar and the foamy egg whites and mix until smooth. Add and blend in the almond extract and zest.
5. By teaspoonfuls, drop the mixture onto the parchment sheets, spacing them at least one inch apart. Bake until they become a very light tan or beige and firm to the touch, about twenty-five minutes.
6. Be sure to cool the cookies on the baking sheets. The cookies should cool completely before they are removed. If they are not cool, some of the bottoms will stick to the parchment. Sprinkle with confectioners' sugar before serving. If storing them, place them in airtight containers.

6

OUR CRAZY FOODIE PAPA

When Papa died in 1972, he had been married to Mama for fifty-nine years, some very happy times and some unhappy. He was born on Mott Street in lower Manhattan, a building torn down many years ago, then brought to Italy as a young boy because of his father's health. He enjoyed his teen years in Italy and talked often of wild excursions to Foggia with other boys his age. When in Italy, he lived in a small village, Ruoti, a suburb of Potenza. When he was twenty-two, he came back to America with his parents, both of whom are buried in Naugatuck, Connecticut, and took a job with the New York City Department of Sanitation. Shortly thereafter, he moved into the Department of Water Supply, where he remained until he retired many years later. As a city employee, he claimed, "I never missed a day's pay," a claim made by most city workers. Papa would add, "If you vote for Tammany Hall, you get and keep the job."

He was ten years older than Mama when they married in 1913 and clung to old-fashioned Italian values about wife and children. For example, we were not allowed to celebrate New Year's Eve outside our home, and smoking was not permitted at any time until many, many years later. He, in the meantime, smoked De Nobili cigars.

Although he did not like priests, he did not discourage Mama from raising us as Roman Catholics. Each of us was baptized and confirmed at St. Albert's on West Forty-Seventh Street. He said priests ate too much and drank too much (wine). One of his favorite stories had to do with serving Mass in Italy—when he poured water into the priest's glass, the priest would move the glass upward, an indication for him to stop pouring; when he poured wine, he said the priest always lowered the glass to be sure it became full.

He acted out scenes about the Catholic Church. He would imitate my mother's cousin who went to church and received communion daily. He described Aunt Margaret as going down the aisle to receive communion with her arms stretched downward in front of her with her hands placed together, thumbs and index fingers of each hand touching their mates' to form an oval. He said Aunt Margaret was demonstrating the look of a vagina for the priest. The only times I saw Papa in church was at weddings, baptisms, and funerals, but he would imitate priests saying and singing parts of the Mass.

Shortly before he died, he told us he wanted a High Mass for his funeral, with three priests officiating. We thought he was joking, but when he died, we thought it best to follow through with his wishes. As I sat close to his casket at his funeral Mass, I kept wondering if we had done the right thing.

Although he wanted to appear irreverent, he was basically a good, kind man. He loved children and would never strike us or any other child. Once, when Mama was scolding one of her daughters, her hand slipped and struck our sister on the head. When Papa saw this, he upset the household, reprimanding Mama and demanding that it should never happen again.

One time, though, I thought I was going to be killed by him for doing something I wasn't supposed to. Papa always had a brief meal before our regular supper—his city job usually brought him home two or three hours before Mama got home from work. He was sitting at the kitchen table, and I was going out the kitchen door, which led to the hallway downstairs. I was about ten years old, standing there in the doorway and picking my nose. He threw a round loaf of Italian bread at me. The bread was spinning at high speed, and I thought it would cut off my head—a picture I have never forgotten. "Don't you ever pick your nose while I am eating!" he yelled, and, believe me, I heeded his command from that time on.

Papa wasn't emotional about any one of his children, but we knew he cared. There were often little rewards from him: a nickel or an Oh Henry! chocolate bar, not for any special reason or to reward outstanding behavior on our part but just because he was in a giving mood, a mood that was part of him all his life.

He loved people and often brought home a guest for supper with no notice for Mama. She usually didn't object to this, and they would pull a supper together, with Mama doing the major share of the work. For them, preparing a meal was not difficult—thanks to our many stored provisions. They could always open a jar of preserved homemade sausage to fry with peppers and potatoes. Papa's special spaghetti dish was made with a quick sauce of olive oil, garlic, fresh ginger, and minced carrot pieces, salt, pepper, and red pepper flakes. We always said he crossed over into Chinatown when he lived on Mott Street, and that is how the ginger got into his sauce, but he always claimed it was a legitimate ingredient in southern Italy. This has been written about by Waverley Root, the noted food authority in his *The Food of Italy,* and he said that ginger is such a popular spice in southern Italian cooking; it is often left out of the ingredient list. This dish was so good we called it Papa's Immortal Quick Pasta with Ginger and Garlic. It is amazing how quickly this pasta can be pulled together. Papa heated the sauce ingredients, and they cooked in less than fifteen minutes. While the sauce was cooking, he boiled pasta with a quick drain and married them by uniting them in the same skillet with the sauce. It became well known by all our friends.

Years later, Craig Claiborne of the *New York Times* heard about this dish, and he devoted his entire column De Gustibus to the recipe. My brothers and sisters and I have received, over the years, many requests for this recipe from people who lost the recipe from the *Times* and were hoping to get a copy from us.

Papa was a collector of people. It never seemed to matter where you were from, what skin color you might have, or your social or economic status. "Signora stracciatella" was a nickname he gave to a neighbor, a woman everyone called Nick because her clothing had the overall appearance of "torn to rags"—that is, "stracciatella." She was in her fifties, lived alone, and made her living working on transoceanic liners. The exact nature of her occupation was never clear to us, but we would guess a stevedore—she certainly looked the part. She wore tattered trousers, a loose navy-blue cardigan, which was often buttoned in a haphazard fashion, and always a wool-knit cap pulled to the middle of her forehead, covering most of her bobbed, shingle-style hair. She looked tough, especially when she held an Italian De Nobili cigar stub between her teeth; and Papa and she would spend hours talking about food, each with the De Nobili stub. I always thought Mama accepted her as one of Papa's buddies. We all accepted her and liked it especially when Papa would call her "La Rosa"—the rose—a genuine gesture on his part to make this woman sound soft and beautiful.

Another of Papa's unbelievable recipes was the one he made with horseradish. When he cooked this, we all were teary eyed—the horseradish made us cry. Papa always said, "Don't blame me. After the tears, you'll love it." And we did. When we made it, we'd always ask ourselves, "Are you crazy!"

This is a tough recipe only because it's not easy to find fresh horseradish in the markets. But if you see it, be brave and try this recipe. One has to be very careful in making this dish. Don't attempt it unless you know fresh horseradish is available. Many paisanos would not cook this often, as it was brutal on the eyes. Papa liked it because it was a challenge (also a competition response to Mama's cooking), and it made a rare and unusual condiment to accompany other foods—chicken, beef, and pork, for example.

Papa was set in many of his ways. During the years that Mama was working, our eldest sister, Mary, put his meal before dinner on the table according to instructions from Mama. Papa ate slowly—every bite of food was tasted and chewed, with almost every bite followed by a swallow of wine, usually homemade. He rarely spoke while he ate. He used a napkin in a special way to swipe his mouth after every bite. He opened the napkin each time and then folded it back before using it again immediately after the following bite. He didn't eat much at these in-between meals, but they were habitual. Often, he was accompanied by "La Rosa."

Papa was a light sleeper. He arose at six in the morning and put the stove, icebox, garbage pail, and Mama, and his six kids into action. He shuffled from bed to bed, pulling off covers as he sang, "La mattina e la madre della giornata . . ." (Morning is the mother of the day). We all thought that being a light sleeper meant that he slept with one eye open. Because the flat was designed so no one could enter a bedroom without first passing through Papa's room, he could be sure that none of his six kids, coming home late, could get past his room, even on tiptoes or knees. If you thought you were getting by, he'd snort, "Questa e l'ora di venire a casa?" (Is this the hour to get home?) The midnight sermons on this subject never changed in composition or delivery, regardless of the trespasser or the hour of the night.

Papa's special piece of kitchen equipment was always on the stove—Mama could use it, and we could also; but it was his *macchinetta* (small machine), or what we called "the Italian coffeepot." Others called it "the poor man's espresso pot." It is known all over the world as the moka pot and was designed by an Italian, Alfonso Bialetti, in 1933, and now included in the permanent collections at the Museum of Modern Art, the Cooper-Hewitt, and the London Design Museum. The design has become an art deco classic. It makes a strong espresso-type coffee, not really espresso but the closest thing to it. It made coffee for our family and guests. Mama and Papa drank it straight; we were allowed a teaspoon of it in a cup of warm milk.

We had three moka pots: two-cup, six-cup, and twelve-cup. Each pot has three parts: a bottom container that holds water and has a pressure valve (Papa always used warm water, as it shortened the brewing time); a middle perforated basket, known as the filter, that holds the ground coffee; and a top container, with another filter at the bottom, and a handle and lid, where the brewed coffee collects as the heat pushes it up through the grounds. Papa and Mama could make their coffee in this classic aluminum pot blindfolded. Later on, when stainless steel moka pots became available, the older aluminum ones were replaced. When half the brewed coffee was in the top section, the pot would gurgle, and it would instantly be moved off the heat source. Of course, there were times when Papa and Mama would hear the gurgling, and each would suggest that the other move the pot from the heat. If one had been keeping score, Mama would win (or lose) for moving the pot off the heat most. This became a source of jokes in the family, as each of us kids would try to imitate the gurgling. Sister Bea may have gotten credit for her gurgling, but she got booed for her unwillingness to clean the pot.

Papa did not use the kind of finely ground coffee needed for an espresso machine; his was coarser, so it wouldn't fall through the filter. When he added the coffee, he always said, "Don't overfill *il caffe*"—meaning, do not compact it. He became dramatic as he screwed the top onto the bottom. He made the task (to achieve a perfect seal) seem harder than it might be, and when he accomplished it, he would look at anyone in his audience and heave a heavy sigh.

Every morning before leaving the house, Papa added an ounce of spirits to the "espresso" cup and left merrily on his way.

Papa was definitely a foodie—I would say totally perdutamente. He loved to cook and was passionate about serving his special food to all of his kids' friends, his coworkers, neighbors, and relatives.

Who else would stuff squid the way he did? His "Calamari at Christmas" (and its variation) was a standout every Christmas Eve. Grandma praised him by saying she couldn't think of a way to improve it. One time, his friend Nick (La Rosa) wanted to learn how to clean a squid. We thought she was joking, but Papa took her request seriously.

He and La Rosa always talked to each other in Italian, and he taught her, "Lay the squid on this flat surface in front of you and stretch it lengthwise from left to right with the tentacles to your right."

La Rosa asked, "What are the tentacles?

Papa showed her, and she tried stretching the body as he described with the tentacles to the right.

"You take a sharp knife and cut just below the eyes because this will free the tentacles," he explained. "See, there are ten of them, and right in the center of those tentacles is the mouth. Pull or cut it off and throw it away."

La Rosa did as he said and did very well, as Papa said *brava* more than he needed to.

"La Rosa, try to pull some of the skin off the tentacles, but don't worry if you don't get it all off. We always use what you remove—we chop it up and put it in the stuffing. Now squeeze the body and pull the head up—the viscera will come out easily and throw it all away."

"Not the body, for sure," said La Rosa.

Papa said, "Of course not."

Papa continued, "Now pull out the transparent center bone—the quill or the chitinous pen—whatever one calls it, and what remains of the squid is called the sack. Wash this well and peel off the outer skin," explained Papa as he showed her how to do it.

"It's so purple and gray and like a membrane—it pulls off easily," said La Rosa with a broad smile of success.

"Wash it well," Papa said as he put it under running water and gave the sack to La Rosa.

She responded, "Well, if we're going to stuff this, we'll have to keep it and the others whole," putting into her mouth the De Nobili cigar she had left in a nearby ashtray.

"*Brava, brava.* You are a conqueror. Now we'll make a stuffing for them".

Papa's Immortal Quick Pasta with Ginger and Garlic

Pasta di Papa con zenzero e aglio

Serves 4 to 6

½ cup olive oil
½ cup finely diced carrot
1 tablespoon finely minced fresh garlic
2 tablespoons finely chopped fresh ginger
2 tablespoons finely chopped fresh scallions
1 teaspoon dried oregano
Salt to taste
¼ to ½ teaspoon dried red pepper flakes

½ cup white wine or dry vermouth
1 cup water
1 pound pasta, such as vermicelli, spaghettini, or spaghetti
4 tablespoons butter
Freshly grated Parmesan cheese

1. In a large pot, heat the water in which the pasta will boil.
2. Meanwhile, heat the oil in a saucepan and add the carrot. Cook about three minutes, stirring occasionally. Add the garlic, ginger, scallion, oregano, salt, pepper flakes, and wine or vermouth. Cook about five minutes.
3. Add one cup of water. Bring to a boil and simmer. Cook the sauce, fifteen minutes, no more.
4. When the pasta water is boiling, salt it and add the pasta. Cook, stirring, until pasta is al dente. Do not cook until soft.
5. Drain the pasta and return it to the same pot. Add the butter.
6. Add three-fourths of the ginger sauce. Toss.
7. Serve the pasta in hot bowls with equal portions of the remaining sauce (about one tablespoon to each serving) on top. Serve Parmesan cheese separately.

A Wild Horseradish Omelet

Rafanata
Serves 4 to 8

½ cup vegetable shortening, melted
1 cup grated fresh horseradish (*rafano*)
1 cup grated Parmesan cheese
1 small raw potato, peeled and grated
2 eggs, well beaten
1 teaspoon baking powder

1. Heat the shortening in a seven-and-a-half-inch skillet. Mix all the other ingredients in a bowl. With your hands, shape the mixture into a ball. Put into the hot shortening. Be very, very careful to lay

it in gently; hot shortening can splatter. Flatten the mixture with a wooden spoon to the approximate size of the skillet. Shortening will come up the sides of the skillet, and that is what is supposed to happen.

2. Over low heat, cook one side until omelet is well done, about five minutes. When the bottom is brown (edges will begin turning deep brown although top will remain off-white or pale cream), remove the pan from the heat and pour off and reserve as much of the shortening as you can without damaging the shape of the "pie."
3. Press a plate that is larger than the skillet against the pan and quickly turn the omelet over onto the plate. Put the shortening back into the skillet and slowly slip the omelet back in with the light side down. Cook another four or five minutes, or until this side is also browned.
4. Then decide which side is better looking and serve that side up. This frittata can be eaten cold, but the flavors are more fragrant and tastier if it is served hot.

Calamari at Christmas with Variation: Potato and Rice Stuffing for Calamari

Calamari Imbottito per Natale
Serves 4

To stuff the squid:

1 tablespoon olive oil
1 tablespoon butter
½ cup onion, chopped fine
Squid tentacles, chopped
¼ cup dry white wine
1 cup fresh bread crumbs
1 tablespoon orange zest, chopped fine
⅓ cup raisins
1 tablespoon grated Parmesan cheese

1 large egg, lightly beaten
Salt and freshly ground pepper
2 pounds fresh or frozen squid (about 8 medium or 12 small squid), whole

1. In a skillet, heat the olive oil and butter and sauté the onion and tentacles until they are lightly browned. Transfer them to a mixing bowl.
2. Add the wine to the skillet and deglaze the pan over high heat. With a rubber spatula, scrape the skillet liquid into the mixing bowl. Add the bread crumbs, orange zest, raisins, cheese, egg, and salt and pepper to taste, and stir together with the onions and tentacles. (This stuffing mixture should be fairly dry but well blended; if it is too dry, add more white wine by teaspoonfuls.)
3. Stuff the cleaned and washed squid a little more than half full. (Do not fill them more than that.) Secure with a toothpick or sew loosely with white thread.

To cook the squid:

2 tablespoons olive oil
2 tablespoons butter
Stuffed squid from above
½ cup onion, chopped fine
1 small garlic clove, chopped fine
2 cups fresh tomatoes, cored, blanched, peeled, seeds removed, and chopped fine (or canned plum tomatoes, sieved)
¾ cups dry white wine
½ teaspoon dried oregano
Pinch of red pepper flakes (optional)
Salt and freshly ground pepper
2 tablespoons fresh flat Italian parsley, chopped

1. In a skillet, heat one tablespoon olive oil and one tablespoon butter. When they are hot and bubbling, add the squid and sauté over low heat. (The squid will enlarge as they sauté, so keep the heat low.) As the squid begin to turn color—they will become

whitish, almost translucent—remove them from the skillet, transfer them to a dish, and set them aside.

2. In a large covered saucepan or heavy enameled pan, heat the remaining one tablespoon oil and one tablespoon butter. Sauté the onions until they are pale yellow (about four minutes). Add the garlic and cook for one additional minute.
3. Add the tomatoes, wine, oregano, red pepper flakes, salt, and pepper to taste. Cook over high heat, about five minutes, stirring frequently. Add the sautéed squid to the tomato mixture in a single layer (if at all possible) and cover the pan. Cook the squid over low heat, thirty minutes, or until done.
4. Serve on a platter garnished with chopped fresh Italian parsley.

Potato and Rice Stuffing for Calamari

Calamari ripiene

Serves 4

2 tablespoons olive oil
2 tablespoons butter
⅓ cup onion, chopped fine
Squid tentacles, chopped fine
1 cup cooked rice
¾ cup raw potatoes, shredded
¼ cup grated Parmesan cheese
2 tablespoons fresh flat Italian parsley, chopped
1 egg, lightly beaten
Salt and freshly ground pepper

1. In a skillet, heat the oil and butter and sauté the onion until it is softened. Add the tentacles and cook for four minutes, or until the onion is lightly browned. Add the cooked rice, potatoes, cheese, parsley, egg, and salt, and pepper to taste. Mix thoroughly and remove from heat. You will have almost two cups of stuffing for your calamari.
2. Follow the rest of the procedure for cooking the squid on the stovetop.

7

THE GREASED POLE

Sundays were special days in our home. If we were at home, as we usually were, except for picnics and outings three or four times a year, we would sit, eat a really full meal, and talk, talk, talk.

Every Sunday morning, Papa made his weekly trek downtown to Ferrara's Pastry Shop to bring back a boxful of Italian pastries that always included *sfogliatelle* and cannoli. Often he would go further downtown to Allen Street for fresh kosher chickens to be brought home alive. Mama would use an old ax to sever the chickens' heads on the stone kitchen windowsill. Other days, vegetables were sold from wagons drawn by horses. The vegetable man, competition for Manuel's Grocery, would yell from the street; and at the sound of his voice, Mama would run down to buy vegetables, knowing they were as fresh as anyone could expect them to be.

And there were other salespeople who traveled to the block. Once a week, another horse-drawn cart came by selling *materassi* (mattresses). On late Saturday afternoons, a Mr. Spagnola came to sell jewelry and collect weekly payments for previously sold items. There was also a linen-and-towel seller who brought goods once a month for Mama to view.

Another monthly event was Papa's picnic.

Papa never missed a picnic given by the Societa Sociale dei Ruotiese—an organization of paisanos from Papa's Italian hometown. Though Papa was the secretary of the organization, it was my task to send out the monthly postcard invitations, a nonpaid job. Not all the invitations sent were for the picnics. Many of them were for "business" meetings—meaning, the business of all male card players playing "scopa" with one hand and drinking beer with the other. Some unhappy times in our household came when Papa returned home with too many beers under his belt. Papa was never an unhappy drunk and would never become violent. But he could become loud and insistent about some point of view about one thing or another, almost always to Mama's annoyance and exasperation.

The picnics, however, were memorable. Food, food, and more food were prepared for these outings. We didn't have the luxury of a car, so all the food, packed in shopping bags, were carried on the subways. The meals we ate al fresco were bountiful: soup, lots of pasta with various sauces, meatballs and sausage, cabbage with spareribs, several kinds of roasted or grilled meats, veal scaloppine, roasted potatoes in olive oil with rosemary or oregano, broccoli with olive oil and garlic, roasted red peppers, a variety of cheeses and fruit, plenty of homemade bread, a large box of Ferrara's pastry, and homemade wine. Three specific foods we had always on these outings were, first, Papa's special dish of cabbage and spareribs cooked together. Friends of ours still talk about this dish and say they make it. Papa said the secret to the recipe was to use Savoy cabbage after it had been hit by the frost, so he would never attempt this dish until late September, October, or November. We used to grow Savoy cabbage at our country place in upstate New York, and Papa would never pick the cabbage until it has been blessed by the frost. Often the cabbage was split, but that didn't matter to him. This remains one of the tastiest dishes we enjoyed growing up American/Italian. Our friends asked for it (and the recipe) all the time. When Papa described making this dish, he always cautioned that when adding the dripping cabbage to the hot oil, do it slowly or it will splatter and you'll get burned.

The second staple was veal scaloppine with fried peppers. Veal of this cut marries beautifully with lemon, orange, Marsala, vermouth, capers, tomatoes, cured meats, cheeses, and a wide array of herbs and spices. The fried peppers add so much to the tender thin veal. Cooking veal scaloppine that has been properly cut is one of the simplest things one can do in the kitchen, and one of the fastest. It is easy in the United States to buy this meat, plastic wrapped, in the refrigerated meat sections in supermarkets, but what is in those packages has not been properly cut. It is best to ask your butcher to cut the scaloppine from the top round, from the upper part of the hind leg, and to cut across the muscle's grain. Cut this way, the meat can be pounded properly. The reason for cutting across the grain is so the meat will stay flat while it is sautéing. This of course can be served at the kitchen or dining table, but don't think you can't carry it to a picnic, eat it in your backyard, or carry it to the beach. You don't need knives and forks on these outings, just some thinly sliced Italian bread to make sandwiches.

The third regular dish was spaghetti with garlic and chili. It is best served at room temperature, so it works very well if you are carrying food to any kind of outing. Easy on the red pepper flakes unless you want it especially spicy.

Mama and Papa made this dish a lot at home. They liked the way it tasted, as did the rest of us, and they both said it was one of the easiest preparations to pull together.

We always wondered what Mama was thinking as she cooked this dish. She cooked it so many times and did it so automatically, there must be something beside the recipe going on in her mind. Sister asked her one day, "What are you thinking about, Mama, as you cook this dish?" Mama answered readily. "Oh, a whole lot of things go through my mind. Comara Lucia was telling me the other day about her unmarried daughter, Filomena, who is now thirty-nine and sees a Mr. B. on the sly. Lucia didn't tell me who he was, but we all know who he is. I was wondering what I would do in Lucia's situation, and I concluded I would leave it alone—I would not interfere. Filomena is old enough to know what she is doing. But I know one thing: Mr. B. will never leave his wife and three children for her. Filomena is a nice girl, but she doesn't do very much. She had trouble completing elementary school, and, let's face it, she's not what one would call attractive. Sometimes I feel sorry for her, but she has to have a life. I think Mr. B is the foolish one. He's an old-style Italian cat, who thinks he can stray and that no one will know and that he can get away with it. Can you imagine, if his wife did such a thing, how he would behave about it? I have no patience with him. I suppose, at some point, it will all dissolve," she said as she stirred one-half pound of spaghetti she had put in salted boiling water a few minutes before.

Mama then prepared the garlic for the dish, checked to be sure she had some hot pepper flakes nearby, and put the oil in the skillet but did not heat it yet. She pulled a string of spaghetti out of the water, bit on it, and shook her head to say it wasn't cooked yet. She stirred the spaghetti pot. And she started again with "You know, Mary, we have to keep life simple—if we have problems, we have to learn to solve them. We have to learn to keep our eyes on what matters. We must get rid of the chaff. If someone hurts you, get over it—there's no gain in trying to get even—you lose a great deal of time that way. You know I love you, kids, and you are my first responsibility.

"We all know life is tough, but it's easier if you solve your problems first, keep your family happy—I want all of you to eat well and grow up strong—and then I can help others more easily."

Mama drained the pasta, saved a cup of the cooking water, and put it aside. She heated the oil in a large skillet, added the minced garlic, and cooked it for a few seconds, just to toast it. She took the skillet off the heat, added the red pepper flakes, stirred them into the oil, and returned the pan to the heat. She added the drained pasta and most of the cooking liquid in the cup and tossed the spaghetti over the heat. She said, "Mary, listen to the pasta cooking. In the south of Italy, they call this dish *cifutti* because as it cooks, it sounds like someone saying 'cifutti.'" She added some pepper and a bit of salt after she tasted a strand of spaghetti. "Mary, Mary, come over here and listen," she said as she gave the pasta another toss. "What does it sound like?"

Mary looked up at her and said, "Cifutti, cifutti, cifutti."

"Oh, get me some grated Pecorino for the pasta," she said in a slightly admonishing tone to her firstborn daughter.

At these annual summer picnics, the main competition was the climb up the greased pole for the provolone, sausages, and other goodies dangling from the top. Grown men, usually the papas, participated in this contest. The pole was thickly layered with grease, and to this day, none of us can figure out how any of them was able to reach the top. But many of them did, including Papa. The task was so difficult, only six or seven men would try it, and no one was able to get more than one or two prizes, so there were always some left for the next contender. At home, when Papa prepared a meal, he made it an event. The meal was usually simple—one dish with Italian bread on the side. First, all ingredients were gathered and set aside. Then Papa covered himself with a half apron, sometimes one of Mama's frilly ones. He was a natural born actor, and when he cooked, he was on stage. When he added an ingredient to the pan, he did so with flourish. He didn't sing; he hummed. When he tasted food as it cooked, he removed the pan's cover dramatically. Before that, though, he would tap the spoon on the counter to get everyone's attention, then he'd taste the food and grimace as if he had burned his tongue. When he was the cook, he made a big deal of serving his food with a clean folded kitchen towel over his left forearm. Mama's parents usually joined our family for the picnics. They did some cooking, after consulting with Mama, and what they prepared was added to what had been cooked at our place. Those lazy summer afternoons were so much fun for us kids. The greased-pole event didn't happen until late in the afternoon, so there was plenty of time to eat, visit, and talk with people who came over to see what Mama and Papa had brought to eat. Then we would have to listen to them describe what they had brought. One of the most interesting parts of the afternoon was usually when Grandpa would take over the conversation. His topic almost always was food. This story about how they killed pigs in his hometown made us sit upright. Most of the women did not want to hear these stories, but we hung on every word. Grandpa said this took place at a neighbor's farm because that farm was set up properly. What he meant was it had a big butchering table, large pots for boiling water over heavy fires, other necessary pots, pans, and bowls, and so on. He described his friend who did the butchering as a man named Giovanni who owned the butcher shop. Grandpa's job was to be one of four men who secured the pig for slaughter—a very difficult thing to do according to Grandpa. We were sure he was right, and we were happy that we would never do that and that this was only a tale of olden times.

"Sometimes, we could hardly hear ourselves over the noise of the pigs—it was as if they knew they were going to be slaughtered," explained Grandpa. "The pig was hauled to the butchering table amid hysterical squeals where the butcher had to find the main artery in the pig's neck. The pigs head was hanging over the table as the butcher proceeded with the small knife. Having found the artery, he made a small but definite cut. Someone held a large bowl underneath to catch the blood." Grandpa further explained that the pig's head went limp, but the pig's heart continued to beat—this was important, as they needed all the blood to drain out. "The pig was in no pain," said Grandpa.

The bowl of blood was given to some women waiting inside the barn building, and the next outdoor task was to pour small pans of hot boiling water over the pig's skin. With more small knives, the men scraped the skin to remove the hairs until pure white pig's skin appeared. Then the head had to be cut off and all the innards removed—not one scrap to be wasted. We sighed heavily, thinking how happy we were to have eaten two hours before. But we were intent on hearing Grandpa's story, for he told it as if it had occurred the day before. He added, they usually butchered two pigs, one after the other.

Then he recounted all the products they made and how they filled their cantina with salamis, coppas, and sausages. We looked at Grandpa as a gladiator with his foot on a freshly killed lion. We were grateful that we would never have to participate in such a slaughter, but we knew it was necessary if we were to enjoy the resulting bounty of foods.

Grandma never added a word. She had not participated except in the actual making of the sausages and salamis. Grandpa did his job; she did hers. There was no argument over this. Sometimes, instead of various roasted meats, we'd bring a whole roasted suckling pig. This size suckling pig was bought at Esposito's on Ninth Avenue, in New York City. It was ordered a day or two ahead. Mr. Esposito and his family sold many of these suckling pigs, which were favorites with the Italians in the neighborhood. Mr. Esposito said people came down from Harlem, from New Jersey and Connecticut, and elsewhere to buy these animals from him.

At these picnics, we would run into a woman, Lucia Colucci, a very large woman with large eyes, one of them slightly crossing the other. She seemed like a pleasant person, but we ignored her because we had heard rumors that she had been Grandpa's mistress while Grandma was in Italy waiting for Grandpa to send the fare to bring her and Mama and Aunt Mary to America. Lucia was unattractive compared to Grandma, who had normal eyes, small features, beautiful pink coloring, beautiful hair that had turned white early in her life, and the most pleasant disposition of anyone in the family. It was also rumored that Lucia was an awful cook, and that in itself made us disbelieve any possibility of a relationship with our grandpa. When you are young, you don't want to believe or think of such dalliances.

As children, we enjoyed these outings. As we approached our teens, we became more selective; and when we tried to get out of going, Mama or Papa would always suggest our bringing along one or more of our friends who ended up thoroughly enjoying themselves. They raved on and on about Mama and Papa's food, the idea of community, and the excitement of the events. Mama and Papa were delighted by the raves, but inside their hearts, they felt they had bested us. By including our friends, they had gotten us to go.

This was how our parents did things. Of course, eventually, we came to understand their technique and would pull out for other events, but rarely would we miss the picnics. Laughing, we filled our bellies with spaghetti and garlic and chili, Papa's spicy Savoy cabbage with spareribs, Mama's scaloppini with fried Italian peppers, and more. Any wonder most of us fell asleep on the subway ride home.

Spicy Savoy Cabbage with Spareribs

Verza picante con costine di maiale

Serves 6

1 medium head Savoy cabbage
2 tablespoons extra-virgin olive oil
8 pork spareribs (about 1 ¼ pounds), cut into 8 ribs
2 cloves garlic, minced
¼ teaspoon red pepper flakes
6 cups homemade chicken broth or 3 cups canned with 3 cups water
Salt
¾ cup freshly grated Pecorino cheese

1. Trim and core cabbage and cut into eight wedges. Put cabbage in a large bowl, add a teaspoon of salt, and cover with cold water. Let stand, thirty minutes.
2. Heat olive oil in a large soup pot over medium heat and sauté ribs until they are lightly browned, about ten minutes. Turn the ribs two or three times to cook all sides. Add garlic and cook one minute. Add red pepper.
3. Bring the bowl of cabbage in water next to the soup pot. Lift the dripping wet cabbage by hand and carefully put it into the soup pot. As Papa always said, look out for the spatter. Add one cup of the cabbage water to the pot. Bring to boil, partially covered, over high heat. Reduce the heat to medium and cook until the cabbage is limp and bright green, about fifteen minutes.
4. Add the broth. Check salt seasoning. Cook, partially covered, until the cabbage is very tender, about thirty minutes. To serve, put a rib, some cabbage, and broth in the soup bowls. Put some cheese on top, and be sure there is some good Italian bread to be served with this dish.

Scaloppine in the Milanese Style with Fried Peppers

Scaloppine alla Milanese con peperoni fritti

Serves 6

To prepare the peppers:

- 3 tablespoons olive oil
- 2 small garlic cloves, halved
- 1 ½ pounds green Italian peppers, wiped clean, cored, seeded, and cut into one-fourth-inch lengths
- Salt
- Pepper, ground fresh

1. In a large skillet, heat the olive oil. When it is hot, add the garlic pieces and brown them lightly. As the garlic cooks, press down on each piece with a wooden spoon to extract some garlic juice. When they are done, remove and discard the garlic pieces.
2. Add the pepper slices and fry them until they soften (they should be soft but not mushy) and somewhat charred. Salt and pepper to taste.
3. Transfer the peppers to a serving platter and keep them warm.

To prepare the veal:

- 1 ½ pounds scaloppine of veal, cut from the leg in slices less than ¼-inch thick (there will be 7 to 9 slices of this size in 1 ½ pounds)
- ⅓ to ½ cup all-purpose flour
- Salt
- Pepper, ground fresh
- ⅓ cup olive oil
- 6 tablespoons butter
- 3 eggs
- ¼ cup cool water
- 2 cups fresh bread crumbs
- ¼ cup grated Parmesan cheese (or Romano)
- 2 whole lemons, each cut lengthwise into 6 wedges, seeded and cored

1. The veal slices should be very thin. Pound them until they are about four by six inches or five by seven inches each. Cut each slice into two or three pieces so that each scallop is now two by three inches or three by three inches.
2. It is easiest to flour the veal pieces only minutes before you are ready to cook them. Put the flour on a dinner plate and dredge each piece of veal.The easiest way to do this is to pick up the piece of veal at one corner with the thumb and index finger, touching as little of the meat as possible. Brush the piece of veal against the flour quickly and, gently on one side then on the other, shake the veal over the flour plate in quick short strokes to remove any excess. Lay the floured pieces of veal on wax paper.As soon as the pieces are floured , sprinkle them with salt and pepper to taste.
3. In the same skillet in which the peppers were cooked, heat half the oil and butter.While this is heating, combine the eggs and water and beat lightly. Also combine the bread crumbs and Parmesan cheese. Put the egg and the crumb-cheese mixtures into wide soup bowls and place the bowls close to the skillet. Pick up the floured veal, one piece at a time, dip it into the egg, then into the crumbs, and place it in the skillet. Repeat this until the skillet has one layer of veal pieces. Cook each piece two or three minutes on each side.
4. Transfer the cooked pieces to the serving platter on which you have put the fried peppers. When each batch is completed, coat and cook the next batch.Arrange the lemon wedges on the platter and serve hot.

Spaghetti with Garlic and Chili

Spaghetti con aglio e peperoncino

Serves 4

½ pound spaghetti
4 tablespoons extra-virgin olive oil
2 cloves garlic, minced

½ teaspoon red pepper flakes
½ cup freshly grated Pecorino cheese
Finely chopped Italian parsley for garnish

1. Bring water to boil in a large saucepan. Add a teaspoon of salt just before adding the spaghetti. Cook to al dente stage, eight to ten minutes. It is always best to consult the pasta manufacturer's instructions about cooking time, but it is also important to test along the way by forking a strand of pasta from the pot and tasting it. It should have "bite" between the teeth.
2. While pasta is cooking, heat oil in a large skillet. Add the garlic and pepper just before adding the spaghetti. Drain the pasta, reserving a half cup of the boiling water. Then quickly add the garlic to the hot oil and cook it less than a minute. Remove from the heat and add the red pepper flakes. Stir skillet then add the spaghetti. Toss lightly but well and return the skillet to the heat. Add a tablespoon or more of the cooking water to the skillet while tossing the pasta. Add salt and freshly ground black pepper if you wish.
3. Serve on individual plates, topping with some freshly grated Pecorino cheese and a sprinkle of parsley. Pass more cheese.

Whole Roasted Suckling Pig

Porchetta

Serves 10 to 12

1 whole suckling pig, 15 to 20 pounds, readied for oven-roasting
Cloves from 1 whole garlic bulb, peeled, ⅔ left whole, ⅓ minced
4 large branches of fresh rosemary
1 fennel bulb with leaves, coarsely chopped
1 tablespoon dried fresh fennel seeds, crushed
1 cup olive oil
½ cup red wine vinegar
1 whole apple

1. Preheat oven to 350°F. Put the pig in a large roasting pan. Liberally salt and pepper the roast, inside and out. Place three rosemary branches in the cavity of the pig along with the whole garlic cloves, fresh fennel, and two-thirds of crushed fennel seeds.
2. Combine oil and vinegar, minced garlic, and remaining fennel seeds and use this mixture to brush the roast before putting it in the oven. Continue to baste roast with this all during the cooking.
3. Bake five to six hours, basting every twenty minutes or so. To test for doneness, insert a long wooden skewer into the roast—if it meets no resistance upon entering, the roast is done. Remove from the oven and, when cooled for ten minutes or so, insert the apple in its mouth and serve.

8

THE MISSING BIRTH CERTIFICATE

One morning, Papa had to go downtown to the Bureau of Vital Statistics to get his birth certificate reissued. The original had burned with many thousands of others in a fire before 1900. He should have taken care of this far earlier in his life, but for some reason, he kept putting it off so that by now, it was a *cause célèbre.* I had been elected to go with him.

Early that morning, he woke me with "C'mon, pa-pa, pa-pa, get up. *E tardi!*"

"Gee, Papa, it's only five fifteen," I complained. "We don't have to be there until ten."

He was extremely finicky about being prompt. Being on time was not enough for him; he had to be early. When I left for my first year at college, he insisted on taking me to Pennsylvania Station in New York City (only a few minutes away from our flat) about three hours before the train's departure. No one, not even Mama, could change him.

He pushed some more. "C'mon, pa-pa, *il caffe e pronto*" (the coffee is made). Papa never called his children by their Christian names but instead referred to all of us as "pa-pa," his term for baby.

From where I lay, I could look into the girls' room, through Mama and Papa's room, and into the kitchen.

Although we complained about our lack of privacy, we enjoyed its compensations. Talking between rooms was a favorite nightly pastime and, as we got older and busier, tended to be the time we communicated most often. Our conversations bounced from wall to wall, room to room so that we were all kept abreast of the latest neighborhood news: who was getting married, who had died, and who got a job.

That morning, I lingered in bed, desperate for a few more minutes. During the summer, our windows were wide open, and West Forty-Sixth Street was the most peaceful place in the world at five thirty in the morning. And then, in a split second, the garbage trucks entered the block, and I listened to the grind of their motors and then clash of an ash can lid hitting the ground. The pause in front of our tenement always seemed to take forever. More cans, more bags full of garbage. Sometimes we could hear the guys on the trucks griping to themselves, "Jesus Christ, the goddamn slobs—all they do is eat."

Papa never seriously considered responding to this, but I remember him once saying, "What do those Irish bastards know about eating?"

The smell of coffee was enticing. The kitchen clock read six twenty when I finally made my way to it, again reminding my parent that we didn't have to be downtown until ten.

"Its a make no difference. We got to be there *oily*," Papa insisted, pronouncing the word "early" as only true New Yorkers can. "How many times I got to tell you, when you got to go someplace, start *oily*. What's one or two hours? This way, you sure you get there on time. I never miss the train in my life. When my mother, she makes me, I was not late."

We had heard this before, and I knew I would hear it again. And it was true. Papa was never late for anything.

The shirt he wore that morning was white, bleached to a dazzling brightness as it hung on the clothesline in the June sun. His hair was thinning on top and gray but still full on both sides. His eyes were blue-gray and his complexion pink. Papa called himself a white Italian, mostly to get Mama's goat because her skin was pure olive, her hair jet black, and her eyes deep brown.

While I drank some coffee, Papa dampened the corner of a Turkish towel and brushed each side of his mouth with short gentle strokes. Between strokes, I heard him mutter, "L'acqua non e calda stamattina" (The water is cold this morning). We were supposed to get hot water every day in our flat, but the landlady only delivered it on Sundays. This frequently prompted Papa to grumble, "Questa Siciliane miserabile" (This miserable Sicilian), to which he added, "She's the cheapest woman on the block!"

When we got to the street, that block was still filled with morning sunlight. Papa complained that he had forgotten his "schnapps"—his term for the shot of whiskey he mixed with a cup of hot coffee and which was guaranteed to get him through any event. We crossed Ninth Avenue, and he headed for the Rivoli Bar for a drink. Although I reminded him it didn't open until 8:00 a.m., he cupped his right hand over his eyebrows, reached high on his toes, leaned his face against the bar's front window, and glared through the large Victorian-lettered *O* part of "Rivoli." He rapped against the window with his left hand, hitting the Victorian *V*. His tap clearly had telegraphic powers because very quickly his friend and fellow drinker, Sam, the proprietor, unbolted the door and welcomed us inside.

Sam was one of Papa's foodies, and the two never seemed to tire of talking about food—unless the subject was the horses. As Papa walked the length of the bar, skimming his right hand over the bar rail, he explained that he needed his schnapps. "You're going to get me in trouble one of these days. You know da cops keep close watch on me," Sam told him as he led us to a mahogany booth in the back where we were hidden from front window. Sam's face was covered with gray whiskers, and his eyes reflected twenty-five years of drinking, bar tending, and preparing food for the bar. His apron smelled of spilled beer and tomato sauce, and when he spoke, tobacco breath overtook the air. It was easy to like Sam because he liked Papa. Before we left, Papa reviewed Sam's menu for the day; I heard Sam agree to his suggestions for menu changes.

Papa and Sam discussed roasting a farmed rabbit in wine to add to the menu for the next few days. The farmed rabbit would not require a marinade, although if Sam bought wild rabbit from Tony's Butcher Shop, he would have to soak it in red wine overnight—and that was too much trouble. They also decided that Sam would make broccoli rabe the way Papa did. This would be just right to serve with the roast rabbit.

He also would offer a soupy dish called stracciatella. Papa made this simple dish in the Roman style, although it was similar to Teresa Lofortes's Sicilian dish. The quality of the beef broth is critical for the soup, and we always believed the delicious soup showcased Papa's creative Italian hand in cooking.

By now, it was 7:45 a.m. We made our way down to the Bureau of Vital Statistics on lower West Broadway, with Papa keeping up a constant conversation about Sam's food for the day and the changes he had suggested. He also pointed out every heavy-pressure fire hydrant below Fourteenth Street, explaining the number, size, and capacity of each. It was his job to keep those between Fourteenth Street and Battery Park in good working order, a job he took seriously. As he often said, he never missed a day on the payroll.

He knew every saloon along the route as well. Papa thought the Clover Bar on Hudson Street had more historical significance than the Flatiron Building. He believed the life in the Empire Café on Bleecker Street had more impact on national affairs than anything that went on at the New York Stock Exchange. He was the visiting chef at these establishments, where he would alter the menus to his liking. He was sure of what he was doing and never hesitated to offer his opinion, which usually was on the mark.

During our meeting with the director of Vital Statistics, Papa was told to write to the village clerk in Ruoti, Italy, and request the records kept when, as young boy, he returned to Italy from America. I said I thought that would be a waste of time, but the director reprimanded me. "My dear boy," he said, "Italy keeps the best birth, marriage, entry and exit, and death records of any country in the Western World—you should know that. Do as I suggest, and when we get the response from them, come back here, and I'll reissue your father's birth certificate." Before we left, Papa told the director how he prepared Savoy cabbage, even scribbling a recipe on a scrap of paper for him. This cemented their relationship.

We took a cab to the Rivoli Bar. Papa wanted one short drink before going home, and Sam greeted us at the front door along with other noontime drinkers. "I got a hot tip while you were gone," Sam said. "Put the money on Wonder Brown in the fifth today."

"No, no, today my money is on Greek Boy," Papa said.

Sam looked perplexed, "Greek Boy, what the hell for?"

"Because I lika Greeks, thatsa why," he said. Papa then decided against the drink, reminded Sam about the menu changes, and put his arm around me as we walked to our block, where the sun hung high. "Hurry up," he said, "We don't wanna be late for Mama."

Mama first wrote a letter in Italian to someone she knew in Ruoti to get the name of the clerk; she then wrote to a Mr. Bartolucci, the village clerk. About a month later, we received a large package with copies of all essential data on Papa's family, dating back to the early 1800s. Each document had red ribbons, gold seals, and authentication by the American Consulate in Naples. Among them was the document showing Papa's entry into Italy and, on it, his date of birth in New York, New York. There was a cover letter from Mr. Bartolucci describing his search and how he had discovered he and Papa were sixth cousins.

We were overjoyed, and the New York Bureau of Vital Statistics reissued Papa's birth certificate. It was safely stored in the bank vault, but from then on, Papa carried a copy to show everyone. Mama and Mr. Bartolucci exchanged recipes and letters for quite a few years.

Papa's Stracciatella

Stracciatella di Papa

Serves 6 to 8

8 cups homemade beef or mixed broth

3 eggs, room temperature

¼ cup freshly grated Parmesan cheese

¼ cup fine semolina or cream of wheat or farina

Salt

Freshly grated nutmeg (use less rather than more)

1. Put the broth in a medium soup pot over medium heat and bring to a boil. Lower the heat and keep the broth simmering.
2. Whisk the eggs in a large bowl. Add the cheese, semolina, salt, nutmeg, and whisk until well blended.
3. Remember, before adding the egg, the broth should be hot and simmering. Pour the egg mixture into the broth, stirring with the whisk all the time as you add the eggs, until the egg mixture resembles snowflakes, two to three minutes.

Papa's Broccoli Rabe

Rabe piccante
Serves 4 to 6

NOTE: Broccoli rabe is a bitter-flavored cousin of broccoli. The stalks are thin and long, and the leaves resemble those of regular broccoli. But broccoli rabe does not have the large, tightly closed heads of broccoli; instead, they have tufts of flowerets here and there throughout the stalks.

4 cups broccoli rabe
¾ cup cooking liquid
⅓ cup olive oil
1 clove garlic, chopped fine
1 dried hot chili pepper (optional)
Salt and freshly ground pepper

1. Wash the broccoli rabe well and cut off the root ends. Remove the strings on the larger stalks just as you would on a large celery stalk. Cut the larger broccoli rabe leaves in half. If you are not ready to cook them, let them stand in cool water.
2. In a large saucepan, bring two or three cups of water to boil. Add one teaspoon salt and bring the water to a rapid boil. Add the broccoli rabe and cook them until they are just tender (not beyond the al dente point). Depending on the size and freshness of the stalks, this will take five to ten minutes.

3. Remove them from the boiling water immediately and transfer them to a bowl. A fork or slotted spoon works best for this. Reserve about three-fourths cup of the water in which the broccoli rabe was cooked.
4. In a large saucepan, heat the olive oil and sauté the garlic until it turns pale yellow. (Do not let it brown.) Add the hot chili pepper (if you wish). Now add the cooked broccoli rabe and the three-fourths cup of its cooking liquid. You must do this very carefully because the hot oil will sizzle and splatter as you add the liquid. Bring to a boil and remove from the heat. (Do not overcook.) Add salt and pepper to taste. Serve immediately.

Roasted Rabbit in Red Wine

Coniglio arrosto al vino rosso

Serves 4

NOTE: This recipe is for farmed rabbit; if you should use wild rabbit, marinate the pieces in a cup of red wine overnight before proceeding with the recipe. Discard the marinade.

2 tablespoons extra-virgin olive oil
1 medium onion, finely chopped
1 clove garlic, minced
1 small sausage link out of its casing
1 to 2 ½ pound rabbit, cleaned and readied for roasting, cut into 8 pieces
2 tablespoons finely chopped fresh rosemary
1 cup red wine
½ cup vegetable broth

1. Preheat oven to 350°F. In an oven-proof casserole or baking pan, put olive oil, onions, garlic, and sausage and bake, stirring two or three times until onions begin to brown, about ten minutes.

2. Add rabbit pieces, rosemary, some salt, and freshly ground pepper. Turn rabbit pieces over to coat them with oil and sausage. Bake fifteen minutes longer.
3. Add wine and bake, uncovered, until most of the wine has evaporated, about forty minutes. As the wine cooks off, add some vegetable broth, a few tablespoons at a time, and baste the rabbit several times. Rabbit bakes in approximately the same amount of time as chicken, so the total baking time should be about one to one and a half hours. The vegetable broth will cook down as well.
4. After the liquid has evaporated, cover with foil. Serve with the polenta offered in the next chapter.

9

THE CAT, THE FIG TREE, AND MAMA GRANDE

Our maternal grandmother and grandfather played important roles in our lives. Papa was at work all day, and Mama worked an even longer day. Our eldest sister, Mary, was in charge during their absence, but the supervision came from our grandparents. They always spoke to us in Italian, and we reported back in English. After years of these discussions, our grandparents' English vocabulary was limited. They were adept at saying hello, goodbye, and no. Yes, for them, was always "si." Our Italian vocabulary, unfortunately, was also limited. But we understood one another.

They lived nearby, and we spent a great deal of time with them because Mama asked us to lend them a hand. Grandmother Beatrice married Grandfather Joseph in Italy in 1886, and eventually they came to America. We called Grandma "Mama Grande," a tribute to her generous spirit as well as the few extra pounds on her small frame. Her silver hair, swept up into a bun, framed pink cheeks and an ever-present smile. She was always dressed in black, long cotton skirt topped with a cotton blouse. She went to church every day, adorned her bedroom with religious statues, and pretended to be unaffected by Grandfather's lack of enthusiasm for the church or its clergy.

Much of her unending domestic activity focused on food. No other warm, just-baked bread slathered with butter—not even our mother's—compared with hers. She cooked on an old-fashioned stove fired with wood and bedded with coal, and one of our tasks was to carry the buckets of wood and coal up from the basement storeroom. In her kitchen, you could always count on a nourishing bowl of soup any time of the day, for there was usually not one but two pots of it simmering on the stove. She made her own sausage, suspending it from broom handles to dry, then nestling it in jars cushioned with rendered pork fat just as Mama did. On Wednesdays, she baked the week's bread; on Saturday, she rolled out a week's worth of pasta. She was especially fond of our mother, and that affection was lovingly transferred to us children. She held us in her arms every single day.

Of course, we also loved Grandfather very much. If there were an Italian Norman Rockwell, he would have painted Grandfather in his knit cap, seated at the table with a big bowl of minestrone in front of him and a bottle of red wine at his side. He would have been holding a big, round loaf of grandmother's bread against his chest, cutting it into thick slices from the outside in! Or he might have been shown hand-grating flurries of Parmigiano-Reggiano directly over his soup. He spoon-fed me my first taste of ice cream. And I was perched on his knee when I tasted my first fig, carefully picked from the precious fig tree he nurtured on his New York City fire escape. He lived to be ninety-six, and in the years we had together, he shared with us not only countless experiences but also the folklore associated with them. For Grandpa, roasting chestnuts was an art, as baking bread was an art to Grandma. Food was a part of everything they did with us, from our first tastes of everyday Italian food to the Christmas stockings they filled with chestnuts, tangerines, apples, nuts, and chocolates from Italy.

One of Grandpa's stories was about the time he was in Italy, working late in the fields, getting home after the sun had set. Tired, he stopped and sat on the ground outside the cemetery's high stonewall. The evening was still, except for a voice on the other side of the wall, "This one is for you," and then a different voice replied, "And this one for you." And so it went: "This for you," and the reply was "This for you." "This for you, and this for you." "This for you, and this for you." Grandpa, becoming frightened, leaped up and ran as fast as he could, believing he had encountered God and the devil dividing souls. When he reached home and related what had happened to his family, his father explained that it was simply Antonio and Pasquale, two well-known chestnut pickers, who were dividing the day's take. Grandpa's message to us: don't frighten easily—get your facts before deciding on anything.

Grandma said Grandpa loved his cat first, his fig tree second, and her third—exaggeration perhaps but with an element of truth. He loved his cat, groomed it constantly, and petted it forever. Their intimate connection seemed inexplicable, especially to Grandma. Grandma was not allowed to discipline the cat nor even feed it. Grandpa was the sole caretaker. He kept a special brush for the cat, and no one else could use it. We thought he overbrushed the cat, but he and the cat seemed content. The cat was always at his side. Only Grandpa fed him.

Many people have never tasted a fresh fig. My first taste was a joyous experience—thanks to Grandpa. It seems incredible that he grew a fig tree on a fire escape in the summer and moved it in front of a very sunny window in late fall and the winter, but he did. We believe it was his connection to the "old country." He knew exactly how to make this tree flourish. I will never forget sitting on his knee and his caring gestures in presenting a prize fig to eat the first time. He snipped the stem end to make a cleaner cut, lightly "brushed" it with a clean kitchen towel, and gave it to me whole to bite into. I liked it. (My sister tells the story of us in Verona, in the Piazza delle Erbe, buying a one-half kilo of fresh figs. The plan was to share them with her and her husband. I wandered through the stalls, bag of figs in hand; and by the time I caught up with them, I had eaten all the figs.)

When Grandpa came to New York, he started an ice business in the basement of a building near his home. He soon learned that the coal business was more lucrative. He supplied restaurants and other businesses with coal for their furnaces and provided the service of keeping the furnaces going. One Sunday, he took my brother and me, ages seven and five, to Moore's Restaurant on Forty-Sixth close to Broadway (about a two-block walk for us). The restaurant was closed at this hour, but he had a key. He needed to stoke the furnace and add more coal. He put us up on a table where we sat and watched him perform his work. When he finished, he opened a door of a very large ice-cold box, reached in with a large spoon, and filled a bowl of the most delicious and creamy vanilla ice cream for us.

I was at college when told that Grandma was ill. Because I had an important examination, I was not called home. A few days later, there was a knock on my door; and as it opened, the first thing I saw was the black tie worn by my older brother. Children of Italian immigrant parents seem to learn early the important signals about life and death. The black tie told me all. Before Jerry spoke a word, I cried, "It's Grandma, isn't it?" She had died a week earlier. Gangrene set in, in her right leg; and because this happened before World War II, antibiotics were not around yet or perhaps she could have been saved. Why didn't my family get me home. At that point in life, it seemed important I know and experience anything having to do with life and death.

Grandpa lived without Grandma for about twenty more years but always with a cat and the fig tree. He never went to a doctor or dentist. He had all his hair, salt and pepper in color, cut short and wore his navy-blue hand-knit cap over his head. He had all his own teeth. He continued to roast chestnuts (always covering them with a towel once they were removed from the oven to facilitate peeling them). He would use a switch on any of my sisters' behinds if he thought their skirts were too short. He found fault with priests and somewhat less with nuns. He ate slowly—soups, pasta, lots of greens, fruits, and cheese. And as time went on, he tried his best to fill our Christmas stockings with a new dime, fresh and brightly colored oranges, and a piece or two of black/blue coal—to remind us of the early days. When we talked of Grandma, he gazed into space, stroked his cat, and said little or nothing. He always kept a jug of red wine on the floor next to his favorite chair. Often we caught him smiling, and we were sure he was thinking of something that had happened a long time ago.

We talked of past events. How on Christmas Eve nights in his home, he created a theater by hanging two bedsheets over a clothesline strung from one side of the kitchen to the other. Each grandchild had to concoct a performance. If we demurred, there would be no filled stocking. We thought that cousin Bea should at least be able to portray Clara Bow doing a simple dance routine, but cousin Bea never participated. She ate a few shrimp, and that was it. Then when we all looked into our stockings, cousin Bea was insulted to find Grandpa had given her only a piece of coal.

The saddest thing of all was that Bea never worked with the rest of us to prepare the Christmas Eve feast: many fish dishes with pasta, fish in soup, fried and baked fish, sautéed calamari slices and whole calamari stuffed with potatoes and herbs, homemade bread, greens cooked with oil and garlic, beans with herbs and olive oil, and freshly cut slices of fennel dipped in expensive extra-virgin olive oil with salt and pepper. All these and the variety of Christmas pastries, *zeppole*, *struffoli*, and more, were there. It was an unfortunate lost opportunity for cousin Bea to learn to cook and eat something Italian.

I was in Washington, DC, when I heard of Grandpa's impending death via a telephone call. The doctor told me personally to come home immediately, that Grandpa was expected to die that evening. His illness, the doctor said, was "old age—his heart is giving out." Grandpa lived another eight months until his heart finally gave out.

Nonno, as we called our grandfather, was also a peach specialist. He said that we should never buy peaches that have no fragrance. We always had tasty peaches in our house, and the attar of peach filled the air. "You should be able to smell them," he would say. Forget the beautiful skins: it is the odor that counts. He was the family member responsible for buying peaches, and it was his delight to plunge slices of them into red wine and eat them at almost any time of day.

He and Grandma had differences over food. He liked pigeons cooked any style, roasted, sautéed, whatever. Grandma would have none of this—she abhorred pigeons. There was a pigeon man on her tenement roof who cared for about one hundred pigeons. She and others in the tenement complained bitterly and loudly to the landlord who rented the space to the pigeon keeper. "Sporco piccione spregevole" (Filthy, despicable pigeons), she would shriek. Throngs of pigeons gathered on our block, there were at least three other cages on rooftops with keepers. The pigeons begged for any scraps they could get. As they ate, they left their calling cards on everyone's windowsills and fire escapes and sometimes on the fig tree's leaves. This would upset Grandma so much she would lose her speech. Grandpa, defending the pigeon, would counteroffer the history of this bird and its meaning to Italian cuisine, particularly its importance to their *provincia* (province, in Italy). He described its status to Roman times and the cooking of Apicius—the first cook in Italy who suggested in his cookbook the art of serving roasted pigeon with a sweet and sour sauce. These days, "squab" is almost entirely pigeons. Its meat is dark with a fatty skin, like that of duck, and lean and easily digested. It is rich in vitamins, proteins, and minerals.

My family remembers two distinct things about pigeons as we were growing up. First, they could be purchased at Piccini Brothers, a specialty meat store on Ninth Avenue and Forty-Fifth Street; and second, that there was a severe shortage of these birds during the lean years of World War II. Europeans, notably Italians, were eating them all the time. Pigeon still appears on Italian menus and in fancier restaurants in the United States and abroad. Papa would bring some home from Chinatown in downtown New York City, where most restaurants offered them on their menus.

Instead of preparing pigeons, Grandma would cook quail with quince. She adored quince and would wrap one quince in a linen towel and put it in her undergarment or handkerchief drawer for the delightful fragrance it imparted to the clothing. Grandma, at times, cooked quail "alla cacciatore" and served it with risotto. And she cooked it as they do in Capri, with peas. The recipe Grandpa liked best is the one with quince. They served this with polenta. For cooking today, it is best and easiest to use organically produced Arrowhead Mills Yellow Corn Grits to make this polenta. It is available in most supermarkets. Also use the buckwheat flour made by Arrowhead Mills. There is more flavor to be had by adding Taleggio, Fontina, or Gorgonzola cheese.

Cooking rabbit was okay with Grandma. She made it often, as it was one of Grandpa's favorite dishes cooked in his red wine. Grandma used wild rabbit in those days, and after she cut the rabbit into pieces (like a chicken), she would put the pieces in cool water and leave it three or four hours until the color of the meat lightened considerably—this was her purification process. Grandma almost always cooked a small piece of sausage with vegetables, and it added a special bounce to escarole, beans, broccoli, or cabbage. On occasion, it was one of the ingredients she used to stuff chickens; and invariably a guest would ask, "Why doesn't my stuffing taste like this?" (You'll probably get your sausage at a supermarket; try for less fat. Note, in this recipe, the sausage is taken out of the casing, cooked, drained, and the fat discarded.)

Grandma would often use one-half pound each of hot and sweet sausage. Or she used all sweet. The hot sausage alone will make a spicy dish. She always put aside the feathery ends of the fresh fennel, which made an eye-catching garnish. The pasta she used was called *farfallette*, a small pasta; but there are many others in the shops, such as *lumache*, *ditalini*, *fusilli*, and *rotelle*. Any of these will work well. Grandma made her *farfalle* for this preparation, but store-bought will do. Visiting them as often as we did, we usually found a pot of it on her stove. It became a favorite food and a connection to our grandparents.

Here are some of their favorite foods:

Quail with Quince

Quaglia con mele cotogne

Serves 4 as a first course, or 2 as a main course

- 6 quinces, wiped, quartered, cored, and pared
- ½ cup sugar
- 1 cup water
- ½ cup Madeira
- 4 tablespoons butter
- 4 quails, dry plucked, singed, drawn from the neck, head and neck removed, and wings trussed (as for squab)
- 1 cup beef broth
- 4 tablespoons Cognac or brandy
- 1 tablespoon lemon zest, chopped fine
- Salt and freshly ground pepper

1. Arrange the quince quarters in a shallow covered baking dish and sprinkle the sugar over them. Add the water and Madeira and cook in a preheated 325°F oven for about one and a half hours. Baste frequently during cooking and test for doneness with a fork.
2. While the quinces are cooking, prepare and cook the quails. Melt the butter in a large heavy-enameled saucepan with a cover. (The pan should be large enough to accommodate the four quails in one layer.) Brown the birds on all surfaces and salt and pepper them to taste. Cover the pan and bake in a preheated 375°F oven for approximately thirty minutes.
3. Remove the pan from the oven and transfer the quails to a large warm serving platter. Keep the birds warm.
4. Remove as much excess fat as you can from the pan in which the birds were baked. To this pan, add the beef broth, Cognac or brandy, and lemon zest. Bring this mixture to a boil, reduce the heat, and simmer for approximately fifteen minutes, stirring frequently and deglazing the pan as you stir.
5. While this sauce is simmering, arrange the cooked quinces around the quails. Then pour the sauce over the birds and serve immediately.

Polenta, Nonno's Way

Polenta al Nonno

Serves 4 to 8

6 cups water
1 ¼ cups yellow corn grits (preferably Arrowhead Mills)
¼ cup buckwheat flour (preferably Arrowhead Mills)
½ cup either Taleggio or Fontina cheese, cut in small pieces
4 tablespoons butter
6 fresh sage leaves, 4 chopped finely, 2 cut in half, lengthwise

1. In a medium saucepan, bring the water to boil. Add some salt.

2. Slowly stir in grits and buckwheat flour. Bring to a boil, lower heat, and simmer, uncovered, over low heat, five minutes, stirring often.
3. Remove pan from the heat. Add cheese, butter, and finely chopped sage leaves. Stir to melt cheese and butter. Then transfer to a shallow bowl. Arrange four half sage leaves to resemble a flower with four petals on the top center of the polenta. Serve now or keep warm in a 250°F oven up to a half hour or so.

10

GRANDMA BAKES BREAD IN THE PUBLIC BAKERY

Most of the Italian immigrant women brought customs from their regions of Italy. Grandma was a prime example. It showed in her routine for baking bread each week, a task that started as early as sunrise. Grandma saved a small part of the dough to be used as leavening for next week's loaves. Julia della Croce, a writer about Italian food wrote that the process of making the dough, allowing it to ferment and transforming it into loaves, is as feminine a ritual as birth. Grandma's birth and early life were in the southern Italian village of Accettura, a region heavy with mysticism, and the ritual of bread making there in the village or town communal oven is imbued with spiritual significance. Grandma, while shaping her loaves, ran her fingers over each loaf, saying, "Father, Son, and Holy Spirit," and actually made the sign of the cross. Mama and others in the family did exactly the same thing.

Grandma and her friends agreed to approach the local professional bread baker who had a large wood-fired oven in the basement of a tenement on Tenth Avenue between Forty-Forth and Forty-Fifth Streets. The entrance to the bakery was through an outside basement door, opened fully during business hours 6:00 a.m. to 6:00 p.m. every day except Sunday. The basement steps were uneven, and you had to be careful on your descent. It seemed easier for the older Italian ladies than it was for others. They had years of practice climbing and descending uneven deep stairs in and out of their houses and properties in Italy. If the basement opening had been higher, they would have entered with pans of dough perched on their chignoned heads. Instead, they carried the pans in both hands in front of them at waist level. The arrangement with the baker was that the women made the dough at home from the initial mixing through one rising. Then only could the dough be brought to the baker where table space was provided for shaping loaves for a second rising. He charged them one cent a loaf for the use of his facilities on Wednesday afternoons. This included the use of the table and the baker's time and tools, as well as the wood used to heat the oven. The baked bread and any bread-making paraphernalia belonging to the women had to be removed by closing time that day.

Grandma made her rising agent at home with a starter or sponge or, as she called it, a *biga*, a mixture of warm water, sugar, some yeast, and flour. She mixed these thoroughly on Tuesdays then put the bowl on an open kitchen shelf, not the icebox, until the next morning (Wednesday) when she made the dough. I suppose the kitchen shelf was cool enough—thanks to her landlord.

This is a basic loaf that can be eaten with soups, used in soups, to make bruschetta, to dip into peppered oil, and to eat with pasta, which is not uncommon in Italy or in our home. You will also toast it for breakfast, laden with butter and jam, and you will make sandwiches with it. It requires a starter or sponge or a biga. You can make this in an electric mixer or by hand.

When I was ten years old, Grandma was sixty-six. Beatrice, pronounced "Beatrice" in Italian, with elongated sounds emphasizing the vowels, was short, plump, full skirt to the floor gathered at the waist, dark color close to black, with a blouse of the same color, the ever-present starched white apron, and white hair with natural gold streaks made a pretty picture.

I had to carry some of her dough to the bakery before catechism class every Wednesday afternoon. She left for the bakery before I arrived at her apartment and would have left the dough for me to carry in a *gonga*, an oval-shaped white enamel pan, about eight inches deep, and covered with a floured kitchen cloth towel. The filled pan was heavy and difficult to carry. To get to the bakers, I rested the pan on top of fire hydrants along the way. The bakery scene was worth a photograph: the ladies, each of the same mold, standing at the baker's wooden tables, shaping their breads; the baker, his face and hair sprinkled with white flour, skillfully loading a loaf on his long-handled peel then sliding it into the oven a hundred times. After catechism, I ran back to the bakery. There is no smell in the world as there was in that bakeshop. My job was to help carry the six baked loaves and the white pan home in oversized shopping bags.

This included one to take to Mama. Grandma knew her daughter baked her own bread, sometimes at the bakery, sometimes at home. The loaf Grandma sent was meant to show Mama how good bread is really made. The aroma of baking bread fired up one's appetite—no matter how much you have eaten for breakfast and lunch or last night's supper. It may have been a chore carrying those pans of dough, but its reward was the intoxicating smells of freshly baked bread. Ask anyone in the family which smells he or she remembers most—the only answer will be Grandma's and Mama's baked bread.

A special treat for us was a thick slice of Grandma's bread, piled with butter and warmed in her woodstove topped with homemade fig preserve. With the bread came a large jug of "coffee"—milk warmed with a teaspoon of real coffee in it. The fig preserve was not only absolutely delicious on warmed bread with butter but also could be a filling for a *crostata* dessert tart. It can also be used in the *panettone* bread pudding or simply on top of ice cream. Was the delicious jam Grandma's trick to get us to come visit? No matter, we went for the bread, the fig preserve, and our special white-haired lady.

Grandma had four daughters. When Grandpa could afford to bring them to America eight years after he had left them in Italy, the eldest daughter opted to remain in Italy. My mother's younger sister by two years, Maria, and her older sister by four years, Rose, were around, and we knew them well. My family has spent many hours mulling over their differences, unable to explain the reasons for them. Mama was an early riser, went to bed late, and had abundant energy to make things (cooking and most of our clothes, for example)—in other words, a real worker. Aunt Rose, having lost her husband early in life, tended to act frail all the time. She didn't like to be touched by anyone and became known as "No Touch!" She may have been a good cook, Mama's style, but no one remembers eating her food. She smiled a la Mona Lisa, but there was no hearty laugh. Her hand was placed over her heart—her standard Napoleonic posture. When she spoke, the message usually covered her state of health with the added possibility of more serious conditions developing.

Aunt Mary, on the other hand, spoke of good health and never placed a hand over her heart. She loved to sleep late and didn't want to get out of bed to see her kids off to school. She seems to have doted more over her husband than her children, was a very good cook, and would clown when in the mood. She was the type who would throw a lemon meringue pie in Papa's face if he challenged her to do so.

Mama and Aunt Rose, though cordial, didn't seem to hit it off. We had been told of one real moment of connection the year before I was born. Soon after Aunt Rose's arrival in the United States, her Italian-born son contracted influenza at the same time as one of Mama's sons. Both boys died and were "waked" in our front room. I was named Joseph for Mama's son who died of influenza and was also named Joseph. Rose's son was Joseph also. Two Josephs, each in a child's casket in the single front room, might have been a reason for total sisterly love, but it didn't last.

When Aunt Rose died, we took Mama to the funeral. On the drive home, we tried to comfort her by expressing sympathy over the loss of her dear sister. She quickly broke in and said, "Well, she never did much and was always sick." When her younger sister Maria died five or so years later, we were with Mama again, saying how sorry we were over her loss; and once more, she quickly opined, "Let's face it, Aunt Mary never got up early."

Grandma loved cooking. She taught her girls everything she knew. The girls took their cooking seriously. What I remember is that each had her own pasta sauce.

Her cellar was as full of canned food (and Grandpa's wine) as Mama's. Another of her jarred foods that we loved was their pickled eggplant. This is good to have on hand. It can be served on its own but will also add a great touch to sliced tomatoes, pickled or boiled beets, all kinds of lettuces in salad as a condiment, on roasted meat sandwiches (such as beef, chicken, or lamb), or with salami and cheese sandwiches.

Here are some of Grandma's special recipes.

Italian Country Loaf of Bread

Pane casereccio alla nonna

Makes 1 two-pound loaf

For the starter, sponge, or biga:

1 cup warm water, 105°F
1-teaspoon sugar
1-teaspoon active dry yeast
1-½ cups unbleached all purposed flour, plus 1 tablespoon for dusting

1. Pour the warm water into the large bowl of an electric mixer that has a dough hook and add the sugar. Sprinkle the yeast over the water and blend on low speed until the yeast is dissolved.
2. Add the flour except for a tablespoon and, on low speed, stir until smooth. With a rubber spatula, scrape down sides of the bowl. (It is best to stop the machine while doing this and start again immediately after scraping.) When the mixture is blended (only a matter of two or three minutes), remove the bowl from its stand. Sprinkle the tablespoon of flour over the top of the biga and cover with plastic or towel. Let this rest for 8 hours or overnight. If you wish, you may refrigerate this overnight, but Grandma let it sit on a kitchen shelf.

For the dough:

One recipe biga
1-cup warm water
1-teaspoon active dry yeast
1-tablespoon salt
3 ½- 4 cups unbleached all purpose flour

1. In a clean bowl of a heavy-duty mixer, add water and yeast as in the biga. Stir in the biga with a rubber spatula. Add 3 ½ cups of flour and salt and continue on low speed until blended. This should take 3 to 4 minutes. The dough will be quite sticky and tacky. If it appears too soft, add remaining ½ cup flour and beat to incorporate. Cover with plastic and let rise for 1 hour or until it doubles in size.
2. Lightly flour a work surface. Turn out dough onto it. (It should fall out in one piece without the help of a rubber spatula, but if the spatula is needed, use it.) Punch down the dough simply by kneading it two minutes. Shape the dough into a fifteen-inch elongated loaf, gently rolling it with the palms of your hands to the desired length. Line a large baking sheet (a cookie pan with sides works well for me) with parchment paper and transfer the loaf to it, laying it diagonally across the pan to gain the longer length of the pan. Again, cover with plastic or towel. Let it rest until it doubles in volume, up to 1 hour.
3. One half hour before baking, heat oven to 400°F. Using a razor blade or very sharp knife, make three or four slashes on the diagonal on top of the loaf, cutting almost one-half-inch deep. As soon as the cuts are made, put the loaf into the oven, spray liberally with water. Bake until the bread is browned and sounds hollow when tapped on its backside, forty to forty-five minutes.
4. Cool the loaf on a rack and then wrap in a large dry kitchen towel.

Pickled Eggplant

Melanzane sott'aceto

Makes 4 pints

About 3 medium-size eggplants to make 12 cups eggplant shoestrings
4 tablespoons salt
4 cups white vinegar
2 tablespoons sugar
½ cup olive oil
2 chili peppers, chopped fine
½ cup chives, chopped fine
4 cloves garlic, halved
2 tablespoons oregano

1. Wash, sterilize, and dry your canning jars.
2. Peel the eggplant with a vegetable peeler, cut off and discard the ends, and lay the eggplant on its side. Cut it into one-fourth-inch-thick slices then put a few slices together, stack them up, and cut them into one-fourth-inch strips (shoestring style). Put them in a colander, salt them, toss them, and set them aside for thirty minutes. (Put something under the colander to catch the drippings or put the colander in the sink.)
3. In a large saucepan, bring vinegar and sugar to boil. Add eggplant pieces and boil, five minutes. (Do not overcook.) Drain the eggplant and reserve the vinegar.
4. Add oil, chili peppers, chives, and oregano to eggplant mixture, and toss well. Fill the sterilized jars, leaving one-half-inch space at the top. Press eggplant mixture to the bottom of the jar to release its juice. If more juice is needed, add tablespoons of the reserved vinegar mixture. Add two pieces of garlic to each jar and seal tightly. This should be stored in a cool, dark place for four weeks before it can be used.

Fig Preserve

Confettura di fichi

Makes about 5 pints

5 ½ cups sugar
1 ¾ cups water
3 tablespoons lemon zest, chopped fine
5 pounds purple figs, stems removed, sliced thick
1 lemon, ends removed, sliced fine
3 cups filberts, skinned, halved, and toasted
½ cup Cognac (or brandy)

1. Combine sugar, water, and lemon zest in a heavy saucepan and cook over low heat for five minutes, or until the sugar is completely dissolved. Then add figs and lemon slices and simmer twenty minutes.
2. Let this mixture stand, covered, overnight.
3. Bring fig mixture to a simmer again and cook it for an additional twenty minutes until it thickens. Add the filberts and Cognac (or brandy). Cook one minute more.
4. Pour or ladle the mixture into the sterilized jars and seal the jars. This preserve may be consumed right away or stored for future use. Brandied fruits, however, develop a better flavor if stored for a minimum of four weeks.

11

SAINTLINESS AND LAMB RAGU

"Aunt" Margaret and "Uncle" Carmine lived across the street from us. Carmine, Mama's first cousin, was not really our uncle; nor was Margaret our aunt. Papa suggested the courtesy titles as a gesture of kindness to them because they were childless and thought assumed it would bring them closer to our family. At times it did, but that was not always the case.

They were devoted to keeping their Italian identity; nothing American interested them. Aunt Margaret's long hair, upswept into a knotted bun, was not bobbed until she was over sixty. Unfortunately, she had poor eyesight and wore very thick glasses, really thick; and once, someone called her "four-eyes." Because Margaret was so religious, my father called her *la monica* (the nun). Uncle Carmine, typical of most Italian men, took the church with a grain of salt and attended church only when his wife insisted—if someone died or was being married. Carmine's English vocabulary consisted of hello, goodbye, yes, and no. They cooked in America the way they cooked in Italy, but that was a plus; her cooking was not affected by anything American. As little money as they might seem to have, they bought top ingredients, and relatives and friends in Italy sent many dried herbs. Margaret made a pasta sauce of lamb, with fennel seed and saffron. We thought it was a unique dish, and she prepared it often. She did something to the lamb we'd never seen before. She put the lamb (in this case, minced) into a bowl of cool water with the juice of one lemon. She said this helped to cut back on the strong flavor of some lamb cuts. She was known for two special foods they prepared at home: rigatoni with lamb, fennel, and saffron, and roast leg of lamb with anchovy sauce. Her pastas were lightly sauced—the pasta did not swim in sauce in the bowl. Social activities were limited; church for Margaret, some card playing for Carmine. They visited my parents and grandparents—it was only a short walk to either flat—showed respect to both couples in the old country style; that is, if you were younger in age or related, even distantly, you paid a short visit to show respect. When we spent time with them, it made us happy that Mama was striving to be more modern by stretching our lives beyond Forty-Sixth Street and being the first woman on the block to assure friends and relatives that her sons would go to college.

On a day-to-day basis, Papa chided Aunt Margaret about her zeal for churchgoing events. I remember one time he asked why she would go hear a priest's blessing at a wake of a person unknown to her. She rarely responded to his questions or accusations. Margaret went to church every day, some days two times. To satisfy a ridiculous curiosity, Papa followed her to church one day to prove to him and us that the church was her actual destination. While our parents were feeding and clothing six children and with little or nothing left for savings, Margaret and Carmine made weekly trips to the West Side Savings Bank on Forty-Second Street and Eighth Avenue. Time passed, and my older brother went to college, graduated, and entered Harvard Law School. Mama borrowed one thousand dollars from Aunt Margaret to help defray the cost of law school and fought with Aunt Margaret over the interest she charged on the loan to be repaid the following year. There were weeks of serious negotiations between the two women filled with impassioned voices (more Mama's than Margaret's) or periods of silence—like at a wake. The argument centered on why in the world Margaret was expecting a full percentage point over the normal bank interest rate. Mama paid it nonetheless, but from then on, there was a subtle coolness toward Margaret, however, not subtle enough to escape us. One time, I heard Mama say "truffatore" (swindler) as she turned away from Margaret. In spite of this turmoil and disagreement over dollars, we were never discouraged from showing love and respect to them. On important holidays, we visited Margaret and Carmine to wish them a Happy Easter, a Happy Thanksgiving, or whatever. Both Mama and Papa appreciated their cooking. They'd compare notes, and Mama, one day, did admit she liked Margaret's rigatoni with lamb.

There were two people in our immigrant world that our cousin Bea, her two sisters, and her mother (Aunt Rose) were close to—our "aunt" Margaret and "uncle" Carmine, who lived across the street from us. Carmine was not only first cousin to Mama but also had been a cousin by marriage to Aunt Rose's husband who had died in Italy. We know for a fact that Aunt Rose and the girls ate at Margaret's several times. (None of our family ever did.) Cousin Bea and her family, when living on Forty-Eighth Street, would come visit Aunt Margaret on Forty-Sixth Street without making "hello" stops at their other and real aunts', Angela (our mama) and Mary (our aunt), who lived below us. These straight-line, direct paths to Aunt Margaret's were a longtime bone of contention between Mama and Aunt Mary (against them) and (for them) Margaret, Aunt Rose, and the daughters. Mama and Aunt Mary could not understand why, if you came to Forty-Sixth Street, you couldn't stop in and see your real sisters. (And they had a point.) God help us if either Aunt Mary or Mama happened to be at the front window and saw the Forty-Eighth Streeters enter Aunt Margaret's building. Aunt Mary would come up to us, or Mama would go down a flight to her—always with the question, "What have we ever done to them to get this treatment?"—usswords, proverbs, anything to get the wrath out of their systems. The connection between Aunt Margaret and Aunt Rose had nothing to do with religion, or with cooking and food. We guessed it had to do with old Accetturese ways established many years before in Italy. We gave a plus to cousin Bea for her tolerance of this and then added, "We have hope for her still," as Papa would always cap us with "Donna hold your breath-a."

A number of years passed, and there came a time when cousin Bea showed some signs of change, especially after Papa died.

Gradually, she confided more and more in Mama. She began to describe feelings of guilt about denying her Italian origins. Mama, in her inimitable way, would always say that it was a good thing to be Italian, sharing with her the blessings of Italian family life, the strong feelings among siblings, the love of art and music, the comfort of living and eating together, the short-term successes of cooking Italian style, and anything else that made up "la vita Italiana." In other words, Mama took cousin Bea under her wing—almost as if she were gaining a daughter.

At sausage-making time, Aunt Margaret was always in our kitchen, not in anyone else's. She was diligent and quiet, and Mama considered her a good worker. In other words, she kept her nose to the grindstone. There was one incident our family remembers to this day. Margaret had a habit of blessing everything, including food. And she blessed everything on sausage-making day. Mama always added her condiments to the sausage before putting any of it through the casings. She did this by putting the finely chopped meat into a large white enamel bowl of a size she felt comfortable handling. Once the meat was in the bowl, she would add the salt and pepper, paprika, and so on. She would mix then check on the seasoning; she sampled the raw meat, just a pinch of it, in her mouth. Aunt Margaret took a sample too. That night, Mama became ill—so ill we had to take her to the emergency room at the Polyclinic Hospital on Fiftieth Street, between Ninth and Eighth Avenues. She was hospitalized for almost two weeks with the worst case of trichinosis on file in the medical records of New York City. Margaret, having tasted the meat, did not become ill. We were happy about that but could not figure out why only Mama became ill. Mama continued for years to make homemade sausage, but she never tasted raw meat again. And neither did Margaret. What Mama did instead was to take a pinch of it and sauté it in a small skillet to well done. When cooled, she tasted it and adjusted seasoning if she thought necessary.

Aunt Margaret cooked simply, and she and Carmine ate simply. She cooked with lamb almost exclusively. If she had pasta with a lamb sauce, she would add a green salad and a piece of fruit and cheese for dessert. They would make the sauce a day ahead and put it in the icebox until needed. They would put a small amount of meat in the sauce then use it to lightly cover the pasta. They varied the herbs and combined them with the oil and wine. It was the same if Margaret roasted lamb with potatoes—there was the salad and the fruit and cheese. Her husband Carmine loved cheese, particularly Pecorino. It was more economical for them to buy a round, which they covered with waxed paper and a kitchen towel and put in the icebox until the next use. Carmine would unwrap the cheese at the table and, with a small knife, cut off a piece and remove the skin if needed. He handled the cheese with loving movements as if caressing it, and when he took a bite, he showed more emotion at that moment than at all the other activities he performed in a day. He was a son of Grandpa's brother who never immigrated to the United States, and he had some of Grandpa's mannerisms. On the whole, he was not as animated as Grandpa, but you'd catch a similarity as he ate. And he loved all the lamb preparations made by his wife.

We used to wonder if there was any connection between Margaret's love and use of lamb and her connection to the Catholic Church. *Agnus Dei*, the Latin term meaning "Lamb of God," was originally used to refer to Jesus Christ in his role of the perfect sacrificial offering who atoned for the sins of humanity in Christian theology (harkening back to ancient Jewish temple sacrifices). Just as in Judaism, sins could be forgiven through the offering and the pouring out of the blood of an unblemished lamb, so Christians believe that they can be cleansed of their sins by the blood of Jesus, the unblemished Lamb of God. In Christian iconography, an Agnus Dei is a visual presentation of Jesus as a lamb, since the Middle Ages, usually holding a standard or banner with a cross. Sometimes the lamb is shown atop a book with seven seals hanging from it. Occasionally, the lamb is depicted bleeding from the area of the heart, symbol of Jesus's shedding of his blood to take away the sins of the world. We would sit next to Aunt Margaret in church and noticed that she would made a soft fist with her right hand and touched her left side as all of us sang or spoke "Lamb of God, you, who take away the sins of the world, have mercy on us. Lamb of God, you, who take away the sins of the world, have mercy on us. Lamb of God, you, who take away the sins of the world, grant us peace." As we chanted each statement, Aunt Margaret would give another thump to her left side.

As said earlier, Aunt Margaret went to church every day. She went to the many churches in the neighborhood: St. Malachy's on Forty-Seventh Street, between Ninth and Eighth Avenues (the chapel for the actors in the neighborhood); the Church of the Sacred Heart on Fiftieth Street, just off Tenth Avenue; and the church we went to most of the time, St Albert's on Forty-Seventh Street, between Ninth and Tenth Avenues, where Grandma used to go every day, even when it snowed, against Grandpa's advice. There was an Italian church on Forty-First Street, between Tenth and Eleventh Avenues. Grandma, Grandpa, and Papa were buried from that church. Margaret knew all the priests and all the people connected with both churches. She did her shopping on her way home from church, and because she did not bake, she would purchase almost every other day a crusty loaf of Italian bread. We used to think that she didn't because she was childless. Who knows, but we felt that her cooking lamb dishes and the Agnus Dei were related. She would bring home for us from the factory where she worked on Forty-Fifth Street, Tootsie Rolls, a one-half-inch-thick cylinder of sweet candy, all this without our needing to say the prayers of Agnus Dei.

There was a gayer side of Aunt Margaret, and that had to do with her role in the various outdoor picnics and religious feasts—events most of us attended as a family. She felt it was her job to follow up with Mama and Papa and clarify the details of date, time of arrival, which members of the family would be going—Lord only knows she tried to get everyone of us to these feasts and celebrations. And we liked that.

There were lots of special feasts and picnics and still are. One was the Feast of the Giglio, called the Feast of the Lilies, which is sponsored every year by the Church of Lady of Mt. Carmel in July, up at One Hundredth Street on the east side (there was quite a Little Italy community there, which was overtaken by the Puerto Ricans who came to New York some years later). This feast has been celebrated since 1903 and commemorates the canonization of a bishop from the southern Italian town of Nola who exchanged his life for a young boy who had been overtaken by pirates in North Africa and was to be sold as a slave. The bishop was finally freed, and upon his return to Nola, everyone in town greeted him with lilies. Aunt Margaret liked this story, as we all do, because now wherever this feast day is celebrated, there is a wide competition among farmers, butchers, deli merchants, and many other occupations for the most sensational display of lilies.

The Feast of St. Rocco is 121 years young. Rocco is the patron saint of Potenza and Matera, therefore really of all of Basilicata. In the United States, young men, perhaps thirty or forty of them, carry the statue of St. Rocco with over two hundred candles on a three-hour walk, and people attach paper money to his garments and any drapery surrounding him. For the last few years, some of the money goes to a children's cancer group, and much of it supports the school connected to the church, at St Joseph's on Monroe Street in lower New York.

Everyone knows the Feast of San Gennaro, patron saint of Naples, held in lower New York every September. This feast lasts over ten days and has attracted people from all over the world. Needless to say, the Italian-style food stands at these feasts are divine: homemade meatballs in a variety of tomato sauces, sometimes in a brown sauce; lamb chops with fried peppers; panini of all descriptions filled with salamis, cheese, and vinegar peppers; sometimes marinated (pickled) vegetables from jars of *giardiniera;* and the many Christmas pastries of zeppole (fritters of dough) and lovely ribbons of fried dough immersed in lightened honey with colored sprinkles, which, by the way, was one of Margaret's specialties. She may not have baked bread, but she would make several large platters of these for the Christmas holidays, and anyone who visited was delighted to eat some.

Papa was the secretary of two important societies representing paisanos from Ruoti, Potenza, his hometown; and Accettura, Mama's hometown. Although Aunt Margaret was from Stigliano, her husband came from Accettura, so she lent a hand here too. Both of these last two were entire-day affairs. Margaret cooked some lamb dishes for these outings—combinations of eggplant and lamb pieces, roasted or panfried, fresh and uncooked lamb chops she and Carmine would carry to the outing where either one of them would grill them on an open fire and present them with a jar of homemade pesto. The pesto was made of nuts and basil, salt and pepper, and good olive oil.

She always took time to discuss what went into the pesto. She was imaginative about this, and we agreed that her fresh grilled lamb chops, dipped into some pesto, were outstanding. These events, primarily because they had religious overtones, were important affairs for her. They were, in fact, the major social events in her life.

For several years, Margaret and Carmine took into their home two, young children of a deceased in-law and cared for them. Not an easy task. Their child-rearing style was considerably more rigid than the way other children in the neighborhood were raised. Their chores and church obligations were numerous. There was a lot of talk in the neighborhood about the discord in that made-up family. Both "adoptees" left home by moving away and marrying in their teens. Years later, we were comforted to see one of them officiating at Margaret's wake in New Jersey. Carmine had died of pulmonary complications years before her death. Poor Margaret; she had moved from her flat on West Forty-Sixth Street into subsidized housing on West Fiftieth, near Eleventh Avenue. As she got older, she became demented, and her dementia was seriously advanced before she died. She was found wandering the streets at the oddest times. We all thought she was in search of a church. But even if she found one, the doors were secured—no longer were church doors opened around the clock. It saddened us that a woman who went to church as often as she did could not find that comfort in the last year or two of her life. But we have been consoled over the years by preparing her delicious lamb and pasta dish.

Rigatoni with Lamb, Fennel, and Saffron

Rigatoni di Ragu di Agnello alla Cugina Margarita
Serves 4

¾ pound of lamb (from the leg or shoulder) minced
2 cups water
¼ cup fresh lemon juice (about 1 lemon)
1 onion, chopped
2 tablespoons extra-virgin olive oil

1 teaspoon finely chopped fresh rosemary
½ teaspoon dried fennel seeds
½ teaspoon saffron strands
½ cup Marsala wine
1 tablespoon butter
½ pound string (such as fettuccine or spaghetti) or small pasta (such as farfalle)
½ cup freshly grated Parmesan cheese

1. Put lamb in a bowl. Add water and lemon juice. Let stand, ten minutes. Drain and dry lamb.
2. Heat a skillet, add lamb, and cook over moderate heat, five minutes. Discard any liquid in skillet.
3. In another skillet, heat oil and sauté onions, five minutes. Add lamb and cook five more minutes. Add rosemary, fennel seeds, and saffron strands. Stir to mix well.
4. Add wine and cook for about fifteen minutes.
5. Cook and drain pasta according to directions on box.
6. Add butter to lamb sauce, stir, add pasta, and toss over moderate heat, one or two minutes, to marry pasta and sauce. Serve with grated cheese.

Roast Leg of Lamb with Anchovy Sauce

Arrosto di cosciotto d'agnello con salsa di acciughe
Serves 8 to 10

5- to 6-pound leg of lamb
2 garlic cloves, cut into 4 pieces, crosswise
1 teaspoon dried rosemary
2 teaspoons fresh ginger root, chopped (or 1 teaspoon powdered)
1 tablespoon salt and freshly ground pepper
¾ cup dry vermouth
6 anchovy fillets, chopped fine
2 tablespoons lemon zest, chopped fine
2 tablespoons shallots (or scallions) chopped fine

Preheat oven to 325°F to 350°F

1. Wipe leg of lamb clean with a tea towel and, with a small, sharp paring knife, cut eight little pockets in the skin of the lamb. Space the pockets evenly over the top of the leg. Insert a piece of garlic into each slit.
2. In a mortar, combine the rosemary, ginger (fresh or dried), salt, and pepper to taste, and grind to a smooth paste with a pestle. In case the herbs are too dry, add a few drops of vermouth to help create the paste. Set the leg of lamb, fat side up, on a rack in a roasting pan and spread paste all over the meat.
3. Place lamb in oven and cook two to two and a half hours, basting with the vermouth and pan juices every fifteen minutes or so. When leg of lamb is done, remove it from oven and take out garlic pieces. Transfer the roast to a serving platter and allow it to sit, fifteen minutes, before carving it.
4. Pour pan juices into a one-cup measure. Skim off as much fat as you can. You should have one cup defatted pan juice; if you don't, add some hot water to make up the difference. Pour pan juices back into the roasting pan, add anchovies, and cook on stove top over medium heat until anchovies are blended into sauce, three or four minutes. Add lemon zest and shallots or scallions. Bring just to the boil, remove from the heat, and serve sauce separately with the slices of lamb.

12

COUSIN BEA AND THE ITALIANS

We grew up with many cousins. It was not unusual for Mama's and Papa's relatives to have six to eight children. Several families lived in our neighborhood and many in Connecticut, but there were also cousins in Philadelphia, Chicago, various cities in California, and in New Orleans. Except for the "lead asses " across the street on Forty-Sixth, we had cordial relationships. One of the more interesting was cousin Bea—she was nine years old when she came to New York from Accettura, an impoverished town set high on a hill in the south of Italy where Mama was born too. As I mention later in the book, this part of Italy is a region described in the novel *Christ Stopped at Eboli*.

Bea came to America with her two sisters and their mother, Rose, my mother's older sister. They were following my grandfather who had left eight years earlier. His American job was carrying blocks of ice on his shoulders to customers in New York City, most of them living in tenement flats three and four flights above the street level.

The first he brought over were his wife and their two younger daughters, my mother Angela, and her younger sister Mary. Several years later, his next to eldest daughter, Rose, made the trip with her three children: Maria, Beatrice, and Filomena. Beatrice, the middle daughter—called Bea—wanted to be American more than anything else and pretended not to be of Italian ancestry. She got through elementary school, studied stenography, and went to work immediately; it took years before we came to appreciate each other.

Bea worked hard at being 100 percent American. Fashion magazines came weekly, and when she stepped out of her tenement on West Forty-Eighth Street, she assumed the air of popular movie stars, such as Clara Bow, Sue Carol, and others. Clara Bow was the it girl of the day, and Bea carefully copied her, applying lipstick in the shape of a heart to emphasize peaks and valleys in her lips and minimize the width of her mouth. Her dark brown hair was bobbed and shingled above her neck, and spit curls came to points on each side of her face, like the ends of a handlebar mustache. She wore little round collars on her shirts and blouses with large silk bows at the top button.

Her mother, our aunt Rose, never lost her Italian identity. She was in her early forties when she arrived in the United States and never stopped wearing black, always kept her hair in a neat bun, and complained of heart palpitations until the day she died at eighty-five. Because she thought her very existence so fragile, she was careful not to let anyone come too close to her.

Mama, after she married, would send over a pot of her minestrone with bread balls or a zucchini stew. We children have no recollection of ever eating in their home. Bea, as a young girl, was not fond of Italian food and lived on sandwiches from Marquart's Deli on the avenue.

Mama would have loved cooking with her older sister. After all, they had the same good-cook mother. Mama tried this one or two times and walked away depressed. Mama said Aunt Rose had no interest in food for herself or her family. All she did was talk about her ill health. She would go on and on about this until Mama would urge, "Rosa, *basta, basta*" (Rose, enough, enough). Then Aunt Rose would talk about her cat's ailments. Mama would pick up her *mezzaluna* and came home, whispering, "What am I going to do with her?"

As children, some of us had difficulty with tomato sauce that was too chunky—thick and icky pieces of tomato we found difficult to swallow. We were shocked by the brains Papa would eat or the *capuzelle* (lamb's head), and as children, we didn't like *sanguinnacia* or *sangue salscicia* (blood sausage). Mama was aware of our dislike of certain foods, and she tried to find food to please us. She would cook a cup of small pasta and mix it with fresh ricotta and a teaspoonful of white sugar. She might add a sprinkle of nutmeg or allspice. That was good Italian food. Mama used the freshly made ricotta, quite different from the supermarket ricotta available today.

Since Bea was born on the mainland of Italy and in a very southern town, she did not like our Sicilian or Calabrian neighbors. "They are all crooks, all thieves," she said once. At first, we feared them also because of a few stories we heard from Grandma; but as we got to know them, we found they worked as hard as Mama and Papa, had families too, and loved to cook. It didn't occur to cousin Bea that we also might have problems with the tenement flat. She never understood that we didn't like some of the more esoteric foods around and that a few people in the neighborhood might bother us too. Yes, we were vocal about these things at our kitchen table, but we got nowhere with Papa. Even Mama would throw in an "Oh my, not again. Please." It was a lesson in patience, understanding, and loving your neighbor. Papa would speak, "Okay, *attenzione*. Let's hold hands and say a prayer before we eat. *Subito!* (Right away!)" He did not do this for religious reasons—it was a ploy to get us off the subject. Cousin Bea was short and pert and wasn't bad to look at. But her desire to deny her immigrant status did not go over with anyone who knew her. How unfortunate that she closed the door on this warm, wonderful, and caring *vita Italiana*. Would she ever be able to reconnect with her past and renew her spirit? Was she capable of taking a nibble of la vita Italiana? Would she ever be able to enjoy making and savoring one Italian dish?

Cousin Bea achieved a city look; therefore, any thought of going to camp or to the country with us was out of the question. She had no idea about *piedi rossi* greens, the ones Mama foraged for in upstate New York. Her mother, our aunt Rose, never ventured forth to do anything worth talking about. Mama was somewhat critical of her inactivity, her lack of vim and vigor, and grew intense over her lack of cooking in Mama's fashion. When we got our new piano, and as Jerry played his violin with Sister Mary at the piano, they were celebrated by that branch of our family as they were by the rest of us. While Jerry and Mary were making music, cousin Bea was adding more spit to her spit curls and more lipstick to her bowed lips.

Aunt Rose's girls were older than most of us, and we weren't friends. People would comment on this, and we always made excuses, such as "Well, they were not born in this country" or "Aunt Rose has a hard time as a single parent" or "Aunt Rose is ill most of the time." Perhaps these responses from us were right on, but we didn't believe them in our hearts. Mama and Papa had spoiled us with their tender loving care.

After a while, cousin Bea and family moved into the new flat on Forty-Eighth Street, between Ninth and Eighth Avenues, a few buildings east of the public school there. This building had four apartments per floor. Each apartment had a small foyer, a bathroom, one bedroom to the left, a kitchen next to the bath, and, to the right, a living room. The girls took the bedroom and arranged for Aunt Rose to sleep on a convertible sofa in the living room. Their rationale was that it was close to the kitchen—little food came from this kitchen, but things seemed to work out. The one and only time cousin Bea reacted to our family cooking was when Craig Claiborne wrote about Papa's quick spaghetti with ginger and garlic. But she would not taste it, as garlic upset her stomach. Papa said loudly, "Oh, you move-a to Fifth Avenue. How nice-a." Their rent doubled, but Marie, the older sister, found a job to help pay for their new lodgings, and they smiled going in and out of their "uptown" more easterly abode. And we were envious of their location and bath. It was their private bath that began a spate of complaints from us, enough to exhaust Mama and Papa—Mama almost to the point of tears. We too wanted to get away from our current living conditions—we were getting tired of the bath situation, the number of steps to run up and down, the trips through the dark and dingy hallways. So we did have something in common with cousin Bea—we all dreamed that one day we would have a large, beautiful home with lawns on Long Island. We were all moviegoers and adored the art deco, lavish, white-on-white apartments used by Carole Lombard, Bette Davis, and Joan Crawford. Why didn't we live better?

After a good and hearty meal and with Mama and Papa back in the saddle, we went on living—in our railroad flat. Papa's friend, La

Rosa, was a total embarrassment for cousin Bea. One time, when Bea returned to Forty-Sixth Street and spotted La Rosa, Papa saw cousin Bea cross the street to avoid her. Papa would not let this go uncommented on—he was her uncle Joe, and he let her know his feeling in most certain terms, adding, "Amico di tutti e di nessuno e tutt'uno" (A friend to all and a friend to none is one and the same).

Cousin Bea put some spit on her spit curls, adjusted her skirt, tweaked Papa's right cheek, sighing, "Oh, Uncle Joe," and started back to her uptown apartment. In a way, cousin Bea tolerated Papa better than any other relative, probably because of his compliments.

Because Aunt Rose thought her very existence so fragile, she was careful not to let anyone come too close to her. She would caution "no touch" to anyone who approached her to say hello, perhaps with a light embrace, Italian style.

Well, this was mysterious to Papa and, quite frankly, to the rest of us as well. Weren't we supposed to be one big happy Italian family? Aunt Rose didn't like Papa's De Nobili cigars, his "shot" in the morning, his beer and card-playing sessions with his "paisanos," or his practical jokes!

They had to understand Papa was a decent, humble, and loving man. He took pleasure in bringing overlarge platters of the food he cooked. Once, someone told Mama to keep her eyes on Papa, suggesting an affair between him and Aunt Rose.

That was all Mama had to hear. Though we considered Mama a cool cookie, her comments and actions were of Italian cinematic proportions. Anna Magnani had nothing on her that day. Mama was always so calm and collected, it was fun to see this exaggerated, flaring side of her. When she was annoyed with Papa, she always spoke Italian to him—in dialect. Mostly, we did not understand the language, although we knew she was berating him, judging him guilty before proven so, using us kids as one reason he should not dally. We all thought, how could Papa possibly be interested in a "no-touch" aunt of ours, a woman whose total personality and behavior were the opposite of Mama's?

Over the years, the rumor reemerged a couple of times. Mama never spoke up—she would simply say, "Hemmmm." This was a way most Italian ladies reacted about a number of subjects. When spoken, "hemmmm" was a deep crescendo, then a silent second, and more hemmmm, another crescendo. They gave the hemmmm, instead of speaking, which took importance away from a subject they did not want to address, much less give any credit to the gossip.

We heard some of these crescendos when someone came with a sample of their food that had turned out poorly or when a woman, as a guest, brought a plateful of burned crostini and someone asked what happened. The reply then was another crescendo. Later in life, we kids learned this technique and used it as we thought necessary. Eventually, Bea married a non-Italian, Jack, a nice-enough life insurance salesman; but truthfully, he didn't know how to spell Italian, much less live it.

At the few Italian family gatherings he would attend, for instance, Grandma's funeral, the only place you could find him was way out in left field. He was trying to figure out who had died. He stumbled over names of cousins, aunts, and uncles. When we actually thought of it, it was he who was the embarrassment to the family. Bea forced him to wear seersucker suits and a straw hat in the summer months, and Chesterfield coats in the fall and winter. His shirts were so tight at the neck it brought overbright redness to his checks and his smiling Irish face—he looked like the many cherubim on the Michelangelo ceiling in Rome—the only things missing were the wings.

After Papa died, Beatrice and several of her friends visited Mama weekly for coffee, cake, and the other Italian dishes Mama could so easily pull together. Gradually, Bea confided more and more in Mama, usually describing feelings of shame about having been born in Italy. Mama, in her inimitable way, always told her that it was a good thing to be Italian, pointing out to her the blessings of family life, a love of art and music, the comfort of dining and eating together, the short-term successes of cooking Italian style, and anything else that made up *la vita Italiana*.

After each of her meetings with Mama, cousin Bea would telephone one of us siblings and gasp over the wonderful fresh zucchini and sausage stew she had enjoyed during her visit with her aunt Angela. She spent quite a bit of time describing in detail her visit with Mama. She told us they talked about when Bea lived in Italy as a young girl and how so much of her time had been spent caring for her ill father. Her sisters, Marie and Filomena, helped, but it seemed everyone expected so much of her. She had to miss school often because of his sickness—respiratory problems. Some of the local people thought her father should be sent to Potenza (fifty miles away) for additional and perhaps better care, but that idea didn't appeal to Aunt Rose. "Where will we live, who's got the money for that, and what if he doesn't get better? It's too far away from Accettura. I think we should stay here," argued Aunt Rose, who, at that time, was beginning to worry about her own health. Cousin Bea said that time was when they began to appreciate Carmine, Aunt Rose's and Mama's cousin—he was so helpful and caring. He gave up many nights of playing "scopa" so he could stay with Bea's father and try to help. Bea added that "Aunt" Margaret, who married Carmine, was not in the picture yet but had she been, she would have been a big help too.

Bea remembered one night when Carmine was there with another friend, and, to try and cheer up the patient, Carmine and his friend took turns playing the "coop-a-coop" (there was no other name for it). The "coop-a-coop" was a primitive instrument made out of an empty can, one that held forty-eight to fifty-four ounces, with a wet cloth cover tied with string over the opened end. The fabric of the cover had a close-tight weave like a piece of a flour sack. In the middle of the fabric was cut a tiny hole (think straw) that would hold a whittled fifteen-inch or so as-straight-as-possible piece of branch.

The "coop-a-coop" was played by holding the branch and moving it up and down—this would create hollow-type sounds, eerie enough to fill the hills and valleys of Accettura (think of a witch on a broom to complete the scene). Mama was surprised that Bea knew of this instrument—only people from Accettura and a few other towns near there did. So cousin Bea reminded Mama that she lived there for years before coming to this country. Mama told us later how much Bea remembered of her time in Accettura, and she was impressed that Bea could talk about it so easily to Mama. Mama was also impressed that when she made the zucchini stew dish with sausage, Bea had seconds. "Can you believe that?" she said. "I don't know why you kids are so hard on her." Mama was so pleased that her estranged niece might finally be coming around. Bea liked to visit Mama. One day, she arrived with her usual packet of one pound of cookies she had found in an Italian pastry shop somewhere between Astoria, Queens, where she lived at the time, and West Forty-Sixth Street. For the klatch, Mama had already arranged coffee cups, a plate for the expected cookies, little white napkins, the cream-colored sugar bowl and cover with roses on them (a freebie from Manuel's Grocery Store coupons), spoons, a fresh fruit plate of oranges and apples, and some chocolates in a pretty small glass bowl. Mama started to pour coffee, and cousin Bea started to pour her heart out for Accettura.

"You know, Aunt Angela, last time, I forgot to tell you one of the things I liked best about Accettura."

"And what was that?" asked Mama.

"There was an old building that looked like a palazzo with a coat of arms—it was in the square, and it had its own chapel. Uncle Carmine was a gardener, and when we were in Italy, he worked there. He used to take Filomena and me with him once in a while. It had a really big farm too, and they celebrated the feast of San Rocco as we did."

"Oh, you mean the Palazzo Spagna—it was built in 1892. We never met the owner because whoever inherited it left Accettura when I was a little girl," said Mama.

"Aunt Angela, I don't think anyone was living in that building when I was there. It seemed deserted. I'll ask Carmine if he remembers," Bea replied.

"Uncle Joe and I knew some of the Spagna family descendants here in America. They came to many of the picnics we had in Long Island for the Accetturese in this area. You missed a lot, Bea, by not coming to them—they were truly wonderful affairs, and everyone made such delicious food and carried it to the picnic. I remember so well," explained Mama with a great satisfied sense of nostalgia.

"I remember a meal that Grandma's niece, Maria, cooked for us in Accettura just before we left. The antipasto—she had Pecorino cheese made from sheep's milk, homemade mozzarella, and red peppers like you have hanging there, but she fried them, so they were absolutely crisp, and they were not hot; and there were all kinds of cold cuts, salamis, and stuff, you know what I mean. They grilled so many meats, chicken and pork, and lamb's liver, which I never ate before. We didn't drink wine in those days, but they had a lot of it. I always liked Maria's house, and I liked her because she always showed an interest in things. You remind me of her, Aunt Angela," smiled Bea. With each visit, Bea became more and more interested in Italian food. She would talk about her early life in Italy and, specifically, about Italian food, spurred by the many dishes she enjoyed at Aunt Angela's home, especially the bean soup with fennel. At such get-togethers, she would seem more relaxed, and she began to share certain confidences about her past.

Mama was taken aback at some of the things Bea said—her description of the food and of Grandma's niece—she couldn't believe that Bea was relating this Italian story so Italian.

Mama answered with "Wouldn't you like to learn to cook something Italian? You will enjoy it, you'll see." And a plan was made.

The plan was that Mama and Bea would cook and then invite Genevieve, a friend of Bea, who had grown up on Forty-Sixth Street but left the neighborhood after she married then lost her husband shortly thereafter. We all remember her but had no idea she was Bea's friend—imagine, we thought, a girlfriend from Forty-Sixth Street. Although Genevieve was not of Italian ancestry, she was of the neighborhood, and that meant something.

Mama told Bea on the phone that they would be using dried beans that needed to be in water overnight. She explained that dried beans needed a couple of hours or overnight for soaking. "Overnight is easier, so they'll be ready when you arrive."

Bea was hardly in the door with her packet of cookies when Mama explained, "The soaking softens them and speeds up the cooking. And it keeps their skins from bursting open during cooking before the beans become just tender. You'll see what I mean soon. We're using dried cannellinis (taking one or two out of their soak and showing them to Bea). They're like white navy beans. Always look them over before soaking and remove anything that looks like a pebble or a bad bean. Now I did this last night for you. If there is anything that looks strange floating on top, remove it. I'll let you do that."

Bea timidly put her hands in the water and removed a few old skins that had floated up. Bea was accommodating—she looked for the garbage pail, raised its cover, and discarded those few bean skins.

"We're ready to start the soup. Bea, do you know anything about fennel seeds?" asked Mama.

"Aunt Angela, of course I do. Don't you remember that when you, Grandma, and Aunt Mary left us in Italy, we used to send you a bag of dried fennel seeds every month because that's what you wanted?" said Bea with a happy face.

"Of course, I remember, how foolish of me. Oh, there's always so much to remember. Madonna."

"Aunt Angela, I know you don't measure things, but I have to. When you add something, can I just take a second and use these measuring cups and spoons I brought so I can write the recipe?"

Out of Bea's pocketbook came an assortment of measuring cups held together with a metal tie—including a one cup, half cup, one-third cup, and a quarter cup. She reached in once again, and out came a set of measuring spoons, also tied with a piece of metal to hold the tablespoon, teaspoon, half teaspoon, and a quarter teaspoon together. Mama gasped and said in Italian, "Madonna, questa e grave" (Gosh, this one is serious).

"Okay, Bea, if that will help you learn. I soaked about one and a half cups of beans."

"They look like a lot more."

"Well, yes, they puff up because they absorbed the water."

Bea watched Mama and measured the following:

¼ cup olive oil,

4 large garlic cloves that Mama minced liked crazy,

½ teaspoons of fennel seeds, and a

¼ cup chopped Italian parsley.

"Is it okay to use the other parsley?"

"But why? You can buy the Italian parsley almost anywhere, and it has a lot more taste."

Mama put the soaked beans in a pot and covered them with water.

Bea figured it was about three inches over the top of the beans. She kept making notes in her steno pad. They lit the gas jet, brought the water to a boil, lowered the heat, and cooked the beans until tender—it took about one and a half hours.

Later, Mama grabbed a large soup pot and asked Bea to put the oil in it and turn on the heat. Then she was told to remove it from the heat and add the chopped garlic, fennel seeds, and parsley and stir. "Back on the fire to lightly brown the garlic," said Mama as she guided Bea through this procedure, adding, "Don't let the garlic burn. It'll taste sour." She asked Bea to add the drained beans to the pot with the garlic in it and then add four cups of broth (they used two cups of beef and two cups of canned chicken broth [low sodium]) and cook it, covered, for ten minutes. Mama showed Bea how to take out about two cups of cooked beans and puree them in a food mill, then the puree was returned to the pot with salt and pepper and to cook another five minutes. Mama showed Bea her food mill with great pride. Before she actually used it, she showed Bea its different parts—it came with small holes for a finer milling or larger ones for ordinary milling. The big holes would suffice in this case. Mama told Bea that she used to use a metal food mill, but in time, it would rust . But now, they had stainless steel ones, and they are truly a joy. "Bea, you must get this kind—it will last a lifetime," she added.

Mama said this soup is delicious with grilled crostini. Taking the soup pot off the heat, they sliced some Italian bread, ran it in under the broiler, both sides, and brushed one side of each with some olive oil. Mama sensed Bea enjoyed painting the crostini with oil.

Just at this point, the doorbell rang, and Genevieve appeared with another packet of cookies. Mama hugged her again and again—it was a few years since they had seen each other.

"Look what Bea and I have made for you. Come have a seat. Would you like a sip of wine?" asked Mama as she placed two wineglasses out for the girls. She brought the soup bowls to the table with two pieces of crostini in each bowl and ladled the bean soup over the crostini. It smelled divine, and everyone seemed so ready to eat and enjoy. Mama added a touch of chopped Italian parsley and some ground Pecorino cheese for the ladies to spoon over their soup.

Later, both Bea and Genevieve asked Mama if they could have another half portion. They got it, fast.

A salad of fresh greens with lemon and olive oil dressing came next, with lots of cookies and good roasted Italian coffee.

Bea said, "Aunt Angela, this is just like Italy, isn't it?" And Genevieve added. "Oh, I am so lucky to be included."

During the last twenty years of her life, Beatrice visited us in the country one or two times a year. She always arrived in a car driven by a friend because I suspect she never got a driver's license, one American rite of passage she missed out on. She wore pretty pale pink or yellow silk suits with matching shoes and bag, continuing to hang on to a bit of French chic. When we ate at the house in the country, she was thrilled with the elegance of the meals and the lovely, pastoral setting; and with each visit, she became increasingly aware of the relaxed Italian lifestyle. She always talked about her early life in Italy and specifically about Italian food and very often the dishes she enjoyed in New York with Mama, especially Mama's zucchini soup. After a few of these lunches, she began to relax and to share confidences.

One lengthy discussion concerned her daughter's problem with weight. "It's all because of the WASP family she married into," Bea said. "Why didn't I tell them at the very beginning that she was half Italian and not one bit French?" She finally admitted that this lie had caused many problems over the years.

Surely, we thought, Bea realizes now that there is no stigma attached to being of Italian ancestry. In our family were executives in major corporations, judges, lawyers, and schoolteachers. We also realized during these long conversations how important Mama had been in Bea's life and how much she helped her accept her Italian roots. At any number of meetings when they shared food and wine, sometimes alone and sometimes with Bea's friends, the two women also shared common human experiences.

In some ways, Bea identified more with her aunt (Mama) than with her own mother. Like Beatrice, Mama left Italy when she was eight years old. Her stories of having given birth to eight children, her three miscarriages, her work in the textile district, and her own forays into American style (such as bobbing her hair and wearing colorful clothing) were of interest to Beatrice. Over time, Bea started cooking Italian dishes, using Italian phrases, and loving New York and the Italians living there.

Pasta and Beans with Fennel and Sausage

Pasta e fagioli con finocchi e salsicce alla nonna
Serves 6

1 can (28 ounces) peeled plum tomatoes with their liquid
1 teaspoon extra-virgin olive oil
1 pound hot or sweet Italian sausage, casing removed
1 pound (2 medium) fresh fennel bulbs, cut in ½-inch dice
2 medium to large onions, cut in ½-inch dice
4 cloves garlic, minced
½ cup chopped fresh flat-leaf parsley
¼ teaspoon (do not use more) dried fennel seed
6 cups homemade chicken broth, or 3 cups canned with 3 cups water
2 cups cooked dried white beans or canned cannellini beans, thoroughly rinsed
1 cup cooked small pasta such as farfallette (small butterflies or bows)
12 slices Italian bread (½ inch thick)
2 cloves garlic, peeled (for the bread)
¾ cups grated Parmesan cheese
Fennel leaves, chopped

1. Drain tomato liquid into a bowl, cut tomatoes into one-inch pieces, and place in bowl with their liquid. Set aside.

2. Heat oil over medium heat in a large soup pot, add sausage, break it up with a wooden spoon, and cook until browned, five to six minutes. Keep stirring as sausage cooks. Transfer to a strainer and drain thoroughly, pressing on sausage with a rubber spatula to extract all the fat. Return sausage to soup pot over medium heat, add the fennel, onions, garlic, parsley, and fennel seeds. Cook, uncovered, until vegetables are tender but al dente, about twelve minutes.
3. Add chicken broth and tomatoes with their liquid. Bring to a boil, lower heat, and simmer, covered, for thirty minutes. Add beans and pasta and cook only until warmed through, about ten minutes. Fill bowls with soup.
4. Preheat broiler. Broil bread slices on both sides until lightly browned and rub one side with the whole garlic clove.
5. To serve, add two pieces of bread to each filled soup bowl over pasta, beans, etc. Add Parmesan cheese to taste (or pass and let others do this) and the chopped fennel leaves.

13

BLACK-EYED KNICKERS

On hot summer days, the only relief we had was to turn on the street hydrants. It was against the law to do this. The outpouring water sprayed to form an arch we hoped it would reach the other side of the street. All of us kids got under it. It was a beautiful way to cool off. Cops were quick to note which hydrants were on in the neighborhood and to turn them off. As they approached, we would disappear. Once in a while, a policeman reprimanded someone, but nothing more serious ensued.

On hotter days in Manhattan, these hydrants were turned on by the hundreds. Newspaper articles, with photos, would appear on the front pages of the *Daily News* or the *Daily Mirror*, the two popular newspapers of those times, with headlines "THIS AIN'T NO CONEY ISLAND." And the plight of the immigrant kids would be written up. As a rule, the hydrants would be on ten minutes or so, but considering the numbers of them turned on all over Manhattan (and Brooklyn and the Bronx), the loss of city water was considerable.

Early every year, parents arranged two-week dates for their kids at camps in New Jersey, upstate New York, and Connecticut. This was before there were Disney Worlds and Six Flags Recreation Parks. One of the most popular summer camps was Hartley Farm, owned and operated by Hartley House, the settlement/community house at 413 West Forty-Sixth Street.

There were other ways we could cool off—thanks to Mama. For several years, I was sent to "cousins" Marie and Rocky on Staten Island for a week's vacation. Their clapboard house, with sides of gray and brown wooden shingles, had a front and a backyard, both with lush green grasses and a large vegetable garden. Again, these "cousins" were not blood cousins but "paisanos"—warm, friendly, loving, God-fearing paisanos. They were close friends of Mama's and Papa's and part of an extended commitment.

Kids on Staten Island were no different from those in the city. They "hitched" too. That meant getting on the back of a bus and riding along with it. When the vehicle slowed down, it was time to jump off. It was not a favorite sport of mine, but when a couple of Staten Island kids asked me to hitch with them, I didn't want to say no. I was the visiting city kid on the block, and they were testing me. On the day I hitched, I was wearing new gray plaid knickers Mama had bought me for this special Staten Island holiday. The hitching technique was to jump on the rear of the bus just as it was ready to move on to its next stop and hope the driver did not notice you. If he did, he would stop abruptly and yell out his window, "Get off this bus, damn you kids!" The free ride was to the next bus stop. We would get off at the same time as the inside passengers, only to hop on again as the bus took off once more.

After two or three stops, we hitched the bus going in the opposite direction by crossing the street to catch the bus going back. In this way, we would end up close to home. On the day I hitched in my new knickers, I fell off the bus and seriously scraped both knees and tore the knickers. I had to explain to cousin Marie, who scolded me, as she nursed my knees and applied bandages. She said she would repair the knickers and put them in my suitcase. I wore other knickers for the rest of the week. When I returned home, Mama opened my suitcase to unpack, held up the new knickers, and I had to explain why they had black eyes (Mama's description and a fairly accurate one). Cousin Marie had sewn on two round, black patches to cover up the torn areas.

Cousin Marie was born in Accettura, Italy, my mother's birthplace. She had the bluest eyes, premature gray hair, and chiseled features. Her face is easy to remember. Later, when we first visited Accettura, we were met by a group of people, among them three men with blue eyes, gray hair, and chiseled features, and I asked, "Fratelli di Marie?" (Brothers of Marie?) And their response was fast and emphatic, "Si, si." Rarely have I seen such a strong family resemblance. When Mama and Papa celebrated fifty years of marriage, "cousin" Rocky, with Marie at his side, led the orchestra that played at the anniversary party. (By the way, this was the last function at the Astor Hotel at Forty-Fifth Street and Broadway. We were in the Versailles Room, Sunday, December 13, 1963. The next day, the hotel furniture and appointments were sold at auction to make way for the new Portman Marriott-Marquis Hotel at Times Square.)

Rocky was no Glenn Miller or Artie Shaw, but the band he organized made a good living playing at functions such as the anniversary party. He played at weddings when I was a ring bearer. Papa recommended Rocky to his many friends. He would say to prospective clients, "You don't have to be Italian to hire him. He does a good job, and you should sign him up now for your next celebration." Rocky had given Papa fifty or so business cards, and Papa left them in places he thought would pay off. He had several cards in the Rivoli Bar, a few tacked to Tony's (the butcher) wall, and in Frank Cardone's Barber Shop on Forty-Seventh Street, just off Ninth, few steps west of the avenue. Only Frank Cardone was allowed to cut Papa's hair, and Papa insisted on the same exclusivity for his three sons.

Marie was a fine cook—she cooked "Accetturese" as Mama did, who arrived in this country a number of years before Marie. Mama always liked Marie and showed her the ways of our neighborhood and the city, even after Marie and Rocky decided to buy a house on Staten Island. In summer, when Marie had an abundance of vegetables, she prepared many dishes with them fresh from her garden. All of us loved her cauliflower and olive salad. As we picked and ate some cauliflower and olives out of the salad bowl, she would add more, toss, and set aside. It seemed this salad bowl was in use all week long. She called it cauliflower and olive salad, but she also added many other vegetables such as very thin slices of raw baby zucchinis, or older zucchinis, she had steamed or boiled, cut them in lengthwise quarters, removed some seeds if necessary, then cut into chunks. She would stir these and other vegetables in the salad remaining dressing in the omnipresent bowl. Sometimes she would add fresh string beans, boiled and then cut into one-inch lengths as she would diced potatoes (cooked), fresh arugula, chopped scallions, chopped fresh mint, and basil. She added more wine vinegar to the dressing and anything else she thought it needed after she tasted it. Eating this with country Italian bread was so good. When we grew up, we continued to make it, always calling it Marie and Rocky's salad. The other recipe Marie made all the time was the zucchini and *coppa* salad, a bit more formal, but as delicious. *Capocollo* is a highly spiced pork butt, cured in the form of a thick (four to five inches) sausage. It is sliced thin, like salami, and can be consumed as a cold cut or in combination with other food where a ham flavor is desired. Capocollo can be made at home or bought at most Italian delicatessens and some supermarkets. Marie used zucchini blossoms, as did Mama, as packages, filling them with ricotta, Parmesan, or Pecorino cheese, onions, salt and pepper, and sautéing them in olive oil with a dab of butter. Another of their food specialties was zucchini *in padella*—fried zucchini slices in a skillet. In padella is a popular way to cook many things in Italy, especially vegetables. Zucchini are a favorite cooked this way. Marie dried the slices well (using paper or cloth towels) after they were sliced. "Zucchini are so filled with water that you see the liquid even as they are sliced, and if they are not dried well, they will not fry well," explained Marie. She added, as an extra touch, a few drops of good balsamic vinegar to the slices after they were salted and fried.

Almost always when I was with Marie and Rocky, Mama and Papa would take the subway to South Ferry and get on the Staten Island Ferry boat with two bags full of food. Mama planned this visit a day or two in advance with a phone call asking about us and the garden. Rocky would meet them on the Staten Island side and drive them to his home. We all knew the main attraction for Mama was the vegetable garden—she couldn't wait to get in it, pick some young fresh zucchini, and cook her zucchini stew with Marie. When she and Marie prepared this stew in early summer, it was the antithesis of a winter stew (although it can be comforting in winter months too and more so if "baccala" clothing is not on the clothesline). Mama brought two or three pounds of Tony's freshly made fennel sausage, and pieces of it could be sautéed quickly, so it was not a matter of long-cooked meats in a dish of zucchini stew. The young, fresh zucchini cooked quickly, and it was not complex food—its depth of flavor was achieved quickly with garden-fresh tomatoes, basil, and parsley. It was not a heavy dish. We thought of it as an elegant peasant dish. It doesn't require a fine wine, just some Gallo jug wine would hit the spot. And it has to be served with good and hearty Italian bread. Mama liked cooking zucchini—she would sauté slices of four or five fresh zucchini and add them to Marie's salad bowl. After she tossed them in the salad, she sampled and added what she thought it needed—more oil, vinegar, salt, pepper, whatever. Mama would look at Marie and say, "La bellezza e la bonte di estate" (The beauty and bounty of summer). These summer vacations took place before Marie had any children.

When I was not there, Mama, and sometimes with Papa, sometimes without, would visit Marie for an afternoon (mostly in the summertime because of the large vegetable garden). Mama was older than Marie, and it was a natural for Marie to think of her as a mother figure. Mama's English (in spite of her malapropisms) was better than Marie's. In a sense, Mama was a city girl in comparison to Marie who had spent most of her time since coming to America on Staten Island. On one of these visits, Marie asked Mama if she knew how to make *focaccia*. Mama said, "Of course, it's just like making bread or pizza." Little did Marie know Mama's thoughts about bread, how much she loved making it—that Mama thought bread was life.

"Didn't you make bread in Italy, Marie?" Mama asked with the look of disbelief on her face. Marie offered a sad reply, "Aunt Angela, you remember that my mother passed away soon after I was born. Yes, I lived in her house with my three brothers, and I cooked a lot, but

I bought bread from the local baker. I have made some loaves, but I never made focaccia."

Mama hugged Marie in a tender way, "Then we'll make it—I'm sure you have enough flour here. We'll need yeast, sugar, warm water, unbleached all-purpose flour, twenty-six fresh sage leaves, some olive oil, and salt. We're going to make a focaccia with fresh sage, olive oil, and salt."

Mama explained that in Florence, the bread is called "Schiacciata"; in Bologna, "piadina"; in America, "focaccia." No matter the name, this lightly seasoned pizza dough bread makes an especially delicious change from grilled bread. It is put on the table and eaten with and without other food. In Italy, a whole focaccia from a bakery weighs several pounds and is sold, cut into manageable pieces, by weight. Various ingredients can be worked into the dough or serve as a topping—cheese, ham, olives, onions, oregano, pancetta, or rosemary. For other occasions, it may be flavored with sun-dried tomatoes or herbs, but one of my favorites is the simple one made with sea salt, an herb, and extra-virgin olive oil.

Marie had all the ingredients in her kitchen and ran outside to the garden to pick twenty-six fresh sage leaves that Mama said they needed. "I don't measure, Marie, but you can put out what we need for the focaccia, and then you can measure and write it down so you can have a recipe," explained Mama. Marie said that was a good idea. Mama filled a one-cup cup with warm water and opened one package (one-fourth ounce) of active dry yeast and sprinkled it over the warm water then added a teaspoon of sugar. As she stirred the mixture, she told Marie it takes about ten minutes for the water to absorb the yeast and sugar. Then Mama put about three cups of flour on the cleared table. She arranged the flour in a circle with high walls (three inches or so) with a well in the center. She asked Marie to finely chop twenty of the fresh sage leaves to be put in the well along with the yeast water, one-fourth cup olive oil, and about one teaspoon coarse salt. Mama stirred the ingredients in the well with one hand as she held the flour in place with the other. Little by little, she brought some flour in to the liquid to make dough. She worked slowly so Marie could understand what was happening. When dough was formed, Mama took it all up and put it on a clean and floured work surface where she could knead it. She asked Marie to do this, first showing her how to knead. Marie did well, as Mama explained that it takes ten minutes of kneading, adding more flour as necessary, to make a smooth and elastic dough.

Mama took a bowl and asked Marie to place the dough inside it and to moisten a clean kitchen towel and cover the bowl.

"It'll take an hour, Marie, for it to rise, but that is okay, as it gives us time to just talk," Mama said.

Almost as if planned, Marie said, "Aunt Angela, Rocky wants to have children, but I am so afraid of pregnancy. My body shakes when I think about it. I'm frightened. I know so little about it. My brothers in Italy never talked about anything like that, and my mother died so young, I feel foolish to say what I am saying."

Mama took a moment and gave Marie a long, caring look before she started to give her counsel and advice, without oil on the forehead, and no charge. Serious conversations always took place in the Italian language, with a good bit of dialect.

Marie said to Mama, "Non capisco il significato del tremestre?" (I don't understand the significance of the trimester). Mama asked her to relax and said, "Trimestre di gravidanza, secong e terzo trimester di gravidanzo (There are three trimesters during one's pregnancy), and each is about thirteen weeks long. Marie, dear Marie, pregnancy is thought to be one of the happiest times of a woman's life, but I will tell you that many pregnant women do have problems with nausea, morning sickness, sadness, anxiety, *or* confusion as I did with all my children, especially, Joey, because he was born twelve pounds, and the midwife, Mrs. Colangelo, had to slap breath into him. But let me tell you, each pregnancy is different—they are not all the same, but you have to remember that your baby is a gift from God. It is the most beautiful thing in the whole world. There is nothing so good as hearing your baby's heartbeat inside your stomach—a truly exciting experience."

Marie, sitting there like a child in school, looking adoringly at her teacher and friend, said to Mama, "Aunt Angela, I love hearing you talk about this, and you are building my confidence."

Mama continued to describe what things Marie would feel in each of the three trimesters, how to handle morning sickness and nausea, how not to feel down in the dumps if that should occur and how your baby develops inside you, month by month.

Then she looked at the bowl of dough and said loudly,

"Madonna, come la pasta e aumentata! (Madonna, look at how the dough has risen!) Did one hour go that quickly? I guess so. Come, Marie, now we have to punch the dough down, shape it in a ball, and put it back into the bowl to let it rise again, until it is double in size." So Marie punched it down, rolled it into a ball, and put it back in the bowl to Mama's satisfaction. Mama said it needed another hour to rise, as she covered the bowl once again.

"Oh, Marie, I used to feel quite a bit of fatigue—I was always tired, and with most of my kids, I did have some morning sickness. But I always waited for the baby to move inside of me. During the second month, some symptoms become more noticeable—my breasts felt tender and I would urinate more frequently. Sometimes I would vomit, but I always thought of the baby to keep my spirits going. My heart beat faster, and the midwife explained to me that my body was making more blood because I needed blood for two. As you know, Marie, I had a couple of miscarriages, and they happened during the first trimester. The fourth month is the beginning of the second trimester. I had less nausea, but I still had some problems with my breasts, mostly soreness. I was always concerned about that, but Mrs. Colangelo would say, "E normale, e normale!" (It's normal, it's normal!) Every one of my kids was breast-fed. For me, that is the most important thing a mother can do for its child. Grandma, my mother (Marie called her Signora Beatrice), said a thousand times, 'Il primo latte, il primo latte' (The first milk, the first milk!)

"When you feel the first sign of the baby—for Jerry, it was like he was tickling my insides, for Mary, it was like butterflies fluttering their wings, for the twins, I had a lot of gas movements. But the important thing, Marie, is that you will find yourself smiling at everything the baby does. Mrs. Colangelo said the baby was always moving inside me—one time I complained to her that Jerry was kicking me, and you know what she said. Yes, it's normal. When you reach the third trimester, you can see your belly moving as the baby changes his or her position. My friend Teresa told me that a friend of hers who was pregnant thought her baby inside her was as dramatic as a movie star, I think she mentioned Marie Dressler. Teresa said her friend was eating spaghetti from a plate on her belly and that the baby kicked it right off her belly. I don't know if that's a true story, but that's what Teresa told me." As Marie laughed, Mama said, "Marie, look at the bowl, the dough has risen again. Let me show you how the focaccia is formed. We can make it in a pizza pan, about fourteen inches wide, or a jelly-roll pan, eleven by seventeen inches." Marie came forward with the pizza pan, just the right size, and Mama showed her how to oil the pan—Mama dripped a few drops of oil in the pan and rubbed her fingers all over until the oil covered the pan's surface.

"Marie, punch the dough down again, easy, easy, and put it in the pizza pan," explained Mama. "Now with your hands, and I'm going to let you do this, spread it out to fit the pan and then spread some oil over the top." Marie did this with a small pastry brush. "Now, decorate it with the six sage leaves."

Marie made an arrangement in the center, slightly overlapping them; Mama thought that was creatively done. "Sprinkle the remaining one teaspoon salt all over and let it rise for one-half hour. When that is done, we'll bake it for about fifteen minutes in the preheated 450-degree-Fahrenheit oven, or until it is nicely browned."

Mama looked at Marie and reminded her that it was important to make the sign of the cross with her hands over the focaccia before she put it to bake. Fifteen minutes later, it came out with a beautiful light toast color, and Mama hugged Marie, saying, "And you're going to make a beautiful baby. Don't wait too long. You want to enjoy your kids while you're young."

During that week of my "summer vacation," and for several other summers, Rocky would have practice sessions with selected members of his band. I felt like a king, eating fresh, fresh vegetable salads with lots of bread and having a band play just for me.

Marie and Rocky would take me and a bushel of fresh vegetables back to the city in their car. They were so thoughtful, polite, considerate, and respectful of Mama and Papa who always had a special meal for them before their return to the "country" in Staten Island. "Marie and Rocky are part of our family," Mama would swear.

Cauliflower and Olive Salad

Insalata di cavolfiore

Serves 6

1 medium-size cauliflower head
1 teaspoon salt
18 black olives, pits removed, cut into ¼-inch bits
6 anchovy fillets, washed and dried well, cut into ¼-inch pieces
½ teaspoon dried oregano
1 tablespoon capers, drained
Oil and vinegar dressing, see below

1. In a large saucepan, bring some water to boil. Cut the cauliflower head into flowerets, discarding heavy stems and any leaves. Make flowerets uniform in size—they should be no longer than one and a half inches in length or width. Add about one teaspoon salt to the water as it reaches the boil then add the cauliflower pieces. Cook them until they are al dente, about ten minutes.
2. Drain immediately and run the flowerets under cold water to stop further cooking. Dry them in a kitchen towel and put them in a large bowl. Add olives, anchovies, capers, and dressing and toss gently.

Note: It is best to make this salad ahead of time (to allow the cauliflower to absorb the dressing) and refrigerate it. Remove it from the refrigerator at least thirty minutes before serving to allow the dressing to reach room temperature and toss again.

To make oil and vinegar dressing:

1 tablespoon minced fresh basil
1 garlic clove, minced
2 tablespoons wine vinegar
6 tablespoons extra-virgin olive oil
Salt and freshly ground pepper

Whisk all ingredients and leave at room temperature until ready to use.

Zucchini Salad with Capocollo

Insalata di zucchini con capocolla
Serves 4

6 small whole zucchini (no thicker than 1 ½ inches)
⅓ cup shallots, chopped fine
1 teaspoon fresh tarragon, chopped fine (or ½ teaspoon dried)
¼ pound capocollo, sliced thin and cut into ¼-inch pieces
¼ cup fresh red pepper, chopped fine (or canned pimiento)
½ to 1 cup oil and vinegar dressing
Salt and freshly ground pepper

1. In a saucepan large enough to cook the whole zucchini, bring some water to boil. Wash the zucchini and add them to the water. Cook them until they are al dente, about five minutes. Drain them and, when they are cool enough to handle, cut off the ends and slice them crosswise into thin rounds.
2. Put slices in a large clean bowl. Add chopped shallots, tarragon, capocollo pieces, red pepper, and half-cup salad dressing. Toss gently, add more dressing to your taste, and adjust the salt and pepper. (Some capocollo is *piccante*, so watch the amount of pepper you add.)
3. This salad may be assembled and dressed ahead of time and refrigerated for as long as overnight to allow the zucchini to absorb the dressing. But remember, you must remove the salad from the

refrigerator thirty to sixty minutes before serving, allow it to reach room temperature, and toss it again.

Fried Zucchini Slices

Zucchine in padella

Serves 4

4 small zucchini, about 1 pound
½ cup all purpose flour
4 tablespoons extra-virgin olive oil
1 tablespoons balsamic vinegar

1. Wash zucchini and trim ends. Slice into one-fourth-inch rounds. Dry them well.
2. Dredge them with flour, removing excess flour.
3. Heat oil in a skillet and sauté the zucchini on both sides, leaving plenty of space between each round. Brown them lightly and transfer with a slotted spoon to paper toweling to drain. Sauté until all the rounds are done. Salt the slices lightly and dribble balsamic over all.

Focaccia with Fresh Sage, Olive Oil, and Salt

Focaccia col salvia, sale e olio

Makes one flat 14-inch round or 11 x 17 rectangular loaf

1 envelope (¼ ounce) active dry yeast
1 teaspoon sugar
1 cup warm water
3 to 3 ½ cups unbleached all-purpose flour
26 fresh sage leaves, 20 finely chopped, 6 left whole
¼ cup plus 2 tablespoons extra-virgin olive oil
2 teaspoons coarse salt

1. Sprinkle the yeast and the sugar over the warm water and stir. Let stand ten minutes.
2. Place three scant cups flour in a large bowl and make a well in the center. Add the yeast mixture, the chopped sage leaves, one-fourth cup olive oil, and one teaspoon coarse salt. Work in the flour until a dough forms then turn the dough out onto a floured work surface and knead until smooth and elastic, about ten minutes, adding more flour as needed. Place the dough in a clean bowl, cover with a moist cloth kitchen towel, and let rise until doubled in volume, about one hour.
3. Punch the dough down, arrange into a ball form, and put back in the bowl. Let rise again until doubled in volume, about one hour.
4. Preheat the oven to 450°F.
5. Brush a fourteen-inch pizza pan or an eleven-by-seventeen-inch jelly-roll pan generously with olive oil. Gently punch down the dough and fit it into the pan then brush it all over with the remaining olive oil. Arrange six sage leaves on top in a decorative pattern to express your creativity. Sprinkle with the remaining teaspoon of salt. Let rise for thirty minutes.
6. Bake the focaccia until nicely browned, about fifteen minutes. Serve warm.

14

THE REAL ESTATION UNCLE AND A CONNECTICUT VACATION

Papa's sister, our other aunt Rose, lived near Waterbury, Connecticut. She was married to Uncle Patsy. Our family visited them in the summer for three or four days, but after one or two visits, Mama realized these visits were not going to work—too much family, too many children. Aunt Rose and Uncle Patsy had four children, and Mama and Papa would appear with their three youngest, me and my two younger sisters. Aunt Rose wanted me there especially because her third child Sonny was male and my age—in fact, we were born in the same year, he in April, and I in May. So for three or four years, when I was ten through thirteen, I alone went to spend two weeks at Aunt Rose's home in Connecticut—another vacation in addition to Staten Island—Mama's way to keep me cool and off the city streets, away from the city hydrants. Mama was close to her sister-in-law. They had the same ideas of family values and bringing up their kids: love them and feed them.

Over the years, they spent much time on their husbands' shortcomings. Leaving one of her children in her care was just another piece of the family circle. Aunt Rose could have been Papa's identical twin. One time, Papa dressed in women's clothes and she in men's, and it was difficult to tell them apart. They were of same height, similar body frames, and their mannerisms indistinguishable. Each picked up a glass or cup in the same way, and they walked the same way. They even wiped their mouths the same. The napkin was first unfolded and stretched fully between two hands, then both hands were moved to one corner, and the napkins were drawn slowly across the mouth, gently patting as it went. Although both have been gone for years, we children all remember this mouth swipe; and at various times, when we are talking about them to younger members of the family, someone will always demonstrate this particular mannerism. Why did this amuse us so? Was it a pretense of elegance from a brother and sister who were born on Mott Street before the 1900s or was it a natural act of gracefulness, a sense of inborn tidiness? It didn't matter to any of us. We decided they were, after all, a class act.

Rose married Patsy, a volatile personality and temperament with major ambitions. He was stocky, muscular, with a strong face. His chin was square. When Patsy talked, his head fell slightly backward, his chin protruded at an upward angle, and he was Il Duce Mussolini. He had lost most of his hair at an early age. His speech always ended with a bang. He could be considered loud, but we viewed him as forceful and emphatic. He was an owner of an inn and picnic grounds called Hollow Springs in the Naugatuck Valley in Connecticut. His home was on this "reservation." It seemed busy one summer we were there, but wintertime brought few or no people to it. Our families were stunned on the day he lost this enterprise to the bank. Aunt Rose cried for weeks, but Uncle Patsy, quick to forget his failures (God forbid you brought up the subject), wanted to move on. His new occupation was "real estation"—he never learned to say "real estate." He was not to be taken lightly. In our immediate family, he was known as the "millionaire" because he did make what seemed to be a million, lose it, make another, and lose that too. However, during any of these downslides, he managed to feed, house, and clothe his family. When he was on top of the game, the sign was a new Panama hat, with a wide black silk ribbon on his bald head.

The combination of his personality with the rise and fall of income wore on Aunt Rose over the years. At times, she was like a cat on a hot tin roof. We noticed how fidgety she had grown. Papa had some of this too, but we decided it was part of his DNA (a nervous biting of his nails—he didn't actually bite them, but they looked as if he did; his folding and refolding of the dinner napkin, or his quietly tapping his thumb to his little finger on the kitchen table). Aunt Rose had similar mannerisms, and we thought her problem was Uncle Patsy in addition to her DNA. She crocheted, she knitted, and she worked over food in great detail. She could have roasted a chicken, but instead, she preferred rolled and filled chicken breasts, an activity more complex and time consuming. She could have cooked a simple pasta-sauce dish; instead, she kneaded dough, cut it into shapes, filled them, secured them, wrapped them around her fingers to make little hats, and so on. Her food was exquisite but took longer to prepare and expended more energy, perhaps to overcome the stress and aggravation over some statement or action made or taken by Uncle Patsy. Her food, small food, intricate, detailed, surely tasty, and finely prepared, must have helped take her mind away from Patsy's melodramatic behavior. Even when he was successful, he spent the money too quickly, and Aunt Rose's fingers would work faster and harder to form the many *cappelletti* she would eventually lower into the flavorful, boiling chicken broth. She cooked as she knitted, allowing her immediate world to get past her; but if you were close to her in the kitchen, you would sense her choked-up feeling of hushed distress.

Papa and Patsy got along, except for one thing. Uncle Patsy had the habit of coughing deeply and spitting out large gobs of phlegm. He would spit it on the street, in a field, or into a kitchen sink, wherever he needed to. His guttural cough was so pronounced, it upset those near him. Nothing stopped him, however, as he felt this behavior to be normal and necessary, and he couldn't have cared if it annoyed anyone. Papa, on the other hand, didn't know the concept spit existed, much less phlegm. Coughing and spitting was simply not part of Papa's physical being. He considered this act of Patsy's obnoxious, and every time Patsy coughed and spat, Papa grunted and groaned and made it plainly clear that he was annoyed. This behavior on both their parts lasted for years. In spite of this, our family went to the "country in Connecticut," and they visited us in the city. Uncle Patsy enjoyed his city visits because he liked to drink beer and play cards with Papa's friends. It gave him an immediate audience before which he could describe his "real estation" life of adventure and risk.

Friends often asked us why they were in Connecticut when we were in New York. The answer was simple. Immigrants usually settled in a given area because a family member or a paisano was there. Papa and his sister Rose were born on Mott Street, Little Italy, in New York City. Because of their father's health, the family returned to Italy. When he recovered, they returned to Naugatuck, Connecticut, a city famous for its high school designed by the well-known architect Stanford White, because an older daughter, married and with children, was established there. Papa, still single and very young, liked New York, so he departed the small Connecticut town for the brighter lights and faster pace of the big city, leaving behind his parents, sister Rose, and the older established sister Louisa. As time passed, Papa's parents died and were buried there.

There are some things one doesn't forget, and one is a first actual lesson in sex education. This happened for me in the country and not in the city. My cousin Sonny, one month older than I, was several years more advanced sexually. One night, after supper, as the sun was setting slowly over the western Connecticut hills, Sonny managed to get us out of the house. Aunt Rose was compliant and thought it was okay for us to play outdoors on the front lawns—after all, it was summer, and we would sleep better for it. Sonny had a different plan in mind. He directed us to other nearby streets then hid both of us behind a bush or a shed or a parked car, wherever we could be in view of a window behind which a girl or young woman was undressing. He knew exactly where to go and where to hide to get the best view of skirts and panties coming off. At such times, there was little conversation between us. Once in a while, Sonny would whisper. "My god, did you see that?" or "Holy cow, what a beautiful ass." At first, I was in shock for fear of being caught. Later, this activity became a nightly routine unbeknown to Aunt Rose or Uncle Patsy who was away from home selling "real estation."

Sonny was a hot-blooded teenager. Every night of my summer visit, in addition to the nightly off-limit viewings, there were other

Peeping Tom activities. We slept together upstairs in a bedroom next to his older sister Mela. We teased her every night by opening the door to her room and "mooning" her in our underwear. Another evening, to Mela's dismay, we covered our private parts with small dishes, stood in the doorway before throwing open the door, yelling, "Mela, Mela!" In spite of her threats to tell Mama, we repeated this bit of foolishness three and four times in one evening. I always slept in my underwear. Sonny liked to sleep nude, always happy to point to the hard part of his body that seemed like a pole holding up a white tent.

Sonny and I had a fine relationship to the day he died. I didn't see much of him, but there was always that wedding or funeral that brought cousins together. Our special feeling for each other transcended time and was the result of the early-life secrets shared only by us, which no one could take away.

It was fun to watch Aunt Rose cook. Precise in her actions, she exuded confidence as she went from one cooking step to the next. She handled chicken breasts as if she was bathing a baby, almost fondling them. Aunt Rose (and Papa) enjoyed young people. They called us *angeli* (angels). During my stay, she'd ask, first, me and then her son Sonny to help her with some cooking tasks—just to be with us or have someone to talk with, to enjoy her *cherubini*. As she started to prepare the filling for the rolled chicken breasts, she'd ask us to chop celery and mushrooms.

These "little birds" can be made with thin slices of beef or veal, and they are good, but Aunt Rose especially liked these made with chicken breasts. She would add roasted potatoes and a vegetable salad to complete this meal. When she was readying the chicken for filling, she let us use her family heirloom meat pounder, a heavy flat metal disk with an upright handle, to flatten the breasts, just two kids playing gladiators in Rose's country kitchen. When she made cappelletti on another day, we were allowed to turn the pasta machine handle, but she would watch closely and retrieve it before an error was made. Cappelletti differ from tortellini in that they contain no meat. We made them at home. But *cappellettini*, another name for little hats, can be found in the refrigerated and frozen food sections in supermarkets and may be used here, but they won't be as good as the fresh ones you make at home. They're actually quite easy to make.

This soup is very popular in Italy, and it is made and served in most homes and restaurants. All of us smiled at the sight of Aunt Rose and Mama wrapping the pasta shapes around their fingers, gossiping a mile a minute, and in no time, there were two gross of the pasta pieces sitting on cloth towels waiting to be bathed in the best-smelling chicken broth. Aunt Rose knew what she was doing in the kitchen, and every one in our family appreciated her efforts to share food and break bread with us. "We all have problems," she would say. "No one is without them, but please let us sit down and enjoy each other and enjoy this food." Then the elders would tell us stories about their parents and their grandparents who were innkeepers in Ruoti, the suburb of Potenza, and how they would sit around and eat at their table, as we do. We asked, "What was the most popular pasta at the inn?" Aunt Rose replied with this question, "Who, who can resist a creamy Gorgonzola sauce? Perdutamente people dream about this—a good reason to use Gorgonzola in cooking. In addition to its good taste is its ability to melt smoothly. This is an excellent sauce for fusilli and other pasta, such as rotelle (pasta wheels). Does this answer your question?"

Rolled Chicken Breast with Prosciutto Stuffing

Laminati petti di pollo con prosciutto ripieno
Serves 6 to 8

To prepare the chicken breasts:

4 whole chicken breasts, halved to make 8 pieces
1 tablespoon lemon juice
Salt
Pepper, ground fresh

1. Bone and skin chicken breasts, taking care not to separate the fillets from the breasts. Wash them in cool water and put them in a bowl

(it is not necessary to dry them first). Add lemon juice and let chicken sit for fifteen minutes. Meanwhile, prepare the stuffing.

2. Remove chicken breasts, put each one between sheets of wax paper, and pound lightly to flatten. Remove top sheet of paper and salt and pepper each piece on both sides.

To prepare the stuffing:

3 tablespoons butter
4 heaping tablespoons shallots, chopped fine
4 heaping tablespoons celery, including leaves, chopped fine
8 medium-size mushrooms, chopped fine
½ cup bread crumbs, unflavored
2 tablespoons fresh parsley, chopped fine (or 1 teaspoon dried)
Salt and freshly ground pepper
8 thin slices prosciutto

1. Melt three tablespoons butter in a skillet or saucepan, add chopped shallots and celery, and cook, five minutes. Add mushrooms and cook another five minutes. Remove skillet from heat, add bread crumbs and parsley, and mix well. Salt and pepper to taste, but go lightly with the salt because prosciutto is very salty.
2. Arrange one prosciutto slice on each of the eight chicken breast halves then divide the stuffing over them. Roll each piece, beginning with the small end. Secure the rolls with wood bamboo sticks, six or eight inches long, just as you would affix a straight pin to a piece of cloth or paper. If the ends of the roll turn up a bit, flatten it by pushing down lightly with the palm of your hand.

To bake the chicken:

2 eggs
1 tablespoon vermouth (optional)
Salt and freshly ground pepper
1 cup flour (approximately)
1 ½ cups bread crumbs, unflavored
4 tablespoons butter

Few sprigs of parsley
Lemon wedges

1. Beat eggs in a bowl with a fork and add vermouth (if you wish) and the salt and pepper.
2. Roll the chicken in flour, dip it in the egg, and coat it completely with the bread crumbs.
3. Use two tablespoons butter to grease the baking tray. Dot the chicken with the remaining two tablespoons butter. Bake at 400 degrees for thirty minutes (longer if rolls are large).
4. When rolls are cooked, set them on an attractive platter or tray, lined up like birds on a telephone wire. Place a few sprigs of parsley across the top and serve with lemon wedges. A squirt of lemon on these birds is delicious.

Cappelletti in Chicken Broth

Cappelletti in brodo di pollo

Makes 80 to 100 cappelletti to serve 6 to 8 in broth.

2 ¼ cups all-purpose flour
¾ teaspoon salt
3 eggs
1 tablespoon extra-virgin olive oil
1 tablespoon lukewarm milk
¾ cup ricotta cheese
¾ cup grated Parmesan cheese, divided
2 tablespoons finely chopped parsley
Freshly ground white pepper
Freshly grated nutmeg
8 cups homemade chicken broth, or 5 cups canned plus 3 cups water

1. Combine flour and salt in a bowl and make a well in the center. Beat eggs, olive oil, and milk together and pour into the well. Mix with a fork or by hand to make a dough. On a floured surface,

knead to make it smooth , about ten minutes. Cover and let it rest thirty minutes.

2. Meanwhile, in another bowl, combine ricotta, one-fourth cup of the Parmesan cheese, parsley, pepper, and the nutmeg. Mix well and set aside.
3. Cut the dough, after it has rested, in six pieces and put each through a pasta machine to get a one-sixteenth-inch thickness, or roll by hand, making as thin a pasta sheet as you can. Cut each piece into two-inch squares and put one-fourth teaspoon of the filling in the center of each square. Fold over diagonally to make a triangle. Press the edges to secure the filling. Although milk in the pasta is better than water in binding pasta, it is still best to press around each edge with the back of the tines of a fork. Bend each triangle around your index finger and press one point over the other. Reserve any leftover pasta to use as *maltagliati* by cutting it in small, odd-shaped pieces, about one inch each. Toss very lightly in flour, shaking out any excess flour. The cut pasta will last for several days, covered, or may be frozen for later use.
4. Bring broth to boil in a large soup pot. Add filled pasta and cook until they are tender—they will rise to the top in a few minutes. Ladle into warm bowls and serve with more Parmesan cheese. If served with warm Italian bread, buttered or oiled, you will have an excellent supper.

Fusilli with Creamy Gorgonzola Sauce

Fusilli in salsa di gorgonzola cremoso

Serves 4

½ cup butter, melted
¼ pound Gorgonzola cheese
1 cup half and half
¼ cup tomato puree (not tomato paste)
¾ cup walnut halves
½ teaspoon cumin seed

1 pound fusilli
1 cup freshly grated Parmesan cheese
1 large ripe tomato, peeled, seeded, and sliced fine, then cubed
Salt and freshly ground black pepper

1. In a saucepan, combine melted butter and Gorgonzola. Stir until the cheese is melted.
2. Add the half and half, tomato puree, walnut halves, and cumin seed. This should be kept over very low heat or set aside until pasta is cooked.
3. Cook fusilli or other pasta until al dente, drain, and return to pot in which it cooked. Add the Parmesan cheese, cream sauce, and tomato cubes. Toss well, season to taste, and serve warm or lukewarm.

VARIATION

Use one pound rotelle (pasta wheels) in place of the fusilli; twelve basil leaves, chopped fine, instead of the cumin seed; and add one ounce of brandy (optional) to cheese sauce as soon as Gorgonzola has melted.

15

AN UNEXPECTED EATING PLEASURE

The firstborn male has a special place in the Italian family hierarchy. Mama always said this was simply not so, and when we suggested that Jerry, our older brother, got the cream from the milk and the white breast from the chicken, she hushed us. "You know I love you all equally—how can you possibly say or think such a thing?" she pleaded. She kept muttering that we all shared the cream, and all of us got the white meat of the chicken. But it is true that Mama went to work in the textile district to earn enough money to support Jerry through college and law school. She worked long hours, and we understood her goal. Sometimes we were not so accepting of it when we were unable to get allowances or other things we thought we deserved.

Jerry was tall, thin, and good looking, with a wonderful shock of dark hair. It was fashionable to wear turtleneck sweaters (the movie stars set that pattern), and he followed suit, with a pipe stuck between his teeth. It was as if he planned a pose—the hair, high collar, and pipe all fit together to make an attractive picture. He was extroverted and made friends easily; he was the most popular guy on the block, and he could cook! Mama, Papa, and his grandparents taught him.

We thought he was interested in the girl who lived in the fourth-floor flat next to the building's owner. She was a Sicilian beauty who wanted to become a schoolteacher. We all wanted this to work out for them, but it didn't. Jerry left for college, and that was the end of the romance we envisioned for him.

None of us kids will ever forget one meal Mama and Papa prepared for Jerry and his college friends. At a point in his junior year, he was coming home for a long weekend with some college buddies, all longing for home-cooked Italian food. That was all my parents had to hear. They started preparing the meal days before the arrival. The antipasti alone would have sufficed as a full meal, but pasta was made from scratch, rolled out by hand, and then hand cut into three- to four-inch lasagna squares to be layered with ricotta, braised broccoli rape, and Parmesan cheese. A hundred pasta squares were made ahead of time and stored in the icebox until their boiling time. No one else made lasagna this way. It was original—Mama conceived of it for a special occasion.

Mama's special Sunday tomato sauce cooked with beef, pork, and veal was made using her jars of home-canned tomatoes and tomato *conserva*. Papa added a special touch; he added some pieces of her homemade sausage for extra flavor. The meats and sauce were to be served without pasta but lots of bread to clean the bowl of its sauce. They prepared platters of fried baccala (salted codfish) steeped in the "good" olive oil, used only on special occasions, and combined with other fish, including shrimp, squid, and octopus. Mama stuffed a veal breast to be roasted with potatoes and rosemary on the "big" day. It is an adaptation of the Ligurian veal dish—where veal is a popular meat—known as *cima alla Genovese*. A breast of veal is filled with a stuffing of offal, vegetables, and nuts. There are a variety of ways to cook this dish, as you may imagine; and Mama made it filled with ground veal and pork, nuts, and cheeses—in other words, without the variety meats, which did not appeal to us children.

You will need a large veal breast from an animal over one year old. Ask your butcher if he can accommodate you. You may have to use a smaller breast. He should bone it for you and create a pocket so it can receive a filling. Ask for the bones so you can make a veal broth to use in this recipe. Of course, Mama made homemade bread and a delicious cake flavored with orange syrup to be served with caramelized oranges, a version of *ciambellone*, a Florentine orange-flavored cake served with a dollop of whipped cream. (The secret of this cake lies in the syrup.)

There are many versions of this dessert, and most of them call for the oranges to be sliced. Mama cooked them whole, dipped in the syrup, and served whole with strips of caramelized orange on top. This is a special dessert.

There was no end to the parents' preparations. Fruits, nuts, cheeses, and roasted chestnuts were to adorn the table after the meal. We saw table linens we had never seen before. In fact, we have never seen such a plan for food in our home—and all this for the firstborn son and his college friends. We were not going to be allowed to sit with them. Mama's plan was to feed us briefly and quickly before the guests arrived, then we were to be sent to the front room—virtually Siberia, or so it seemed at the time. We helped our parents with the chores, and we kept asking about the time of arrival and who exactly were these people and why we couldn't sit with them.

The meal was to be served at the kitchen table—we had no dining room. This meant every square foot of space was needed for the preparation of the meal, including the first bedroom. Papa was kept busy shuffling between the pasta board and his bed. As Mama completed cutting the lasagna squares, he was there to carry them to his bed. We suggested that perhaps Jerry was married and was bringing his new wife home. That was all we had to say, and Mama's blood began to boil. Mama showing irritation was a rare occurrence in our home, and Papa thought we had gone too far. Surely, some tough discipline would have taken place, except that the phone rang at that moment.

Mama picked it up, and, within seconds, her face had turned white, and she started to cry. We heard part of the conversation. Jerry's plans had been changed, and he and his friends were not coming for dinner or for a visit at all. We thought, "That brother of ours waited until the appointed dinnertime to tell Mama they were not coming—did he think she would prepare only *pasta e fagioli*?"

Mama, quivering and with wet eyes, quickly announced a change of plans. Her other children would join her and Papa for the dinner. You could hear a pin drop—the moment of silence was exhilarating. The underlings had won out. So we sat and ate for hours with laments from our parents over what Jerry and his friends were missing. Oh how we enjoyed every bite. Never before had we had such a feast. This was a fantastic treat, and each of us learned the true glory of sharing great food. It would be difficult to achieve a comparable eating experience in the future. It became family folklore and a story told over and over again. And every time we told the story, the pain in Mama's face was visible.

Jerry finished college and law school and then came the atomic bomb—his plan to marry and live in Kentucky. On top of that, the girl was non-Catholic. I think Mama never got over this. Her dream was to have a well-educated son, married to the girl next door, who lived close to the family, and made babies that Mama could tend to nearby. All Italian families lived close to each other. Kentucky was as far away as Japan. This son, first born, altar boy par excellence who never missed a Sunday Mass and who continued to pray daily with a string of beads, was married on the *other* side of the altar rail (the penalty if you were marrying a non-Catholic) in a Catholic church in Kentucky, miles from where he was to live. I know. I was there. I was his best man.

Why would an Italian Catholic settle in a community where Italians and Catholics were on the fringe of society? Jerry never learned to drive. To get to Mass on Sundays, his wife drove him twenty miles. While he was at Mass, she would food shop. His wife, called "Boone" because she was a distant relative of Daniel Boone, did not object to their two sons being raised as Catholics; so over the years, she transported the three men in her life twenty miles one way and twenty miles home each Sunday for Mass.

In spite of the ethnic and religious differences of voters in the area, Jerry was elected county attorney nine times before he was elected county judge. The only explanation we could find for Jerry's defection was something Mama said many times, "Love is blind, love is blind, and love is blind." The expression became part of her vocabulary. In this way, she began to understand and accept the loss of her firstborn son and his new life in Kentucky where Jerry became known as the judge who cooks. The Louisville *Courier Journal* published a major food story about him and described in detail the contents of his kitchen in a separate building on his farm (named Barrister's Lodge). He cooked and entertained his friends from the court (lawyers, judges, court staff, et al.) just as Mama and Papa did at home. His wife was not included in the Lucullan feasts. The scene was Italian with prosciutto, salamis, and cheeses dripping from the ceiling, and food on this stove was like ours at home.

When he was in public schools before college, he always asked Mama for foods he loved. One of his favorites was tomatoes and peppers, stewed together with onion, garlic, oil, basil, and some wine. This was made at times with one or more sausage links, cooked first, usually sliced before the tomatoes and peppers were added. Red pepper flakes could be included for more spice. We called this Jerry's dish, and when we did, everyone knew what we were talking about. In time, Jerry cooked this himself; and when he set up *his* kitchen in Kentucky, this was the first thing he cooked. Boone, his wife, would smile and say, "Jerree, I jes love it. It's so Southern." Jerry answered, "Yes, my love, southern Italian." Not exactly true, as most regions in Italy have a version of this. In the Veneto, they cook *Papriche stufate* (stewed sweet peppers); they use yellow bell peppers with tomatoes, garlic, oil, salt and peppers, and chopped parsley. Jerry never varied his cooking methods. He was in heaven, mopping the plate with great Italian bread. He cooked earthy dishes and featured cannelloni beans, garbanzos (*cece*), pastas with fiery sauces, and included in his repertoire all of Papa's great dishes. He was known to entertain twelve people at a time. Some Kentuckians thought he was employed by the Italian government to promote Italian food. He knew instinctively that people, even Kentuckians, would love Italian food, and they did. When he called us from Kentucky, his first question was always "Any new recipes?" He found Italian food boutiques across the river in Cincinnati, Ohio, and once in a while, but rarely, we'd send him something he needed. He found a butcher who knew the proper way to slice veal cutlets. After sautéing the veal, he'd cover it with his tomato and pepper concoctions. Both of his sons became good cooks, and only the other day, his younger son Michael called and asked, "When are we going to Italy for *cinghiale?*" (wild boar; it makes a fantastic sauce for pasta)

Mama's lasagna for this meal was not made Accettura style. All her life, Mama made efforts to learn to cook foods from all over Italy. She learned about different tortellini from waiters at Barbetta's on West Forty-Sixth Street, New York, but also from people she met on her travels.

When we took her with us—she was eighty-seven at the time—to France, we were all at a huge market, with a permanent canopy of metal and glass, in Northern Burgundy, and we lost her! Where is Mama! Good God, where is she? We checked all the nearby stands but couldn't find her. We were ready to call the local police when we spotted her across the expanse of the market—two women talking a mile a minute. We said that can't be Mama because she doesn't speak French, and no one here knows Italian or English. It was Mama, one hundred yards or so away. Undisturbed, she said she had met this Italian lady from Emilia Romagna in Italy married to a French man. So began a series of food discussions and reports between Mama and her new friend Liliana as they compared Bolognese recipes. Mama took advantage of opportunities like this. Liliana came to our rented house one day, and she and Mama cooked a meal for us.

The recipes here are some of the food cooked for the no-shows Jerry and his college friends. We were perdutamente the night they didn't show. The food was phenomenal—a meal we could never forget, a meal that defines "perdutamente."

Lasagna Squares with Braised Broccoli Rapa

Quadrati Di Lasagna Con Broccoletti

Serves 8

- 2 bunches fresh broccoli rape
- 3 tablespoons extra-virgin olive oil
- 2 large cloves garlic, minced
- A pinch of red pepper flakes
- 24 fresh pasta squares, each about 4 inches square
- 2 tablespoons butter, melted

1 to 1 ½ cups fresh ricotta cheese
Nutmeg

1. To prepare broccoli rape, wash it well and trim the ends. Remove strings on the larger stalks as on large celery. Cut larger leaves in half and let all leaves stand in cool water until ready to cook. Heat two or three cups of water in a large saucepan. Add one teaspoon salt and bring water to a rapid boil. Add the rabe and cook until just tender; depending on size and freshness of stalks, this may take five to ten minutes. Drain well.
2. Heat three tablespoons oil in a large skillet. Add the minced garlic and cook one minute. Add the rabe and move it around in the oil and garlic. Add the pepper flakes and cook two or three minutes longer. Remove from heat. Keep warm.
3. Bring water to boil in a large saucepan. Add a tablespoon of salt just before it boils. Cook pasta squares until al dente, six at a time. After a few minutes, they will rise to the top, and that indicates they are cooked. Using a slotted spoon, remove the pasta, drain well, and place in a large bowl. Add the butter to the bowl and stir the pasta to coat it. Repeat this until all the pasta is cooked.
4. To serve, set out eight plates (shallow bowls with rims are best) and put a buttered square of pasta in each bowl. Add a good tablespoon of ricotta to each square and then cover each with a second square. Put a tablespoon broccoli rabe on top of each and cover that with another pasta square. Add a bit more butter to the top and a sprinkle of nutmeg. If there is more broccoli rabe, add a bit to the top of each serving. Serve right away.

Angela's Sunday-Best Stuffed Breast of Veal

Petto di vitello facito all'Angela
Serves 10 to 12

One 1-pound Italian bread, one or two days old
1 cup milk

6 large eggs
1 ¼ pounds ground veal and pork
1 pound fresh ricotta cheese
1 cup freshly grated Parmesan cheese
½ cup finely chopped flat parsley
3 large cloves garlic, minced
⅓ cup golden raisins
⅓ cup pine nuts, toasted
Salt and freshly ground pepper
One 8-pound breast of veal
1 cup veal or chicken broth
1 cup dry white wine
1 cup diced, canned tomatoes
1 large onion, thinly sliced

1. Preheat oven to 450°F.
2. Break bread into chunks and put them in a large bowl. Add milk, toss to moisten the bread, and let stand twenty to thirty minutes. Squeeze bread dry and set aside.
3. Whisk eggs in a large bowl. Add ground meat, ricotta and Parmesan cheeses, parsley, garlic, raisins, pine nuts, and some salt and freshly ground pepper. Add the bread and mix with splayed fingers. Combine these ingredients well but don't overdo. Do *not* mix in a food processor or other mechanical device.
4. Fill the pocket of the veal breast. Do not overstuff, as the filling will expand while it cooks. Secure the opening all the way by sewing with needle and thread.
5. Put the filled veal breast on a roasting rack in a large roasting pan and roast thirty minutes until the meat is browned. Remove from the oven and lower the heat to 300°F.
6. Add the veal or chicken broth, wine, tomatoes, and the onions to the roasting pan. Cover with foil and continue cooking three and a half to four more hours. Remove pan from oven and let the veal rest, covered, twenty minutes or so. Slice one-half-inch thick to serve.

Orange Ring Cake

Ciambellone all'arancia

Serves 8 to 10

To make the cake:

1 cup butter, softened
1 cup sugar
4 egg yolks, room temperature
1 cup sour cream
2 tablespoons finely chopped orange zest
2 cups all-purpose flour
1 teaspoon each: baking powder and baking soda
4 egg whites, room temperature

1. Preheat oven to 325°F. Cream butter and sugar until well blended. Add egg yolks, sour cream, and zest. Beat until light and fluffy and a ribbon forms in the batter when the beaters are raised.
2. In a large bowl, sift together flour, baking powder, and soda. Fold this into the batter. Beat egg whites until stiff but not dry and fold them in.
3. Pour batter into an oiled (use vegetable) and floured nine-inch tube pan. Bake one hour. Remove cake and let sit fifteen to twenty minutes. When the pan is cool enough to handle, very carefully loosen around the edge of the cake with a sharp knife and invert cake onto a cake platter.

Orange
Cut four thin slices then juice, see below.

To make the syrup:

Juice of 1 orange
Juice of 1 lemon
¾ cup sugar
¼ cup orange liqueur

Gently boil these ingredients in a small saucepan until the mixture turns to syrup, about five minutes.

To assemble and serve:

Cake, above
Syrup, above
1 cup heavy cream, whipped
Thin slices of orange, seeded, cut in halves

Spoon the syrup over the cake and let it soak in. Cut into one-half-inch pieces and serve each with whipped cream and a half orange slice.

Caramelized Oranges

Arance caramellizzate

Serves 6

6 oranges 1 ½ cups sugar
⅔ cup water
2 tablespoons kirsch or brandy

1. Zest three of the oranges and slice the zest as thin as possible and put aside. Carefully peel all six oranges and remove pits.
2. Combine sugar and water in a saucepan and bring to boil, stirring most of the time to make a syrup. Boil until the sugar is completely dissolved. If the sugar boils up to the top of the saucepan, quickly remove the saucepan from the heat source and, as the syrup recedes, put back on the heat.
3. After cooking the syrup seven minutes add kirsch or brandy. Cook one minute longer and remove from heat. Dip each orange in the syrup for two minutes. Remove and place on a plate. Reserve the syrup in the saucepan.
4. Put the strips of orange zest into another saucepan and cover with water. Bring to boil, lower heat, and simmer ten minutes. Drain well.
5. Cook the drained zest in the syrup until caramelized.
6. To serve, place an orange on a plate and top with the candied zest.

16

BYE, BYE, BLACKBIRD

When Mama worked, our oldest sister, Mary, was the designated mom. She was tougher than Mama—a lot more demanding in her requests. If she was seated in the kitchen next to the icebox and wanted some fresh cherries out of the icebox, she called one of us from the front room to get them. Why couldn't she reach in and get them herself? we wondered. We knew she could have done this without getting off her chair. Because we liked her, she was able to get away with many unreasonable requests. Mama assigned her many chores, and she delegated to us. She commanded; we complied. She ordered us to stir a tomato sauce, move a pot on the stove, or take something out of the oven. This was her modus operandi that carried into adulthood.

The reason Mary became a great cook is directly related to her serving as surrogate mother. Though she asked us to do this or that, she was ultimately responsible for whatever food was produced. Mary learned to prep many foods that Mama could throw together as soups or stews at the last minute. Mary did not disappoint. She learned to make pasta sauce so Mama could quickly boil the pasta, sauce it, and serve it to us soon after getting home from work. If Mary made meat loaf, Mama would add a last-minute salad. If Mary needed help, Grandma lived in the building next door and would teach her whatever she needed to know. If Jerry was home from college, Grandma and Mary would come up with a cooking solution. If Mary needed an ingredient, she had the vast resource of Manuel's Grocery Store a few flights down. If she really liked a food, she mastered its preparation. For example, she loved fresh shrimp and learned to shell, devein, and boil them to perfection, to be added to olive oil, lemon juice, and rosemary, her favorite combination of ingredients. She would explain, "Fresh lemon juice has the ability to quicken the intoxicating scent of rosemary on shrimp and some other fish. You know what rosemary can do to lamb and other cuts of meat, but in this recipe, my unusual touch is rosemary, with the help of lemon, on shrimp."

She also loved scallops, both sea and bay varieties, and caressed them with great tenderness as she combined them with pancetta and fresh chicory. She learned by trial and error. She put the pancetta-wrapped scallops in the skillet on their sides to brown the pancetta. "Don't worry about the scallop—look at the pancetta. If that browns, the scallop will be cooked," she said to us once, teaching us her little trick.

She carried on, "Pancetta and bacon are the same cut of pork, except that pancetta is not smoked as is bacon. It is cured in salt and spices, and it is shaped like a salami." As a rule, it is thinly sliced to order. It is available in some supermarkets and almost always available in specialty food shops. Mary gave us some advice, "If you can't get pancetta, use thinly sliced prosciutto or, as a last resort, thinly sliced bacon."

Many believe someone is either a cook or a baker—not both. The reasons are vague. There was nothing vague about Mary's ability to cook and bake. She would explain the difference, "You don't have to measure things when you cook—you can add a pinch of this or that, and you're more creative. *But* when you bake, *measure everything precisely,* and you'll be okay."

In addition to her cooking skills (thank you, Mama), Mary was the best-looking gal in the neighborhood, and the neighborhood guys were always sniffing around her. This annoyed us, her siblings, perhaps because we didn't understand their intentions; perhaps because we did. She was our other mother, and we wanted her attention. We thought she was beautiful.

She had an innate sense of style. She was Chanel before we knew who Chanel was. She wore the slouch hat worn by Ingrid Bergman in *Casablanca* before the movie was released, and she wore Jackie Onassis's pillbox hat before she did. Before Mary married, she arranged for all her trousseau undergarments to be made by hand of French silk, all with hems hand rolled. Her future sister-in-law, Marion, worked in a high-class lingerie firm, and Mary milked the contact. All of us thought the garments were the most beautiful things we had ever seen. We complimented her about her fashionable wardrobe as often as we did her cooking skills.

We thought Mary, as eldest girl of the family, was, like Jerry, the oldest boy, favored too. Papa seemed partial to Mary, although he said this was not so. There were clearly two times Papa did not favor her. The first was when she brought home a pair of shoes with spiked heels (she paid for them). Papa lifted them in the air and struck Mama's pasta board—the strike was so hard some of the thin strands of pasta on the board coiled, and we thought the heels had broken. He cussed in Italian with words that suggested only trollops wear such shoes. The next week, Mary wore the shoes as if she were in a Gucci ad. The second disagreement was over a silver cigarette case in Mary's purse. Papa needed a tip for a delivery boy and, with Mary's permission, went into her purse and discovered the case filled with cigarettes (Mary had forgotten they were there). The Italian cussing was considerably more intense this time, and for a day or two, our home was like a funeral parlor.

She knew whom she would marry years before vows were exchanged. Her wedding dress and veil were fashioned by hand also and took months to make. The wedding took place at St. Malachy's Roman Catholic Church on West Forty-Eighth Street, just off Broadway. The reception was at the Palm Garden on Fifty-Second Street and Eighth Avenue, a large banquet hall built for 250 to 300 people. Many elaborate Italian weddings were held there.

Weddings in the spring or early fall featured bridesmaids with same-color dresses with shoes dyed to match. They wore hats of various designs, some sculpted to fit around their heads or down one side of the face. Others were large willowy wisps with wide brims and ribbons flowing down the bridesmaids' backs to the lowest vertebrae. The bridal parties normally included six to eight bridesmaids, the same number of ushers, a maid or matron of honor, a best man, two little flower girls, and a ring bearer (little too). I was a ring bearer once a year (sometimes two times) from age six to twelve—dressed fully in tails, top hat, and black patent leather shoes. At my first ring-bearer job, I was asked to sing with full orchestra "Bye, Bye, Blackbird," a song made famous by Al Jolson. I was brought to the stage, with maximum lighting, and sang one line and cried out, "I can't sing anymore. My collar is too tight!" I walked off to thunderous applause.

Sit-down dinners were unheard of and unaffordable. Typical weddings in those days meant a banquet hall filled with large tables seating ten people. Each table was dressed with white tablecloths and surrounding ordinary folding chairs. Each table was assigned to a family. There were as many children as there were adults, sometimes more. The tables were arranged so there was ample space in the center of the hall for dancing. The area in front of the stage, which held the orchestra, was kept free for other activities. That was where Mary and her new husband, Sonny, did the Peabody, a fast, rip-snorting dance where the male holds his partner in front of him but out to his right side. When they danced, he moved forward, she backward. The Peabody was the rage before the Lindy Hop moved it aside.

Several days before the wedding, our family started to prepare hundreds of sandwiches for the reception. They were each wrapped in white waxed paper and placed on a tray—one tray for each table. The contents of the sandwiches were not marked. If you opened one, and it was not what you hoped for, you would pass it around until there was a taker. Each sandwich not spoken for was carried home. For the sandwich fillings, Mama and Papa went to Manganaro's at Thirty-Eighth Street and Ninth Avenue for a grand variety of Italian cold cuts and cheeses. The rolls were a special order from Zito's Bakery, across the street from Manganaro's. Hundreds of them, round yeast dough rolls covered with poppy seeds, had to be carried home in supersize sacks just before the sandwiches were to be made to assure their freshness. Other sacks were filled with sweet and hot salamis, *soppresatas*, *mortadellas*, and whole *caciocavalli* cheeses thinly sliced by the Manganaro staff to Mama and Papa's specifications and satisfaction. Imported prosciutto was too expensive even for a wedding, so it was not part of their order. They would also buy two-gallon-sized jars of pickled peppers and other vegetables, which had to be dried with kitchen toweling before being added to the sandwiches. If they had been wet, they would have dampened and ruined the sandwiches. The rolls for the sandwiches were either buttered or oiled (to keep them fresher, per Mama). They also ordered bottles of catsup, mustard, and mayonnaise, to be used if only anyone asked for it at the dinner. Never did we add mustard, mayonnaise, or catsup to the rolls.

There were also trays of fancy Italian pastries topped with white sugar-coated almonds and many wedding favors picked over by the kids. You would want to kill some of them for their ferocious attacks on these cookie trays. These trays of excellent pastries were special-ordered from Ferrara's, downtown, and they were delivered to the Palm Garden on the day of the wedding, one tray for each table. Individual pastries were carefully selected before the trays were composed. Mama didn't want too many plain sugar cookies, usually centered with a piece of dried cherry. She wanted the rich sfogliatelle, the succulent cannolis, the chocolate and white iced-covered cream puffs, and, most of all, the *ricciarelli*, almond cookies made famous in Sienna, so soft, so moist, so tender, and delicious with pine nuts sitting on their crowns. Gloriously decorated and in competition with the bride, the trays wore lacy doilies, curly ribbons, and artificial lilies of the valley; other confections were wrapped in shiny silver and gold paper. The tray on the bride's table had a miniature bride and groom on top. These trays were important, for they took the place of the wedding cake and, truthfully, cost more than a cake. They were large trays because the hosts wanted each family to fill a large sack with pastries to carry home as a remembrance of the wedding.

To complete the culinary picture, there was a large pitcher of beer poured from a keg (the kegs were kept in one corner of the banquet hall), a bottle of rye whiskey, (everyone drank rye those days, either in shot glasses or with soda and mostly with ginger ale), a jug of red wine (in the jug that came from the store—a popular brand name was Carlo Rossi), and soft bottled drinks for the children. There were no flowers on the tables—they were not needed, as the pastry trays were decorative enough to make a strong splendiferous statement.

The mother of the bride was responsible for making the large white satin bag with a pull string for the cash gifts. None of us remembers a time when a gift was other than cash. Everyone knew weddings were expensive, and everyone knew how much the cash was needed. Mama spent a long time making an appropriate bag for Mary and acted annoyed when we suggested that the bag seemed rather large. Each time we looked at it, it grew larger. In those days, there were no gift registers; everyone gave cash (rarely, very rarely a check) in an envelope. These envelopes were known as *Ma-low-pas* (I am sure this pronunciation was for the English word "envelope"—the word for envelope in Italian is "busta"; "ma-low-pas" was the same kind of word as "baa-cow-za" was for backhouse). When the party was over, the mother of the bride took the satin bag home for safekeeping until the newlyweds were back from their honeymoon, As soon as the bride returned from her honeymoon, she was given a full list and accounting of all the "gifts," by name and amount. Most families kept copies of these lists as a reference for future gift giving. Common practice was to give someone else's daughter the same amount her family gave your daughter when she married.

The fun part of the wedding was the tarantella dance. Older people would strut their stuff. Most ladies would slightly raise their skirts, holding the uplifted skirt in one or both hands—the hands always placed low on the hip to achieve the correct position. The arm hung loosely, and the elbow was slightly bent and placed on the hip without moving up or down. Some women would use a handkerchief, held squarely between both hands, swinging it to the right and then to the left, to excite her partner the way a bullfighter uses his cape. When the tarantella was in full swing, the Palm Garden rocked. At Mary's wedding, it was special when Mama and Papa did their number. People were inclined to overapplaud because they were the parents of the bride and also because they were paying for everything. Weddings took place on Sundays, and people went directly to the banquet hall after the midafternoon church wedding ceremony. In this way, people could be home by 10:00 p.m. Monday morning came sooner than one wished.

Mary and Sonny, her new husband, went to Havana, Cuba, *the* place to honeymoon. Their new apartment was in Long Island City, and for a year or two, it served as a fine "honeymoon cottage" for the newlyweds.

There, Mary experimented with new recipes, dishes she thought would become her as a young bride. One that fascinated her was the soufflé (*soffie* in Italian), but she would complain that sometimes "it is in style," and sometimes "it isn't." This brought forth from Mama "If it's a good dish, it never goes out of style!" so Mary experimented and conceived of a broccoli and ricotta soufflé that was unusual. In time, she could make this blindfolded, or so it seemed. She said if you understand the basics of it, anyone can do it. A base has to be created, in this case broccoli, ricotta, eggs, and cheese. Then the base has to be lightened and given "air" so the mixture can rise as it bakes in the oven. This is achieved by beating egg whites to soft peaks and being careful in folding them into the base. The one disadvantage to this dish is that it can fall if too much time lapses from oven to table. Our sister was very capable of showing her annoyance when we yelled, "Hurry, hurry, or it's gonna collapse," as she took it from the oven to serve.

With the success of the soufflé and because a baby was on the way, Mary and Sonny moved back to our neighborhood for a good reason: they needed Mama's help.

And Mama helped. It was as if Mary had moved back in with the family. Before we knew it, the baby was born. Back to heat the bottles, back to feed the baby, and back to dinner with the folks. That's how Richard, their only child, grew up. As a teenager, he was handsome, did well in school, and showed artistic and athletic ability. Every member of the family considered him outstanding by any measurement. But as a teenager, he was missing meals at home; soon thereafter, he was dating a woman twice his age, perhaps more. They would appear on the lawn clad in riding clothes as we were enjoying al fresco summertime suppers. They were a Ralph Lauren ad. Who was this femme fatal? No one knew for sure, but it didn't matter, for the breakup was imminent. Mary's soufflé fell fast and harder than anyone could imagine. She stopped baking them—she said once as she brought one to the table, "This will fall fast, just like my son." No one said a word. We waited, and the soufflé fell.

We were a family who wanted to be together, to eat together. Mary was included, as was her husband, Sonny. Mary told us she had the Jackie O. disease, lymphoma. Mary was strong, our second mama, and she wouldn't succumb to the disease. If Mary were living today, she would find satisfaction in her grandson who is now executive chef at a well-known restaurant in Baltimore, Maryland. In one of his public interviews, he was asked how he became interested in food. He said, as young boy, he spent many hours and days with his grandmother in her kitchen learning to cook, and because of that, he pursued a career in cooking.

Mary was a fantastic cook. Later in life, we called her Martha Stewart. She entertained others and us with grandiose meals at holiday time. In her home, her aim was to provide good dinners for her husband (and son). Mary told us that her husband, after eating our family's homemade meat loaf every Monday evening for more than twenty-five years, said he could eat it twenty-five years longer. At those meals, Mary also served her Italian cake—he'd been eating that for a long time too. In her sadder moments, Mary said life brings sorrow and joy into a family, as it should be. But we must never forget what matters.

Shrimp in Olive Oil and Lemon Juice with Rosemary

Gamberi in olio d'oliva e succo di limone con rosamarino

Serves 4

1 pound large shrimp, 16 to 20 shrimp
½ cup extra-virgin olive oil
Juice of 1 lemon, about 3 tablespoons
½ teaspoon finely chopped fresh rosemary
Salt and freshly ground pepper
4 sprigs of rosemary, 3 or 4 inches long

1. Bring water to boil with some salt in a saucepan and cook shrimp until pink, about two to three minutes after the water returns to

the boil. Drain and rinse under cold water. Peel and devein the shrimp. Dry them well with kitchen toweling and put them in a glass bowl.

2. Combine the oil, lemon juice, rosemary, and some salt and freshly ground pepper. Mix well and pour over cooled shrimp. Allow to marinate twenty to thirty minutes. Toss again.
3. Place a rosemary sprig on each of four plates. Carefully arrange four or five shrimp on each plate, slightly overlapping the rosemary and with each shrimp hugging another, side by side. Spoon some of the dressing (marinade) over the shrimp and serve right away.

Scallops and Pancetta on Chicory Hearts and Radicchio

Capesante e pancetta su cuori di cicoria e radicchio

Serves 4

3 tablespoons brown raisins
½ cup *vin santo* or white wine
2 small heads radicchio
2 small heads chicory
16 large fresh sea scallops
Salt and freshly ground pepper
16 small slices of pancetta (or 8 cut in half, lengthwise), or its substitute, to fit around the curved side of each scallop
4 tablespoons extra-virgin olive oil
½ teaspoon finely chopped fresh rosemary
⅓ cup walnut pieces, toasted
4 fresh lemon wedges, seeds removed

1. Combine raisins and vin santo or wine in a small bowl and allow to stand for one hour to plump the raisins. Drain, reserving the wine, and set soaked raisins aside. Trim radicchio heads of their first layer of outer leaves, core the heads, and cut them in half. Slice each half very thinly. Remove green leaves from both heads of chicory to reach the yellowish, white inner hearts. Cut off stem ends and finely slice hearts. Set aside.

2. Rinse and dry scallops. Add some salt and freshly ground pepper to them and wrap a piece of pancetta around each scallop, securing it with a toothpick.
3. Heat three tablespoons of oil in a large skillet. Add rosemary and stir, sautéing it about one minute. Put the scallops in the skillet on their sides, rotating every now and then, to brown evenly. Also, sauté scallops on their flat sides. Cook until the pancetta begins to brown. Sautéing scallops should not exceed five minutes, and it is necessary to stay at the stove during this procedure. Transfer scallops to a dish and set aside for a minute. Do not clean the skillet.
4. Add remaining oil in the same skillet. Add radicchio and chicory slices, walnut pieces, and raisins to the skillet. Toss constantly, over medium-high heat, to wilt the greens. If mixture seems too dry in the skillet, add a teaspoon or two of the reserved wine. Sautéing the greens from start to finish should take about three minutes.
5. To serve, remove the toothpicks from the scallops. On each of four plates, add a portion of the sautéed greens. Arrange four scallops on each plate, on top of the greens. Add more salt and pepper and serve with a lemon wedge.

Broccoli Ricotta Soufflé

Souffle di broccoli e ricotta

Serves 4 to 6

3 tablespoons unsalted butter
2 tablespoons olive oil
½ cup finely chopped onion
1 cup finely chopped cooked broccoli
1 pound skim-milk ricotta
3 large eggs, lightly beaten
½ cup freshly grated Parmesan cheese
Salt and freshly ground pepper
4 egg whites
¼ cup bread crumbs

1. Butter a one-and-a-half-quart soufflé dish and sprinkle with crumbs, shaking out any excess. Preheat oven to 375°F.
2. Heat butter and oil in a skillet, add onion, and sauté over moderate heat, stirring, until soft. Stir in broccoli and cook two minutes longer. Transfer mixture to a large bowl and add ricotta, whole eggs, Parmesan, and salt and pepper to taste. Mix well.
3. Beat egg whites in an electric mixer until they hold soft peaks. Fold one-third of the whites into ricotta mixture then fold in remaining whites gently but thoroughly.
4. Transfer the broccoli mixture to the soufflé dish, running your thumb around edge to make a groove. Bake thirty-five to forty minutes, or until puffed and golden brown. Serve immediately.

Mary's Italian Cake

Torta italiana di Maria

Serves 12

To prepare the sponge cake layers:

1 cup cake flour
¾ teaspoon baking powder
¼ teaspoon salt
2 eggs, room temperature
½ cup cold water
1 cup granulated sugar, sifted
1 teaspoon vanilla extract
½ teaspoon lemon extract

1. Line two round eight-inch layer pans with liberally buttered wax paper. Preheat oven to 350°F.
2. Sift flour, baking powder, and salt together in a bowl.
3. Separate eggs; place whites in a small bowl and yolks in a large bowl with the cold water. Beat egg yolks and water with an electric beater, a whisk, or whatever, until yolks are fluffy and tripled in volume. During this process, add the sifted sugar a spoonful at a time. Continue beating until yolks form a heavy ribbon when the

beater is lifted and the mixture is thick enough to mound slightly (about ten to fifteen minutes). Stir in flavorings. Add flour mixture all at once and fold it in with a rubber spatula.

4. Beat egg whites until they form moist, stiff peaks when the beater is raised. Then with a rubber spatula, fold them into the yolk mixture until completely blended.
5. Pour cake mixture into prepared pans and bake in preheated oven for twenty-five to thirty minutes, or until done.
6. Remove pans from the oven and invert them on a cake rack until the cakes have cooled then lift off the pans and peel off the wax paper.

To prepare the filling:

⅓ cup semisweet chocolate pieces
¾ cup granulated sugar
1 pound ricotta
½ teaspoon powdered cloves
2 tablespoons anisette liqueur
2 tablespoons fresh lemon zest, chopped fine
2 tablespoons fresh orange zest, chopped fine

Melt the chocolate in the top of a double boiler over hot water. Stir in the sugar and beat until well blended. Add the ricotta, powdered cloves, anisette, and lemon and orange zest.

To assemble the cake:

2 cake layers
4 tablespoons sweet vermouth
1 recipe ricotta filling

Split the cake layers crosswise to form four layers. Place one layer, cut side up, on a cake plate. Carefully sprinkle the cut side with one tablespoon vermouth. Then spread with one-third of the filling. Repeat this procedure with the next two layers. Top with the last layer, cut side down, and sprinkle with the remaining one tablespoon vermouth. Chill the cake for four or five hours.

The final touch:

1 cup heavy cream, whipped
1 tablespoon sweet vermouth

When it is time to serve the cake, beat the heavy cream until it forms stiff peaks. Fold in the sweet vermouth. Decorate the cake with this mixture as you wish. You may frost the sides and pipe on (with a pastry tube) rosettes or garlands or anything you wish. Or simply spread the cream over the top and sides smoothly but not too evenly.

17

LOVE IS A BLIND DATE

Charlie was four years younger than Mary, but he acted much older. He had a "steady" when he was twelve years old and went with her for a number of years. We didn't like this particular girl, and we found every opportunity to deride her. It made no difference to him, until when he was twenty; he went to visit relatives in Connecticut, had a blind date, broke off the relationship with his old girlfriend in a week or so, and married a new lady, a great cook, about a year later.

Growing up, Charlie erased the year of birth on his birth certificate and substituted a different one to meet the age qualification for a driver's license—he was driving a car when he was thirteen. He also drove a wagon with two horses, owned by the St. Francis French Laundry shop on West Forty-Sixth Street, across the street from where we lived. Its deliveries were made in this wagon, and Charlie had a secret part-time job as driver.

The Ninth Avenue El was still up in the days. I asked him to teach me to drive a car. In order to go around the block, which was part of his training course, I had to steer around the pillars of the elevated train. This was not an easy task, and every time I tried to do this, he would think I was going straight into these cast-iron pillars. After several tries, he yelled, "You stupid son of a bitch, you fuckin' stupid son of a bitch." I stopped the car, got out, and let him take over. I did not get back into the car. I just walked home and wouldn't talk to him for weeks. Charlie never taught me to drive a car; I learned from a friend about ten years later.

Charlie was an immaculate dresser. He never wore knickers. He was in long dress pants by age eleven. He had double-breasted suits, a spiffy collection of dress shirts, and an array of ties that could have come from Saks Fifth Avenue's window display but didn't. He kept this haberdashery and suit assortment in a stand-up closet under lock and key in our bedroom. No one had access to this treasure trove except Charlie. He forgot the key one day, and I found it on the dresser in our room, just at the time I needed to borrow a tie.

I thought I had put one over on him because I took the tie, used it, and put it back before he needed the key to open the closet. Later, I found out I was wrong. The next time he saw me in a tie, one of my own, he came over to me, grabbed it, and punched a hole in it with a hole puncher we used for school papers. He didn't say a word.

He did not like school; I did his homework for him. To keep me quiet about it, he paid me ten cents a week for something I liked doing. For months, I handled his assignments and wrote "separate" fifty times in his lined notebook. I did the same with "occasion" and dozens of other words he had to write fifty times. I did his math work, answered questions in social studies, even wrote compositions (that's what they called them then), all for ten cents a week. After the tie incident, I decided to raise my price to fifteen cents. He never blinked an eye—he knew it was a bargain.

We knew he had laid his first girlfriend in his early teens. She made the mistake of writing him a letter about it, and Mama found that letter in his pants pockets. She and Papa conferred and met with Charlie. That girl was not allowed into our flat. The truth of the matter is that she never did enter our home even before the sex incident. Charlie continued to meet with her on the sly but then, as I said, dropped her like a hot potato when he went to Naugatuck, Connecticut, that fateful weekend, and he met the woman who was to spend her life with him. Charlie was home only at meal times. He loved steak. Like Mama, he was a worker. He didn't want college, went to a trade school instead, and later started a business of his own, fathered three children, and, through it all, held his wife's hand as he gazed lovingly into her eyes. Mama never once said, "Love is blind." She adored Ida, Charlie's wife, from the moment she met her, because Ida was a great cook and introduced us to many Marchigiana recipes. She was born in Fano, Italy (a city on the Adriatic coast in the province Le Marche), and brought a whole new world of Italian food into our home. Charlie may have been critical of his wife's brothers—he called each one "short arm," because they never reached into their pockets to pay for anything, but he loved his wife, Ida. We all did.

Ida was a young lady when she, her brothers, and their parents migrated to the United States. The men in the family had technical abilities, found good jobs, started their own businesses, and, in short time, built a beautiful red brick home in Connecticut that had a separate room for saints and religious memorabilia to comfort Ida's mother. The basement held a virtual winery—Ida's father, Aldo, loved his wine—he made a rather strong vin santo, and one or two glasses of it would make you drunk. Upon entering their home, Aldo would have you in the basement drinking his vin santo before much else happened. It was not easy to walk up the stairs into the large and pristine kitchen, where they made *porchetta*, *brodetti*, vincisgrassi, macaroni dishes, stuffed olives (really big, fat olives), pizza rustica (egg pasta filled with green vegetables, cottage cheese, sausage, and herbs), and pizza con formaggio all'anconetana; the Pecorino they call "formaggio di fossa" (aged in a cave).

Before Charlie married Ida, Mama would go spend some time with Ida and her mother just so they could cook together. It was pleasant because Mama wanted to learn, and they wanted to teach their cuisine. One of their special cheeses was called *caciotta*, made with sheep's milk, and Ida's mother, Barbarina (means "little Barbara"—funny name because she was a large woman), told Mama that Michelangelo loved this cheese, caciotta; he nibbled it while he worked and later bought property near Urbino (in Le Marche) for sheep to graze on, and they produced a steady supply of it for him. Pesaro, the neighboring town to Fano and much larger in size, was the birthplace of world-famous musician Rossini, and Pesaro commemorates his birth not with a fish dish but one of meat, Tornedo alla Rossini. Ida and her family made it with a piece of round steak cooked in a casserole with ham, mushrooms, parsley, pepper, and lemon—quite different from the way it is served in New York, Rome, London, and Paris: a grilled filet mignon with a slice of foie gras on top.

For years, Ida made her *brodetto* with the fish she could get in Connecticut, where she lived. When her mother's sister, her aunt Giudetta, would visit the family from Fano, she would enjoy Ida's brodetto and describe the fish she used at home. Like the original brodetto, this fish dish was spread all over the Mediterranean by the Greeks—Livorno has its *cacciucco*, Liguria has its *ciuppin* (or *buridda*), Sardinia has its *cassola*, Sicily its *ghiotto*, and the *bouillabaisse* in Marseilles, France.

There are purists who list the necessary fish for brodetto, but Ida said more than once, "In actuality, most brodetti eaten in Italy use the fish they have available in their localities. And so be it in the United States." Giudetta lived to be over one hundred—Ida and her daughter Carolyn journeyed to the one hundredth birthday party in Fano, where a story about Giudetta was revealed. Young, with nine children, she needed a sewing machine, and she decided to write and ask Il Duce Mussolini for one. Yes, he sent her one, and the story became folklore. Aunt Giudetta was healthy (she rode a bicycle in Fano until close to one hundred), thoughtful (she always brought Ida certain cooking items, such as dried wild fennel, sea salt, anchovies in salt, delicious jars of jams, and jellies made in Le Marche), and kind. She brought two beautiful hand-knit wool bedspreads for two twin beds, the beds in which she and daughter slept in on one visit to our country place in upstate New York.

Ida emphasized the importance of cooking the fish head(s) to make a good flavorful broth and to be sure to use your best extra-virgin olive oil in making brodetto. She liked adding cinnamon sticks and bay leaves. "Don't leave them out, for sure," she would warn. "Cook the squid whole and then slice it—this will make them tenderer," she also advised.

She said to stand by the pot as the brodetto cooked and check with a fork to see if the fish flakes—if it does, the fish is cooked. The drama of this dish was not only in its preparation but also in its serving. Ida wanted all of us seated at the table, and as she entered with the brodetto, she wanted silence. Her eyes had to meet ours, and only then would she take off the lid. The splendid smell of the fish jumped out of the pot as if a genie was working its magical vapors that soared four feet into the air, only to hit the ceiling and evaporate. "In Fano, we used to go to the fish market to buy the fish. You had to smell it, smell it, fresh from the sea," she would say again and again.

She, as much as Papa, taught us to like octopus, another of her family's specialties. She usually served it as an appetizer with fresh shrimp, garlic, olive oil, and parsley. These days, octopus is sold precleaned, but when Ida was a young girl, she had to clean it herself. She described a way to tenderize it. After cleaning it, she would put it in boiling water, holding it by its mantle, and keep it submerged for twelve seconds, and she would count one to twelve as she demonstrated the procedure. And then do it again and a third time. "You will see the difference, for sure," Ida promised.

Official statistics claim that the "Marchigiani" eat more meat than any other Italians, and it shows in and outside Fano, for a local going to a restaurant is basically an excuse to feed oneself enormous plates of charcoaled-grilled meats, "grigliata mista di carne." Others include stuffed pigeons (*piccione ripiena*) and rabbit cooked with fennel (*coniglio in porchetta*). It is a known fact that the Marches sell a lot of meat to the other provinces, for they develop and raise a special strain of Chianina beef cattle, the meat used for *bistecca alla Fiorentina*. Ida and Charlie prepared their own grilled porterhouse steak, his most favorite food, in the Italian style at home. If you ask either of them for the recipe, they will talk more about the preparation of the fire than cooking the meat itself. All of us in our family imitate and follow their rules, and they are right about this. However, the porterhouse itself is greatly important too, and it should be a thick piece of meat. Charlie emphasized his point about looking for the "beads of sweat," as he called it—this is a sign that the meat is rare and beautifully cooked and time to take it off the grill.

So the happy marriage continued in spite of Charlie's constant complaints about his short-arm brothers-in-laws. For a period of time, every time Charlie complained to us at home, Papa would answer him with a saying that was neither in Ruotese or Accetturese (our dialects), and to this day, we don't know which dialect it is, although we suspect it is Sicilian, and we wonder if anyone ever used it to get a point across to Papa himself.

"Amicu can non ti duna, parendi ca non ti mprests, fuili comu la pesta" (Friends who won't give, relatives who won't lend you a hand, avoid them like the plague).

Happy marriages may also be hit by one of life's tsunamis when least expected. This couple worked hard to get their firstborn through college, and the younger son too. Ida worked in a major plant of Peter Paul, the large candy-making company in Naugatuck, Connecticut. For all we know, Lucille Ball's TV candy-making episode for *I Love Lucy* could have been filmed there. The speeding belt that carried thousands of chocolates for inspection before being wrapped did not tempt Ida as it did Lucy. (This was one food Ida did not have to taste.) Ida had long hours, was paid very little, and she was in a hurry to get her boys through college and married. They graduated and married.

Then a volcano exploded when Charlie was told he had a strange form of lung cancer a year or so before his and Ida's fiftieth wedding anniversary. He began to lose weight, and the shadows under his dark, gray Italian eyes resembled dark clouds covering half his face. He was brave at the formal anniversary dinner party with over one hundred relatives and friends. The celebratory dinner in their honor was Italian and perfect, but there was an undercurrent that good and happy food could not cover up—the sadness of Charlie's illness was on everyone's mind.

In the wreckage of his last year, he was sent home with the hospice crowd, who came to their home smelling of dead people, with blood stains on their white uniforms, echoes from funeral parlors, and always with an appetite for food (they asked for and got gargantuan lunches). Ida and her daughter were there every minute—Charlie smiled once and asked for a porterhouse steak, but his stomach couldn't hold orange juice. He was down to half his normal weight, barely able to hold on to the rail of the hospital bed Ida put in her kitchen.

Our throats were so parched we couldn't sing "Ave Maria" at his funeral Mass. It was a cold February day with snow flurries that fell into his grave. Instead of beautiful flowers on a happy Italian dinner table, we were throwing roses over his coffin as it was lowered.

It was not easy for Ida living without her Charlie. She managed for a number of years, cooking suppers and dinners for her kids who came to visit frequently—her brodetti were short-term cures for their lingering grief over the loss of their father. Ida depended on her cooking and those meals to get her through the lonely weeks—she would harness her abundant energy to prepare vincisgrassi (a special lasagna preparation) and other time-consuming Marchigiana dishes. She spent more time reminiscing about her mother and father and their ways in the kitchen. She lived close to a brother and sister-in-law who were good cooks, and they continued with the family eating rituals as though their parents were still alive. It was comforting for all of them.

Then another family tsunami struck when her daughter was told her mother had Alzheimer. Carolyn, the daughter, had grown suspicious about her mother's behavior at home—a burning candle close to the draperies, an electric frying pan turned on with no food in it, a pot on the stove from which the boiling water had evaporated, the pot heating to melting on the range, and more. Did anyone make brodetto anymore? Who was cleaning the octopus? After two or three years in assisted living, Ida had to be placed in a facility devoted to treating Alzheimer patients. We all visited Ida, but in short time, Carolyn said not to go see her. She remembered no one, not even her daughter, and we are not to remember her that way. Now, we think of them both around the dining table—Ida coming into the room with her infamous brodetto, focusing our eyes so we could witness the magical burst of wonderful smelling vapors, the way life is supposed to be.

A Fisherman's Chowder from Fano

Brodetto Casalingo

Serves 8

¾ cup extra-virgin olive oil
2 leeks, white part only, carefully cleaned and thinly sliced
2 ribs celery, trimmed and thinly sliced on the diagonal
4 cloves garlic, minced
4 pounds various fish such as flounder, any kind of snapper, sea bass (non-Chilean, as it is too oily), trout, tilapia, cleaned and scaled, preferably with bone in, cut in large chunks, ready for cooking, with heads reserved
1 pound cleaned squid, left whole
Salt and freshly ground pepper
¼ cup white wine vinegar
2 small onions, thinly sliced
2 cinnamon sticks
4 bay leaves
2 tablespoons finely chopped Italian parsley
16 slices bruschetta

1. In a large saucepan, heat one-half of the olive oil and sauté the leeks and celery until the leeks become opaque, about five minutes. Add garlic and sauté one minute longer. Add fish heads, squid, and vinegar; turn up heat to cook off the vinegar, three or four minutes. Add some salt and freshly ground pepper and water to cover the heads. Bring to boil, lower heat to a simmer, and cook forty-five minutes, partially covered.
2. Remove the squid and set aside. Strain the sauce and set it aside. Discard the heads and other solids. Do not rinse the saucepan in which the sauce cooked. When the squid have cooled, slice them across the body to make one-third-inch-wide slices.
3. Heat remaining oil in the same saucepan and sauté the onion until it is opaque, about five minutes. Add the fresh fish pieces, cinnamon sticks, bay leaves, and one and a half tablespoons chopped parsley.

Stir the fish in the saucepan; add the cooked squid and the strained liquid. Over medium heat, cook the fish until it begins to flake, about fifteen minutes. Remove the bay leaves and the cinnamon sticks. Put two bruschetta slices in each of eight bowls, spoon the fish over the bread, and add the sauce. Dot with a little fresh parsley.

Octopus with Wine, Garlic, Oil, and Parsley

Polipo con olio. aglio e limone
Serves 4 to 6

- 1 pound shrimp, shelled and deveined
- 1 small octopus, about 1 pound, no larger, cleaned by fishmonger, or see below
- 1 large onion, peeled and chopped
- 1 large carrot, trimmed and cut into small dice
- 2 ribs celery, trimmed and strings removed, cut into small dice
- ¼ cup finely chopped fresh Italian parsley
- 4 lemons
- ⅓ cup plus 2 tablespoons extra-virgin olive oil
- 4 radicchio leaves, rinsed and dried

1. Prepare the shrimp and octopus ready for cooking.
2. Bring a large saucepan of water (about three quarts) to boil, adding about one-third of the onions, one-third of the carrots, and one-third of the celery pieces, a good dash of salt, and two of the lemons cut in four pieces each. When it has reached the boil, add octopus and shrimp. Remove shrimp with a slotted spoon and set aside to cool as soon as they are cooked and have turned pink, about three or four minutes. Do not overcook or the shrimp will toughen.
3. Continue to cook the octopus and the vegetables until tender, about forty-five minutes to over one hour. When the octopus is tender, remove it carefully and allow to cool. Discard the liquid and its contents.

4. While the octopus is cooking, heat two tablespoons oil in a medium skillet. Add remaining onion, carrots, and celery pieces and sauté until tender, about ten minutes. Transfer to a bowl. Add salt and freshly ground pepper. Add shrimp. Cut octopus in small bite pieces, one-half to three-fourths inch, and add to bowl. Squeeze juice from the remaining lemons and add to bowl, with the olive oil. Toss lightly. Add parsley and toss until well mixed. Check for salt and pepper seasoning and even adjust the lemon and oil flavoring to your liking.
5. If individual servings are to be made, spoon some on a radicchio leaf, or put the radicchio leaves on a platter and spoon octopus and shrimp over them.

To prepare octopus for cooking:
Most fish shops sell octopus precleaned. If it hasn't been cleaned, ask your fishmonger to do it for you. If the answer is no, then turn the octopus inside out as you would a swimsuit. Remove the beak and the viscera from the mouth and also the ink sac. Rinse it very well under cool, running water. There is a little trick to tenderizing octopus—after cleaning it, put it into boiling water, holding it by its mantle. Count to twelve and remove it. Do this two more times before adding it to the saucepan in step 2 above.

Grilled Porterhouse Steak

Bistecca alla fiorentina
Serves 4

1 porterhouse steak, about 3 pounds, trimmed, at room temperature
4 tablespoons extra-virgin olive oil
4 cloves garlic, peeled and cut in half lengthwise
6 wedges fresh lemon, seeded

1. Build a charcoal fire and allow it to reach the gray-ash stage. Gently tap the coals to shake off the ash. Move coals slightly so they are about one-half inch apart to moderate the heat.

2. Using less than a tablespoon of oil, brush steak lightly on both sides. Put remaining oil and garlic in a small saucepan or skillet and heat until garlic turns light brown. Do not let garlic get darker. Remove from the heat, discard the pieces of garlic, and set the oil aside.
3. When the fire is ready, place steak on the grill as close as possible to the heat source. Sear for two minutes on one side only to seal in the juices. Raise the grill about four inches from the coals and continue grilling until tiny bubbles of juice appear on top of the steak, three to five minutes depending on the thickness of the steak. Turn over the steak with tongs and liberally add salt and freshly ground pepper.
4. Repeat grilling procedure for the second side, two minutes close to the heat source and then raise the grill rack and grill the steak a couple of minutes more to achieve a rare steak.
5. If you wish to use a gas-fired grill, heat it and follow the same procedure for oiling, salting, and peppering the steak as above. Grill five to seven minutes per side, depending on thickness. Be sure to let the steak rest for several minutes before slicing.
6. To serve, let steak rest a couple of minutes. Reheat flavored oil. Slice the meat against the grain, put some slices onto each plate, and spoon some of the garlic-flavored oil over the meat. Add a lemon wedge to each serving; the lemon is to be squeezed over the meat as a final touch.

18

WOMEN'S PROBLEMS AND MEATBALLS

One lengthy discussion with Mama on another visit was Bea's concern about her daughter and weight.

"It's all because of the WASP family she married into," she said.

Mama showed a truly sympathetic ear. Why shouldn't she? Any woman with a problem interested Mama. Her own life was filled with problems, sometimes about money as she had had with her son's school bills or about Bea playing hooky to go see Frank Sinatra or about Charlie's involvement with that girl. "There is no such thing as a woman without problems," Mama declared.

She looked at Bea and said, "We all have problems, and you can't let them get you down. If we know we did wrong, we have to admit it to ourselves—that's very important. If the goods are damaged, then dry-clean them, wash them, repair them—do the best you can, and God will understand. *Aiutati che Dio ti aiuta*," Mama told Bea—Help yourself and God will help you!

"Did I ever tell you about my job at Murray Rothstein's Dress Factory on West Thirty-Sixth Street, just off Eighth Avenue?"

Bea started to say, "No, you haven't," but Mama just went on . . .

"I was there for about ten years. I started to work there a year or two before you came to this country. Talk about problems. They were all women, pieceworkers, trying to make a few extra bucks as I was, all with problems. Murray was a tough boss but a fair one. He had trouble keeping away the ILGWU, that's the In-ter-na-tion-al Lad-ies Garment Wor-kers Un-ion. (Mama said this very slowly, enunciating each syllable to be sure she did not malaprop it.) Most of the companies in the building had the union, but ours didn't. When I first starting working there, I met a woman who spoke little English and came to me and said, 'That son of a bitch, he won't give me a few hours off to take my sick kid to the clinic. We should have a union here,' said this weeping lady. 'Can you help me, Angela?'" Mama said she would, if Rosalie, the weeping coworker, would not call Mr. Rothstein a son of a bitch. "'He has plenty of problems too.'"

Mama told cousin Bea she hardly knew Mr. Rothstein but went to talk with him and explained the woman's problem, saying, "'Mr. Rothstein, you don't want a union here, do you?' He looked at me with wild eyes, like a cat whose back is curled and paws ready to pounce on one's face. "'Angela,' he said, 'a union would destroy this company, and I mean that!' he cried."

Demurely, Mama explained in a simple, quiet way, hoping to convince Mr. Rothstein that she is correct about this important matter, "'I know, and we don't want to pay union dues either. Mr. Rothstein, you don't mind if I call you Murray, do you?'" Being assured that he didn't, Mama continued, "'Then we have to care about the problems our women have. If we solve them here, the union will never get them to sign up—why should they? What can they do for them that we can't?'"

"'Angela, tell me more" . . . and Mama did.

"'Let's make common sense here, Murray. Rosalie wants a few hours off for her sick child. She did not ask to be paid for the time she was away. Let's ask her to make up her time. If she can't, then I'll get someone else into shop to do so.'"

"Bea," said Mama, "this little plan worked—the kid was not seriously ill, and Rosalie was back at work in three hours, and she made that time up by working Saturday morning, which was okay with Mr. Rothstein."

"Every other day there was another problem. Let's talk to the boss first," Mama said, "and then we can figure out how to handle it. I became Murray's right-hand person—the girls called me the 'problem solver.'"

"Aunt Angela, how could you get your own work done?" questioned Bea.

"I usually handled this stuff during lunch hours, so I wasn't cutting into my piecework. I have to admit that almost every week, I brought Murray something to eat. It didn't matter what I brought him—he always said it was so good. I made more lunch for him than I did myself. He would take his packet of food and go to his office. I usually had some broccoli rabe with a nice piece of my bread, and that was more than enough for me. And so it went on for years. When I left, Murray had a beautiful party for me and drove me home in his chauffeured limousine. (When Mama pronounced 'chauffeured limousine,' and it came out correctly, she crowed.) He hated to see me leave the shop—and I can't tell you how many times I wonder if the I-L-G-W-U got in there. I have nothing against unions—our shop was not that big. Why couldn't we solve our own problems? I call this woman power, not union power," Mama said as she got off her soapbox and came closer to Bea.

"Woman power," said Bea. "I really like that idea."

"Bea, you're going to have to have a serious talk with your daughter. I think it's too late now to say she is half Italian. Instead, I would ask her to open her mind and find something she likes about Italian things, a food, a place, or a fashion designer. Ask her to talk positively about it. Find something Italian and talk about that. Give her a copy of *The Leopard*—ask her to read it," proselytized Mama. She went on, "Tell her it was translated into fifty-five languages and sold more copies than *Gone with the Wind*. In fact, you should read it first. You'll love it, and then *you* talk to her about it and give her a copy.

"Bea, there's a good Italian saying—'Chi la fa l'aspetti'—He who wrongs someone has to expect something in retaliation. And perhaps, she and her husband—what was it you called him? Something like a bug?—a wisp, a wasp, anyway, maybe they should plan a trip to see the Vatican in Rome. They will never forget that beautiful place. It's like being in heaven. I was there two years ago with Rose and Elvira (the landladies), and we spent two weeks in Rome—we didn't want to leave. Well, Rome wasn't built in a day, and this problem isn't going away in a day. But it will go away. Be patient.

"Beatrice (Mama pronouncing it the Italian way), I always liked that name. Let's make another time to cook something else. What shall we cook? Who are you going to invite?"

"You know, Aunt Angela, when I lived in Italy, I used to help make an easy tomato sauce for spaghetti and meatballs. I forgot how to make it. Can we do that?" answered Bea with a contented look on her face.

On another day, between cooking sessions, cousin Bea called Mama to say she had some free time and if she could come over. She knew there was no time to cook, she said, but a little visit with Aunt Angela would please her. She was alone, and she had a box of cookies. "I'm alone, is it all right?" Mama assured her that it was fine and that she would put some coffee on.

As Bea entered the apartment, Mama greeted her with

"Do you remember the Fanelli family—they lived on Forty-Sixth, very close to Ninth Avenue, on the other side of the street? The building has a stoop—four steps up, a nice building. Mrs. Fanelli had six kids like me," Mama asked Bea.

Bea said, "Oh, they had a son who wanted to go to college. He was your Jerry's age and good friends with Jerry."

"That's the one, and guess what?" Mama rambled on, "He is now a judge in Washington, DC—a very successful man. The family doesn't live here anymore, but I ran into Mrs. Fanelli on Ninth Avenue, and she brought me up to date on her children. She lost her husband about ten years ago. They had a hard time when they lived here. He was a shoemaker, a really nice man from Accettura. Their kids did well."

Mama poured coffee and asked Bea to have a cookie, one of the ones she had brought.

Mama continued, "And did you know the Mianos? They lived on Tenth Avenue—they had a boy and a girl. They were from Potenza, and Uncle Joe was a good friend of the father. His son went to college, and now he is the top man in an important company on Madison Avenue in New York."

"I didn't know them, Aunt, but how wonderful that the son could become so successful," admitted Bea.

Mama thought that surely Bea should realize that many successful people were of Italian ancestry, immigrant Italians, and Mama liked to talk about them and the social acceptance of many people in our country of Italian origin. "In our own family, there were officers in major corporations, a judge, several lawyers, and schoolteachers. Aha," said Mama as she slipped into her dressing room, opened a drawer of a small bureau, and pulled out a composition book with a marbleized black cover, one of the ones with white pages and a red line at the top. All the kids used them in school. Mama's was a scrapbook overflowing with newspaper clippings, printed invitations, announcements, and some personally written letters all on one subject: Italians who had made it. Bea couldn't believe what she was witnessing. It was as if she had entry to Aunt Angela's most personal diary.

Before she opened the book, Mama said to Bea that she surely was aware of Mayor LaGuardia, one of the most popular mayors in the United States. "You know about Columbus and other explorers of Italian descent and about the results of their discoveries? You know Ferrari? He makes sculptures for Chicago. When I was there with Uncle Joe to see his cousin Rosa Palumba, we saw many pieces of his work—beautiful. Well, he's Italian who lives in and loves America," she continued as Bea sat there as if at a tennis game, waiting for the next point to be made, the match point.

Mama turned the page. "And what about the architects Venturi and Soleri? The artist Francesco (Frank) Stella? The photographer Francesco Scavullo? The Ghirardelli *cioccolata* people from Rapallo who became rich and famous in San Francisco, California?" Mama turned a page then another. "Bea, listen to this, the close friend of Thomas Jefferson was Filippo Mazzei. He was a doctor who bought guns for Virginia during the Revolutionary War," Mama explained.

Mama was completely carried away. With each name, Bea raised her eyebrows in surprise as if she were participating in a class at New York University in Italian/American cultural affairs. Overall, she was impressed with Mama's cherished notebook.

Mama carried on, "Let me read you this: Arturo Toscanini, the son of a tailor, was born in Parma, Italy, in 1867. He studied at the *conservatorio* in Parma and Milan. Eventually, he became the musical director of La Scala in Milan and became the world's most famous conductor. He was at the New York Metropolitan Opera from 1908 to 1915. Although he went back to Italy, he returned to live in the United States in 1938 and conducts the New York Philharmonic-Symphony orchestra."

Cousin Bea listened with great interest. She knew this was an important subject for Mama, who continued to read short biographies of people such as Enrico Fermi, who worked on the Manhattan Project developing the atom bomb, or Rudolph Valentino, the eighteen-year-old Italian who emigrated to California . . . Mama did not need to finish that sentence as Bea chirped in, "Oh, Aunt, I've seen some of his movies, and he was wonderful. What a pity he died so young."

Mama could have gone on and on but stopped there, as she realized Bea might have come for a different discourse.

Not really.

Bea simply wanted to spend a little relaxed time with Mama over a cup of coffee.

"Aunt Angela, I was so impressed with your fiftieth anniversary celebration last year at the Astor Hotel. It was one of the finest events I've ever attended. I hope I thanked you and Uncle Joe for everything you did for me, my mother, my sisters Marie and Filomena that day. I even remember that cousin Marie and Rocky were there, and Rocky's band played so well. I actually danced with your Jerry."

"Yes, Bea, it was one of the most wonderful parties of my life. My kids did it all—there wasn't anything they wouldn't do, and they wanted the whole Italian family there, and those close friends who were not Italian but people we really like, such as our doctor, Dr. Lazarus, and his nice wife. His father used to take care of us when we were sick. His office was near Tenth Avenue on Forty-Fourth Street. When he passed away, his son took over and has been our family doctor ever since. We are so lucky to have him still. You know, Bea, that was the only party where someone else did the cooking. The hotel people would not let us bring our own food—it had to be catered." (Mama had difficulty with the word "caterer." She wanted to pronounce it as in "Katherine," not as in "Kay," but she pulled it off, and Bea knew what she meant.)

"Aunt Angela," Bea answered, "but at your seventieth birthday party, not so long ago, I was there, you remember, and all the food was cooked by your children. We all talk about it. Imagine stuffing more than sixty artichokes, making over sixty veal shanks (*osso buco*), rice cooked the Milan way, the most beautiful fresh lettuces from the garden with sliced fresh tomatoes—even the tomatoes were peeled before slicing—I will never forget that. I went home and tried it. There were the beautiful trays of Italian pastries from Ferrara's, and each table had its own birthday cake made like—I forget the name, but it means pick-me-up."

"Oh, Bea, you mean tiramisu. The kids made six of them in round circles and put candles on them, and as everyone sang Happy Birthday, the cakes were brought to each table by each of my six kids. What a party. I shall remember that always."

"Me too, Aunt Angela. I don't know why we never did things like that in our family. I remember in Italy some birthday parties when I was a little girl but not many since being in this country. I have to go, Aunt, but I'll be back tomorrow for our cooking session." She kissed Aunt on each cheek, hugged her, and left.

"Don't forget tomorrow at ten o'clock. Remember, we're making meatballs, and remember Frank Sinatra—he is Italian too," Mama reminded cousin Bea.

The next morning:

"Let's make meatballs," said Mama to Bea before she had a chance to lay down the cookies or take her coat off.

"I've been thinking about this all night, Aunt, and I can't wait to see how they're made."

Mama began by telling Bea that there were no deviations allowed to the rules about making meatballs.

"You have to start with freshly ground meat with some fat. You will lose the taste without fat." Mama had already put the meat in a large bowl so Bea could see it. Tony the butcher knew exactly what Mama wanted, and that is what she always got for meatballs.

"Buy the meat from Tony and ask him to give you meat for meatballs, just like he grinds for your Aunt Angela, who lives across the street," Mama added. "This is one and one-half pounds of beef and pork with some fat in it," as she pushed a finger into the meat, "and remember the fat adds a lot of taste."

On the table, Bea could see some eggs, Parmesan cheese (already grated), some bread slices with no crusts, some unpeeled garlic, almost a head of it with two or three missing cloves, salt and pepper, a bottle of milk, and some dry oregano.

Mama wanted to add everything right away to the bowl with the meat, but Bea asked her to please stop before each ingredient went in so she could measure. They both were patient with this procedure, and Bea wrote in her notebook. Following her entry for the meat and its quantity, she wrote: one-third cup freshly grated Parmesan cheese, one large egg (Aunt said if the eggs are small, use two of them), two large cloves garlic, peeled, really minced fine—Mama let Bea do this on a wooden board. She showed Bea how to hold the point of the knife down with her left hand and hold the handle with her right hand and move the knife up and down just like a chopper. Mama said she would have given the mezzaluna to Bea for chopping, but she knew Bea did not have one at home. Bea smiled.

"Oh, Aunt, I'm not sure I can do this."

"Of course you can. I'll put my hands over yours, and you'll get the feel of it right away. See what I mean, just hold the point of the knife down with your left hand, lift the handle with your right, and go up and down like a seesaw."

Bea was trying hard, and she seemed to be making progress. "I think I'm getting it. Have I chopped enough?"

"No, do it some more to get it chopped finer. I'll tell you when to stop." When it was finely chopped, it was added to the meat.

They sprinkled everything in the bowl with salt and pepper. Then Bea made her measurement of milk, which came to one-half cup, and of about one cup of one-half-inch bread pieces, no crusts, cut from Italian bread.

"Now," Mama said, "it is important to mix the bread and milk together, so we need another bowl, not so big, it's just for the bread and milk. Just stir with a fork to moisten the bread, and then we can add it all to the meat."

When that was mixed, they added about one tablespoon dried oregano, which Mama put in the palms of her hands over the bowl, and rubbed her hands together to crush the herb to release its perfume. Bea noted that most carefully. The last ingredient was about one-fourth cup of finely chopped fresh Italian parsley, and Bea, the new "pro," was given that to chop, which she did well, and added it to the bowl when Mama motioned her to do so.

For a moment, Bea's attention went across the ocean. The sun on the water was bright; she started to cup her hand over her eyes but pulled it back.

She saw herself as a little girl in the stucco house, running on dirt in the one room that didn't have a concrete floor. There were a couple of chickens roaming around that room too, making lot of cackle. She went into the other room and saw Grandma and her mother at the large, old wooden kitchen table, bent over a bowl, making meatballs just as she and Aunt Angela were doing.

She smelled garlic and grimaced, but she thought, "I like the smell of oregano," and began to smile. She looked around the room, and her face saddened. Why was there so little furniture, and why is the room dark? Where was the light? Where was the air? Why was there only one picture on the wall, and did it have to be of Jesus? Why aren't there fancy curtains or a sofa with gold, silky material? Why can't this house be like the palazzo in the center of town? Why did Papa have to die? Will we ever see him again? She wafted through space and returned to the scene just as Aunt Angela was explaining the importance of not overmixing the meat.

"Just toss it lightly—see my opened fingers—keep them open and just toss three or four times, and the meat is ready for shaping. If you toss and work the meat too much, the meatballs will toughen. The light mixing gives it air and lightness."

Mama made a ball of the meat, pressed on it lightly to expand it, and then explained to Bea that she had to visualize the meat divided into four sections and, with a knife, then actually did divide it. "From each of the four sections, we will make three or four meatballs, with wet hands." Mama got a bowl of water and brought it to the work area. "Let's make them a bit larger today, Bea, so that means we'll make three out of each fourth. "Mama started first, put her hands in the water, and grabbed about one-third of one of the divided fourths of meat and started to roll lightly with her wet hands. She asked Bea to try one—she did, and though hers was not as shapely as Mama's, Mama took the ball out of Bea's hands and rolled it one or two times in her hands to get a full and rounder shape. They worked together and made twelve meatballs that Mama set on a cookie sheet, nicely spaced one from the other. "Sometimes I use a pizza pan, and it works as well as the cookie sheet. Whichever you have on hand will be okay." And Mama added, "These could be frozen now and, once frozen, moved into bags or a container to hold all of the balls together. This way, you can use one or two or more as you wish." But today, they were baking them. Mama had already put on the oven to 350 degrees.

"There are two things I forgot to say, Bea. If you freeze them on a tray, you should cover them fully with wax paper until they freeze and before you move them to a container, and, in the old days, we used to fry them before adding them to the tomato sauce. Now, to be modern (Mama sounded a bit sarcastic as she used the word 'modern'), everyone is so afraid of cholesterol, they would rather bake them. But that's okay too. Grandpa lived on fried meatballs for almost ninety-seven years, so there can't be too much wrong with frying them." As she startled Bea with that important fact, Mama continued, "After they bake for twenty-five minutes, we'll put them in a bowl, cool, and refrigerate them—they can stay for a week or so."

"Promise me you'll be back in a few days, and we'll make an easy tomato sauce. If you invite someone, we can have spaghetti and meatballs with a special tomato sauce, real Italian style."

"You are truly fantastic, Aunt Angela. I'll call you tomorrow, and we'll set a date. I hope I'm not taking too much of your time."

"No way, Bea, it's a pleasure. It makes me feel younger when I show you these things, and I know you appreciate it."

As Bea left Mama's apartment, she crossed the ocean once more. She saw herself in tattered clothing running across a crowded piazza, busy with people, street vendors, crying babies, and haggard mamas, papas who seemed drunk—all this in Accettura, her old hometown. She saw the Spagna family crest on the palazzo door and knocked. The man who answered was wearing a handsome velvet jacket with pants of the same and a bright patterned red and white scarf tied around his neck and inside his shirt. He looked at Bea, and said, "Che povera ragazza (What a poor little girl), come qui, per favore" (come here, please), as he took her hand and led her inside the palazzo.

It was Mama Angela, who, over the last quarter of Beatrice's life, helped her see Italians as they were. Through close meetings, with food and some wine, sometimes alone with Mama, sometimes with some of Beatrice's friends, they shared experiences that were common to people regardless of their ancestral backgrounds, and sometimes, because of it.

Homemade Italian Meatballs

Polpette Italiana fatte in casa

Makes 12 meatballs

1 ½ pounds ground beef and pork (¾ pound each) with some fat
⅓ cup freshly grated Parmesan cheese
1 large egg, lightly beaten
2 large garlic cloves, peeled, minced
Salt and freshly ground pepper
½ cup milk
1 cup ½-inch bread cubes from Italian bread, crusts removed
1 teaspoon dried oregano
¼ cup finely chopped fresh Italian parsley

1. Put meat in a large bowl. Add cheese, beaten egg, garlic, salt, and pepper. Turn on oven to 350°F.
2. In a smaller bowl, combine milk and bread cubes, toss lightly with a fork, and add to meat.
3. Put oregano in one hand and rub both hands together over the meat bowl to release perfume. Add parsley and with splayed fingers and mix lightly to combine ingredients. Do not overmix.
4. Empty bowl onto clean workspace and gently pat into a disk. Divide disk into four parts.
5. Form three meatballs out of each fourth of meat. Do not overwork. Set meatballs on rimmed cookie sheet or pizza pan.
6. Bake twenty-five to thirty minutes. Remove from oven, use immediately as you wish, or cool and refrigerate them (up to five days). These may be frozen, cooked, for up to four weeks.

19

YELLOW SILK DRESSES WITH DAINTY FLOWERS

Sister Beatrice was two years younger than I, and we grew up together. She had jet-black hair, cut Buster-Brown style, dark eyes, and just enough baby fat to appear healthy. We thought she looked Chinese and asked Papa strange questions about his trips to Mott Street, the street bordering Chinatown in New York City. This chitchat became a family joke and displeased Mama. Bea was bright and irritated us when she went to the bathroom just at the time of doing dishes, or feigned a headache when it was time to help Mama press the laundry. She was always alongside me regardless of what I was doing, work or otherwise. We had an innate ability to get along with each other. We were a Laurel and Hardy duo, often to Mama's displeasure if Mama was trying to achieve a serious objective, such as getting the entire flat cleaned in a couple of hours on Saturday mornings. Bea and I had the same group of friends; we knew everything about each other and found it easy to agree or disagree about whatever. We were each other's shadows.

When we were very young, after Mama put us to bed, Bea would come over to my room. She sat on my bed, hugged me, and kissed me a thousand times with puckered lips on my cheeks. The kissing sounded an alarm for our older cousin who came into the bedroom to ask what we were doing. When she saw us, our cousin laughed, told us to go to bed, and left us, but Bea continued with the puckering sounds until Mama came to move her to her own bed. We never lost that closeness, which became more intense as we entered adolescence and fought off Mama and Papa to earn our independence. She stuck with me, and I with her, at times in defiance of Mama, who seemed to forgive me more easily than Bea. I think she expected her daughter to be more in line with her thinking. I felt this tension between mother and daughter.

Louise (Luisa), the youngest, was delivered in a hospital. Since the rest of us were all delivered at home, we thought of her as an oddity. How unfair can siblings be? My earliest recollection was a visit in a yellow-checkered taxicab to the French Hospital in the west thirties in Manhattan. A cousin piled us in the cab that drove us to the hospital to see Mama from a window on a high floor. She didn't have Louise in her arms, but we knew it had to be Mama, for no one else knew we were coming that Sunday afternoon at 4:00 p.m. to wave to. I never knew why Mama chose to have Louise at the hospital. Mrs. Colangelo, a midwife who lived in Astoria, Queens, who dressed like a Navy WAC, hat, bag, and all, delivered the rest of us. She was a friend of the family who dropped by to see Mama even if Mama was not pregnant at the time. She was a paisana, and that explained it. She delivered other babies born on Forty-Sixth Street, and she was considered our prime deliverer; Mama (and Papa too) would always ask her to stay and have something to eat. There was usually a soup or stew sitting on the stove, or some spaghetti that could be put together with a fast sauce for her. She always accepted the invite. She liked our food and could converse easily with both our parents. If Mama happened to have a stuffed artichoke on hand, she would be ecstatic. And in this way, Mama was always updated on who was being born to whom and when. Perhaps it was Mama's idea at the time that it was fashionable to go to the hospital to have a baby. Customs were beginning to change.

When the rest of us were born, we were wrapped in fabric. We must have looked like mummies. This was done to straighten our legs, and they wrapped us around our heads, shoulders, and arms, mid body, down the legs. The only exposed part of our bodies was the face. The wrapping was called *la fasciatura*. To change the wrapping, we were unrolled from tens of yards of fabric, only to be rewrapped anew. Although Louise was born in a hospital, Mama wrapped her, mummy style, once she was at home. Born blond and blue eyed, she looked like Papa's side of the family. She was a quiet, pensive child. Mama dressed her and sister Bea in dresses and hats made of yellow silk printed with dainty flowers, with matching ribbons. They looked very Park Avenue, and everyone in the block said so, particularly the non-Italians. The Italian ladies didn't say too much because they felt guilty; they were not doing the same for their daughters. There was something special about Louise. In elementary school, she won a citywide painting contest sponsored by the then-famous department store, Wanamaker's. As good as she was at art, Bea and I preferred her culinary skill. Louise was a born cook and is probably the best cook in the family. We used to ask her to make her delicious banana sandwiches. She had to make them before we were put to bed and bring them to the bedroom without Mama and Papa noticing. Once the parents were asleep, Louise would divvy a banana sandwich between Bea and me. They were delicious—just a sliced ripe banana on thin slices of Mama's homemade bread. We slept well, and Louise appreciated the pedestal on which we put her for these nighttime snacks. Louise enriched her life by learning to cook as Mama did, often going outside the box and creating her own dishes. She is strong, the way Mama was, and she can let the trials and tribulations of life roll off her like raindrops. Never formally trained, she nonetheless pursued her culinary skills. She coauthored three food books with me. Her husband, John, is a passionate cook, and together they've fashioned many special food preparations—at times totally perdutamente.

There was an early tragedy in Louise's life when the Hollywood-created Jean Harlow died. The blond bombshell, or platinum blond as some called her, was Louise's favorite movie star—Louise was almost nine years old when Jean Harlow died. The New York papers covered it on the front page: "Harlow Dies at twenty-six." Louise cried for a week; we never realized the power Harlow had over her—in retrospect, we think it was the glamour Harlow offered in a time when everyone was living through a miserable depression, even a child had to reach for something out of the ordinary. In trying to forget Harlow, Louise found comfort in making banana sandwiches and more, as she cooked alongside Mama. She had no interest in college and went to work right after high school. She had plenty of time between when she got out of school and the time Mama returned from work, so many of her cooking lessons came from sister Mary in addition to Mama. Louise always had an admiration for Mary—this lasted a lifetime, so learning from Mary was easy. As Jean Harlow became a thing of the past, one of the first things Louise mastered was making bread, and then she became an expert pasta maker. It seemed she and the kitchen went together like pasta and *fazool.* Anything Mary could cook, Louise could cook too. Anything Mama cooked, Louise cooked too. This foundation was set early in her life.

As she grew up, people noticed her good taste in clothes; and when she was fully grown, we called her Ava Gardner. There were some men who interested her, but she didn't decide on any of them until her John came along, and they soon became a cooking duo. John loved innards, and Louise knew how to cook them. He also loved clams, oysters, mussels, eel, and they developed a battery of those dishes. They went as lovers to the Italian market in the Bronx for imported prosciuttos, salamis, and fresh seafood, freshly made pasta, and, most of all, fresh ricotta, the kind that was made that morning, sold in three-quart tins with holes so it dripped and had to be wrapped properly. To this day, they make biweekly trips to the Bronx for some of their food, including mussels and oysters of a size you could choke on. They knew the names of most of the vendors and exchanged Christmas gifts with some of them and recipes with them all.

John always said that oysters should be tightly closed and odorless and that fresh oysters should be consumed as soon as possible after they are bought. If you need to keep them a short while, store them in plastic bags in the refrigerator, making small openings in the bag (snip with a scissors after tying the bag) to let air inside.

John loved to show people how to shuck oysters. He'd say, "Hold each oyster in your hand and protect the hand with a kitchen towel. The flat side of the oyster should be up, and the hinge side should face out (as he showed with his hand and an oyster shell). Then put the tip of an oyster knife into the hinge. Twist carefully to free the top shell. Now, to help do this, run the knife along the underside of the top shell. This will cut the muscle. Please do *not* cut the small muscle that holds the edible oyster to the bottom shell, as it will cause the oyster to curl and lose its flavor. And throw away the top shell. "One last point," and he said this at a snail's pace, "try to do this slowly and carefully to avoid losing the juices inside the shell."

Then the oysters were baked and consumed. Each time they were served, someone asked about a secret ingredient. John was quiet about this, and Louise acted so indifferent to the question; we became suspicious. Finally, one day, when she felt a bit looser after a glass of wine or two, she confessed, "Well, if you really want to know, I'll let you in on the secret. It's something called *colatura di alici*—an anchovy juice, with an amber color and a fresh taste and smell of the sea. Mama and Ida know about it, and I learned it from them. It's been used in the Naples area for years, but you can buy it in New York."

"You're kidding" was the reaction from those of us who were ignorant about this.

Louise went on, "It's made by marinating anchovies in salt—fresh anchovies without heads or entrails—surely, you've tasted this along the Amalfi Coast. They add it to spaghetti cooked with garlic, olive oil, and red pepper flakes, and with clams, mussels, and other seafood. Just a drop of it goes a long way! I got the idea to use it with baked oysters. Just a tiny drop of it on the oysters in the half shells before other ingredients are added and baked."

"Well, I have to get some of it if that is your secret taste," said one of Louise's friends. "How is it made?" Everyone present wanted to know more about this.

Louise answered, "Wait a minute. I'll go get the info sheet that came with the bottle I bought in the Bronx. It's a long procedure, but I'll try to summarize it for you. Put the cleaned fresh anchovies in a bucket and salt them plenty and leave them for twenty-four hours. Then they have to be transferred to a chestnut or oak wood barrel, making head-tail layers, again covered with salt. They have to be covered with a wooden top with weights added in order to press the anchovies for forty-eight hours. Liquid will develop and the base of the colatura is formed. Oh, I forgot to tell you that the anchovies have to be fished in the period from April to the end of July. When the forty-eight hours have passed, the juices in the tub are bottled and left in a sunny place for four months—to concentrate the liquid. But wait a minute," she said, "there still is another important step," as everyone gasped.

They were interested, in spite of the gasp, so Louise went on with her description, aided by the information sheet: "The trick here is to return all the juices to the bucket that had the anchovies still in them. A little hole is made in the bottom of the wooden tub, and the juice eases out slowly. One last important step is to drain the colatura through linen fabric to finely strain the juice. And there you have it."

"Well, we'll never go to the trouble to make that—Good Lord, four months in bottles—and where in hell do you keep the salted anchovies all that time? But I know one thing. I will buy a bottle of the colatura and use it as you did on the baked oysters. What a great idea, and what a great tasty secret," one friend said as she applauded.

Later, John said to Louise, "I don't know why you had to tell them all that. It was our little secret. "Oh forget it, John, we have bigger fish to fry. I didn't tell them that I put a drop or two on a grilled tuna steak, or a drop in spaghetti with garlic and chili, or on scallops and pancetta—the one with the chicory hearts,"` she said laughingly as she put away the information sheet and the secret bottle.

Italians treat eel as a delicacy, and it is cooked all over Italy, especially in towns and villages along the hundreds of miles of coastline. It may be stewed, baked, or grilled, or one ancient way to cook eels (only newborn tiny eels are used) is to put them in large basins of seawater and leave in the sun until all the water has evaporated. A dash of vinegar is added and *ecco!* an eel dish is ready. John does not cook it that way. He mostly uses a variety of herbs such as thyme and basil in his recipe. When grilled this way, the flesh is sweet and firm. Eel must be freshly killed and skinned at once, and a fishmonger will do this. In the United States, conger eel, also known as sea eel, is common on the Atlantic coast. John says, "This is one of my favorite things."

There were two or three violent years when Louise had severe stomachaches, with serious upchucks. It was painful to watch her during one of these episodes as her face turned green. They checked her gall bladder, looked into her stomach, checked blood again and again, and found nothing. She lost five, ten, and then fifteen pounds until one doctor thought he found the cause of her problem and perhaps that meant she could start eating again: gallstones that were so hidden they didn't show on the tests. Once the stones were removed, they resumed their trips to Arthur Avenue in the Bronx and to all the special food shops they had discovered before and during her illness. They lived the saying: a couple that cooks together, stays together.

Sister Bea and her husband Richard never cooked together; he was too busy doing other things. We thought he was mostly of Irish descent, but he claimed he was part Scotch, English, and German in addition to Irish. Okay, we agreed he could be Irish and German; we did not see signs of anything else. In those days, it was customary (and wrong) to think of a nationality with certain behavioral characteristics. Therefore, he was hardheaded as the Germans. Bea met him during WW II. He was in uniform and could have been considered good looking. She brought him home for dinner a couple of times. He tried to behave properly—meaning, he should have said no to the third drink—but didn't. A few months went by, and they decided to marry. Mama and Papa gave their opinion, yet knew it was Bea's call. Before they married, he got a job at the big blue company, IBM—they were offering vets entry jobs as typewriter repairmen trainees. He took the job. At that time, Bea was earning over a hundred dollars a week as an area sales manager for Dorothy Gray Cosmetics and oversaw a great area, Twenty-Third Street to Fifty-Ninth, that included most of the major department stores, all with ground-floor boutiques devoted to the major cosmetics companies, Elizabeth Arden, Revlon, and so on. Bea was good with people. One day, I saw fifty or so copies of an Italian recipe, and I asked Bea what she was doing with them. "I give a copy to each of my girls—they love the food and the recipe. They usually report back to me that they cooked the dish and liked it," she said. One Christmas, she actually brought samples of her famous Christmas pastries to her outstanding performers. They loved it. Before the wedding, Mama and Papa did the usual inviting of the groom's parents for dinner at our kitchen table. The food was splendid, and they ate it up. There were also doggie bags for some leftovers, which seemed to please them more than the dinner. The war was over, and we didn't want to say too much about Richard to Bea that we all had been through a lot, both those of us in the service and those left behind. Richard seemed overpossessive of sister Bea and didn't seem as bright as she was. We didn't want to spoil it for her. She was sharp—she earned that kind of money because she was "on the ball."

The dinner during Christmas week:

Jerry and Boone came from Kentucky to see Mama and Papa and the rest of the family. Bea knew they had not seen her apartment, so she invited them, Louise, and me. Bea prepared a lovely soup (see end of this chapter), and she had several trays of her Christmas cookies on large platters, one on the center of the dining table and two others in the living room. She loved sprinkles on them, and she liked adding a red ribbon bow to the side of the platter, sometimes right on top, so they looked especially festive for the holidays. She told us later, as we were eating the soup, that she got the idea of adding crumbs of dried amaretti cookies to it as a holiday garnish. She had the cookies on hand, and she used them not only in this soup but also in other finely strained pureed soups. We thought it was a great idea, and the highly flavored crumbs were an interesting counterpoint to the silken asparagus and leek soup. Before dinner, we had a drink and some warmed olives, real big olives, with a touch of red pepper flakes, oregano, and pieces of fried pancetta. The dinner, conversation was about Social Security, still a fairly new concept in our lives. Richard said he liked the idea for himself, but he didn't want to pay anyone else's. Bea hurried the food because of the snow and ice coming down in droves. Bea got up, came over to Louise, and whispered, "The weather is really bad and it's very difficult to get a cab downstairs". We got up and left as soon as we ate the soup, never having a taste of the Christmas pastries. But wise sister Bea had pre-packed several dozen or more for us to take home. When we got outside, it was snowing heaps, and we were not dressed for snow—another aggravation. We tried to protect Beas's fritters and wished we could have been of greater help to her that night. In our discussion, we agreed that Bea made a fabulous soup and Christmas pastries of handmade dough, cut into fancy edges, curled, and fried and powdered with sugar and cinnamon looked so tempting.

We gathered around Mama's kitchen table, had a cup of coffee, and devoured Bea's crispy Christmas confections.

Bea found solace in her cooking times. She was freer, after Richard died, visited us more frequently, cooked and supped with us, and learned some new recipes. She would be so happy to know that her two daughters are marvelous cooks who enjoy Italian food and that one of her granddaughters, Jennie, studied cooking for two years after college, and worked in the famous TRU Chicago restaurant and with one of the leading food magazines. Another granddaughter, Melissa spends weekends with her great-uncle to learn to cook Italian. What a great thrill to receive a phone call from her after one of her dinners and hear, "They just loved the zucchini stew with the sausage, and the fig bread pudding was a raving success."

Asparagus and Leek Soup with Crushed Amaretti

Crema di asparagi e porri

Serves 8

4 leeks, to make 2 cups thinly sliced
4 tablespoons butter
3 or 4 boiling potatoes, peeled and diced ½ inch to make 2 cups
2 cups asparagus pieces, 1 inch long, using tender parts only
1 ½ quarts chicken broth

Salt and freshly ground pepper
1 to 2 cups light cream
4 amaretti cookies, crumbed
Oil for deep-frying leeks for garnish

1. Cut the leeks in half, lengthwise, and wash them well, separating the leaves with your fingers as you rinse them under cool running water to remove any sand. Drain the leeks and cut them crosswise into thin slices. Reserve about one-fourth cup for garnish.
2. In a large saucepan, melt the butter and sauté the leeks very lightly. Dry the potato cubes and add them to the saucepan, toss them with the leek pieces, and sauté for four minutes. Add the asparagus pieces, the broth, and a little salt and freshly ground pepper. Bring to boil, lower the heat, and simmer thirty to forty minutes until the vegetables are tender.
3. Put the mixture through a food mill, or rub it through a fine sieve. Return the pureed mixture to the saucepan and add the cream to achieve a desired thickness. Simmer until the mixture is warmed.
4. To serve, heat some oil in a small saucepan and fry the reserved one-fourth cup leeks until crisp. Remove with a slotted spoon to a kitchen paper towel. Ladle some soup into individual warmed bowls, sprinkle a bit of the crumbed amaretti on the center, and top with a bit of the crisped leeks. Serve right away.

Mussels in Garlic Butter in Shells or Ramekins

Cozze in burro aglio in conchiglie o stampini
Serves 6

3 dozen mussels, fresh (see note)
½ pound butter, softened
1 tablespoon oregano
2 tablespoons fresh parsley, chopped (or 1 tablespoon dried)
2 medium-size onions, chopped fine
6 cloves garlic, chopped fine

2 tablespoons lemon zest, chopped fine
Juice of 1 lemon
½ teaspoon crushed red pepper (or 6 drops Tabasco)
1 teaspoon salt and pepper, ground fresh
2 tablespoons Marsala (optional)

To prepare mussels:
Wash and scrub the mussel shells thoroughly. A small, hard-bristled brush is helpful here. Remove the "beard" by pulling it out. Soak the mussels for about thirty minutes in enough salted water to cover them. Some mussels contain sand, and the soaking helps to rid them of it.

To prepare the garlic butter:
Cream the softened butter. Using a rubber spatula, work the oregano, parsley, onions, garlic, lemon zest, lemon juice, red pepper, salt, pepper to taste, and Marsala (if you wish) into the butter. Mix until all the ingredients are well blended.

1. Shuck the mussels. Discard half of each shell, keeping the mussel in the half that is more level and will hold more of the garlic butter. Add one dollop of the butter mixture to each mussel shell. Put the filled mussel shells on a baking tray and store them in the refrigerator until you are ready to heat and serve them.
2. At least ten or fifteen minutes before serving time (and as much as one hour before), remove the mussels from the refrigerator. Then when you are ready to serve them, bake them in a preheated 450°F oven for ten to twelve minutes, or until the butter sauce bubbles.
3. Serve the mussels piping hot (six shells per person). If some of the sauce has spilled into the baking tray, spoon it over the shells after they are on their serving plates.

Note: Canned mussels may be used if you wish. Drain the mussels and discard the liquid. Place six mussels in each of six large shells or ramekins. Divide the butter mixture equally among them. Refrigerate and/or bake as directed.

Salad of Squid Rings

Insalata di anelli di calamari

Serves 6 to 8

To prepare the squid:

4 cups of water
2 teaspoons salt
1 bay leaf
2 pieces lemon zest, about 1 by 2 inches each
2 pounds fresh or frozen whole squid, washed and including tentacles

1. In a saucepan, combine the water, salt, bay leaf, and lemon zest, and bring this to a boil. Add the squid. Cook over medium heat for ten to fifteen minutes, until the squid are tender. Halfway through this cooking time, add the tentacles.
2. Drain the squid and put them in cold water to stop further cooking. Drain again and cut the squid bodies into thin rings, approximately one-fourth inch wide. Chop the tentacles into one-half-inch pieces. Set all the squid pieces aside. Cover them completely.

To prepare the salad and dressing:

1 garlic clove, quartered
½ teaspoon sugar
¼ cup fresh lemon juice
⅓ to ½ cup olive oil
¼ cup fresh green pepper, chopped fine
1 medium-size red or purple onion, sliced very thin
2 inner celery stalks, including leaves, sliced fine
2 tablespoons fresh flat Italian parsley, chopped fine
Salt and pepper, ground fresh

1. While the squid is cooking, combine garlic, sugar, and lemon juice in a large bowl, mix well, and allow to stand thirty minutes or longer. With a wooden spoon, press the garlic pieces against the

side of the bowl to "bruise" them and thereby extract some of the juice, then discard garlic pieces.

2. Add olive oil and mix well. Then add the green pepper, onion, celery, parsley, salt and pepper to taste, and the squid rings and chopped tentacles. Mix well and serve.

A variation:

An interesting variation is to add freshly cooked peas instead of, or in addition to, the green pepper. Use one cup peas (or a little less), increase the amount of olive oil and lemon juice, and adjust the seasoning to taste.

Grilled Eel with Wine, Brandy, and Thyme

Anguilla arrostita al timo (in gratella)

Serves 6

6 pieces of eel, each 3 inches long, about 3 pounds
1 cup dry white wine
3 tablespoons brandy
4 tablespoons extra-virgin olive oil
Juice of 1 lemon
1 tablespoon chopped fresh thyme, or 1 teaspoon dried
2 tablespoons chopped fresh basil, or 1 tablespoon dried

1. Rinse and dry the eel pieces and place them in a glass or ceramic dish in one layer.
2. Combine the wine, brandy, and two tablespoons of the oil, lemon juice, thyme, and some salt and freshly ground pepper. Mix well and pour over the fish. Marinate in the refrigerator for two hours and be sure to bring to room temperature, about one-half hour, before grilling.
3. Split each piece of eel lengthwise and pat the basil in between the halves. Thread on three skewers and, when the fire is ready, grill fifteen minutes, turning carefully and basting with the remaining oil. The eel is done when it turns white and a wooden skewer can be inserted with no resistance. Serve hot.

Baked Oysters

Ostriche in forno

Serves 4

2 dozen fresh oysters
Drops of colatura di alici (anchovy juice), optional
½ cup finely chopped Italian parsley
½ cup freshly made bread crumbs
2 cloves garlic, minced
Freshly ground pepper
Extra-virgin olive oil for sprinkling
2 lemons, cut in wedges, seeds removed

1. Shuck the oysters. Arrange the half shells carefully (do not spill the juices) in one layer on one or two large baking pans.
2. Preheat oven to 350°F.
3. Add a drop of the colatura to each oyster in its shell. Sprinkle some parsley over each oyster. Combine bread crumbs and garlic. Mix well and sprinkle this over them. Liberally sprinkle with black pepper.
4. Carefully spoon about one-fourth teaspoon olive oil into each shell. Bake ten to twelve minutes. Serve six per person with two or three lemon wedges.

20

THE ICEBOX ZIA, THE HEALER, AND THE TRIPE LADY

Maria Giuseppe, my father's aunt by marriage, was called Zia Zeppe. She was not a fat woman, but she had a large frame and was tall and seemed strong. She wore the perennial long, black cotton skirt with a blouse of the same color. She brought this outfit to life by donning a colorful apron slipped over her head and tied behind her back. Her pile of graying hair was meticulously coiffed into a bun. I wouldn't label her attractive—her ears and pockmarked nose were too large, but she had a direct look-you-in-the-eye manner and a caring attitude. I never knew my paternal grandfather or his brother, her husband, but he was responsible for a slew of children, all of them much older than I. The youngest, Dominic, tried to bugger me; and perhaps for this reason, I never felt good about her offspring. But I liked Zia Zeppe.

She and Mama were "apron ladies." They had almost as many aprons as they had forks, knives, and spoons, and they were all homemade. Every old curtain in both abodes was examined to see if they had potential as aprons. The same can be said for bedspreads, old dresses, and material that Mama brought home from Mr. Rothstein.

"Yes," Mama would say to her aunt (Zia Zeppe), "we can get two out of this piece—one for you and one for me." They both sewed well, so this was an easy thing to do. There were lots of ladies in the neighborhood who worked at Mama's dress factory, and they would bring home material and sometimes give it to Mama to do with it what she wanted, but no one got as much fabric from the dress shop as Mr. Rothstein gave Mama.

Zia Zeppe would comment, "Angela, I like-a that one zo much, it's a nice material."

"Well, of course," Mama would say, "we'll make an apron for you with that piece." They concentrated on white fabric mostly, but sometimes a fancy print would stand out. One of their favorite aprons was made of a white cotton with eyelets. It stood up and sparkled when washed and starched, especially if it had ruffles, a pattern *di rigeur* for both of these ladies.

Zia Zeppe lived across the street, one flight up, and was always in view at her front room-window, leaning over the sill or seated on a red painted chair in front of the entrance to her tenement building. We called her the icebox lady because she was thrilled to have the largest white refrigerator on the block. She called it the "ice-a-box" to the day she died. As you entered her kitchen door, she would go to the ice-a-box, open the door slowly, dramatically, with a smile and, say, "C'e tutta cosa—tutta" (There is everything here—everything). She pointed to and often removed some of the contents to show you—the sausage, the fresh mozzarella, a tin of fresh ricotta, the many eggs, and fruits of all kinds. The ice-a-box seemed to soothe her and made her a happier person. It may have helped her get over daily small family problems. She frequently opened and closed that refrigerator door. It gave her a special status because no one we knew had a larger fridge. She had not set her sights on a house in Long Island or a new living room "suite" or a new bureau. She didn't yearn for a washing machine and had no toaster. She felt rich with that refrigerator sitting in her kitchen. Its mere presence overcame all the things she didn't have in this country or in Italy. She settled for this refrigerator economically, socially, and psychologically. When she wrote to relatives in Italy, she wrote about the refrigerator and described its contents, summarized as "C'e tutta cosa." When her children visited her from Astoria, Queens, or Long Island City or Brooklyn, she compared refrigerator sizes with them—hers was always the biggest and, therefore, the winner. Along with the fridge, its contents met her basic needs. She thrived on making beef rolls because the meat was special and more expensive than most people would pay for their meat. She made mushroom stew because mushrooms in a stew—it took a lot of mushrooms—were also expensive and something other people weren't buying. When others used mushrooms, they used three or four of them for flavor. Not Zia Zeppe; she depended on mushroom stews for social status. When she made it, everyone knew. Word got around, and it made her feel important. She knew they were artificially cultivated in sheds, cellars, and airy caves. She would say in Italian to anyone interested, "Mushrooms are abundant and available all through the year. My stew is very tasty because the fresh mushrooms are accented with some dried ones."

And the same for her eggplant mold—few of her contemporaries would take the time and the trouble to make this beautiful dish lovely to look at and better to taste. If she was making it, and you happened to pop in on her, you got both treatments—the fridge and the turned-out eggplant mold, filled with peppers, tomatoes, eggs, and death-by-cheeses.

Her mother Zia Angela lived with her. Smaller in size than her daughter, Zia Angela was pixielike. Her hair was white and gold, and when I was ten years old, she was one hundred. We were told that she had difficulty holding her urine, and one time, standing on the street outside her home, she parted her legs, walked away, and left a puddle. We once heard someone say that she never wore underpants.

Mama and Zia Zeppe liked to cook together, mostly to help one another. We suspected the real reason for them cooking together was more because they wanted to share experiences and get caught up on local gossip, not all of it savory. They would always say to each other, in Italian, "Non do mai retta alle chiacchiere" (I never listen to gossip), to release themselves from any guilt about sharing a piece of "news."

There were many males named Joseph in both families; therefore, St. Joseph's day, celebrated each year on March 19, was not only a big affair at both homes but also this feast date was celebrated all over the city and all over Italy. If there is one food that symbolizes this saint's day, it is the zeppole, a piece of fried dough that is sugared after it's cooked. Kids love them, parents love them, and there never are enough of them to go around. Zia Zeppe liked them so much, perhaps because of the alliteration: Zia Zeppe's Zeppole.

One day before St. Joseph's, she and our mother decided to make a batch of them. (There is no point in giving the actual amounts of ingredients they used because you will not want to make so many. This is their recipe reduced by two-thirds, and that seems to make sense.)

Combine two and a half cups of tap water and one-half cup white wine in a pot and bring it to a slight boil. (This means you see little bubbles at the bottom of the pot, and not a raging boil). "Propio come la vita," laughed Zia Zeppe (Just like life). This made Mama laugh as she quipped, "Forse un grande punto di ebollizone" (Perhaps a greater boiling point). In a bowl, combine two and a half cups of all-purpose flour sifted with a good pinch of salt. Then put all the flour into the pot and stir like crazy with a wooden spoon.

Mama used to do the stirring, as her Zia complained, "Non posso fare, non posso fare" (I can't do it, I can't do it).

Mama stirred until the dough formed a large ball. Zia Zeppe was watching and said now was the time for the pot to come off the stove. She had prepared a part of her countertop with a bit of oil, spreading it over a one-foot square of surface. The dough was put on this space, and Mama began kneading the dough, just as her aunt said, "Non dimenticare di batterlo" (Don't forget to beat it), an unnecessary instruction for Mama. "Io uso il mattarello" (I'll use the rolling pin), Mama replied. And as her aunt pleaded, "Non posso fare, non posso fare," Mama beat the dough with the pin for about ten minutes. When it was flat and smooth, Mama cut it into strips and rolled them one at a time into ropes about the thickness of your index finger. She cut the strips into six-inch lengths and pressed the two ends together to make a ring as she put each aside. Again, the aunt said, "Oh, sembrano cosi belli" (Oh, how pretty they look).

To cook them, the women used a small frying pan, about one-half inch deep, with peanut oil mixed with some olive oil (three-fourths peanut, one-fourth olive oil). They never measured the heat point of the oil (it should be around 375 degrees) and cooked two at a time, three to four minutes, per side, or until they start to turn brown. If they could get a third in the skillet, they would add it; but mostly they didn't, as two of them would cook in a shorter time.

As Mama tended the frying zeppole, Zia was adding cinnamon powder to a cup of sugar, which she put on a large plate so the zeppole could be sugared after being drained on some paper towels.

As Mama arranged the sugared zeppole on a large plate, Zia looked at them and said, "Anima di soddisfazione" (Soul satisfying).

One day, Zia Zeppe told Mama that her daughter Angelina and her family were coming for dinner, and she wondered if Mama would help her. They decided they would make the vegetable-stuffed beef roll that was a specialty of Zia Zeppe, who would gather all the ingredients, and together they would calmly work in unison until the dish was prepared, usually in the ready-to-be-cooked stage. Sometimes, Mama couldn't stay too long, as she had a family to feed, but she was willing to give what time she could.

As they cooked, Mama said in Italian, "Oh how I detest the expression 'figliola' (little girl). The connotation of the word is not especially pleasant." She admitted that Papa called her that sometimes, and she felt a married woman with six children should not be so addressed. "Why does he call me that, Zia?" she posed to Zia Zeppe who answered right away with a broad smile.

"Angela *mia*, so many Italian men do that. They say it to remind you they are the boss. They are in charge, and don't you forget it is what they mean. Gerardo (her husband) did the same to me, and I would remark, 'Che catzo di parole e quella?' (What kind of f——g word is that?) His only reply was always 'Sta zitto, tu' (Stay quiet, you).

As they were combining the partially cooked vegetables in a bowl, they switched the conversation to the little black girl who worked for Zia Zeppe for an hour or so and then came over to Mama's for a couple of hours, usually on Saturdays. Zia Zeppe's family was grown and out of the house at this time, and it was getting difficult for her to sweep under her bed, reach high for some cleaning, and iron large white sheets for the bed. Zia Zeppe had trouble conversing with the girl, but at the start, Mama instructed her—she knew what had to be done at Zia's. When she came to us, things were different. All of us could communicate with her, and as we were helping Mama with the Saturday morning chores, Miss Prissy, as we called her, kept a lively conversation with us all. We called her that because she reminded us of the character in *Gone with the Wind*—remember her famous line, "Hones', Miz Scarlett, I didn't do it," as she returned from being absent too long just before Melanie was to have the baby. She was under five feet tall, weighed less than a hundred pounds, was sprightly, and wore a tam (a black beret) the whole time she worked. Under the tam were some braided extensions—little clusters of fake hair that would show under her hat. Every once in a while, one would fall out, but she paid no attention to that. She'd pick up the switch and put it back where it belonged. Mama would complain to us, "You're talking too much. Stop it now." She never said a word to Miss Prissy. We think Mama couldn't stand the high pitch of her voice if it went on too long, and that's why she asked us to shush. Both Mama and Zia Zeppe were kind to her—she never left empty handed—there was always a little care package of leftover spaghetti with a meatball or whatever was on hand. "I sure love that Eye-talian food!" she would screech at high pitch. One time, she spent an hour or so explaining to Mama the similarities between "Suddern and Eye-talian cookin'." She would comment, "Well y'alls put pork fat when you cook beans, don'tcha? And y'all like garlic with tomatoes and peppers, like we do. Now, ain't that raight? And y'all roast yer meat with pork fat. We do."

On the first floor of the very next tenement lived Zia Anna Maria. *Life* magazine should have photographed the two Zias when both were at their windowsills. This Zia was more formal and a bit more elegant because of the hand-crocheted lace shawl over her shoulders, once in a while casually stretched over her piled up hair. Other than this, the Zias could have been sisters. I have no idea whose Zia she was; it was not uncommon to refer to any older woman (in black with piled hair) as Zia, even if you weren't related. The special feature about this Zia was her "secret" ability to heal. I had a severe headache one time, and in spite of rest and castor oil, the headache persisted. Mama marched me across the street, up one flight of stairs, to Zia Anna Maria; I was placed in a kitchen chair next to the Zia. She gently put three or four fingers on my head, barely touching me. She poured a few drops of oil into a small saucer, dipped one finger in it, moved the oiled finger to my forehead, and made a cross—her touch was as light as a feather. In Italian, she whispered several short paragraphs. Mama stood close by, never saying a word. When Zia Anna Maria touched my elbow and moved it slightly upward, I knew she wanted me to stand and leave. Again, in Italian, she spoke softly to Mama who gave her some money she had held in a closed hand the entire time we were there—in toto, perhaps five minutes. As we went down the flight of stairs and left the building, my headache seemed to have left me. Mama used Zia Anna Maria at other times for my sisters and brothers and one other time for me. My wrist was sprained and achy for several days before we crossed the street to this Zia. The gentle touch on my wrist, a light application of oil, and some Italian prayers—I always thought of her words as prayers, as if she were reaching for a higher authority. Did she have real power? Was she God's delegate on earth? What exactly magical know-how did she have, and where did it come from? We all stopped the questions—we got nowhere. If she made us better, that was the real proof. Why did we always feel better when we left her?

As far as we knew, Zia Anna Maria lived alone in one sense; in another, she didn't. She had many callers during the day—in-between callers, and weather permitting, she advertised her talent by sitting at the front windowsill. The Zias, of course, were excellent cooks. They were definitely of the old school. They came to this country as older people, and with them came their bags of kitchen tricks and tools. Both ladies had mezzalunas from Italy. Many of their spices and herbs were sent from Italy. They each had their own versions of how to roast a chicken or cook fish. No one could tell Zia Maria Giuseppe how to roll and stuff a slice of beef. When Pino Luongo opened his Le Madre restaurant on East Seventeenth Street and brought real live Italian mothers from Italy to work as chefs, he could have saved time, money, and headaches by simply hiring these already US-based Zias.

"Tripe: (1) The light-colored, rubbery lining of the stomach of cattle or other ruminants used as food.
(2) Something of no value, rubbish".

The American Heritage Dictionary

There's a strange phenomenon in our family—in that we think of a person in terms of his or her food quotient. What do they eat? Can they cook? Do they like Italian food? What don't they eat? Will they eat anything served them? Do they guzzle wines and liqueurs? Do we want them to sup with us? You will hear, "Oh Lucia, Delmonte is so thin. She eats nothing. She is difficult about food" or "That Mario, he'll eat you out of house and home. He eats everything, especially meat. Last time, he ate the entire mozzarella meat loaf—mozzarella is not cheap, believe me!"

There are a number of ways the Italians prepare tripe—the method is usually dependent on the way the mother, grandmother, and great-grandmother taught their daughters to make it. Some people do not add tomatoes but will add a taste of cinnamon. Others cook it in white wine with different herbs, and others add cabbage and potatoes to the dish. Mama's cooking style included some of her homemade paste, spiced with some pancetta, garlic, and onion and topped with Pecorino cheese and chopped mint. Mama would say, "Yes, Jean Ducas, yes, my friend Jean. She likes my tripe. My kids don't like it, but she's crazy about it, and I love making it for her."

Jean, a very old friend in the country and the city, is a natural-born eater; Scotch by heritage, American in real life, with a husband who deserted her (and their three children) for a somewhat phony-type socialite, his secretary. When we first encountered Jean, she was in the throes of the divorce. She was furious about her husband and what was happening to her and her family. She made it clear she did not like the home breaker. She found substantial solace in food and our family. When she ate with us, everything seemed forgotten (for the moment anyway), and Mama felt Jean would feel better if she left us with a we-love-you-food package. Mama thought these food packets energized

Jean, who, happily or not, had to move out of her lovely country home. She asked if we would help dig out her peony plants. When we said yes, we didn't realize how many there were. She wanted them all out of the ground and moved and replanted to her new rental house, a mile or so down the road. We were sure she was in violation of her rental lease, but Jean enjoyed breaking rules. We suspected she wanted to keep us at her house because she knew each time we appeared, there was another large pot or oversized bowl of Mama's minestrone, lasagna, or vegetable casserole. One day, Mama asked Jean what she would like to eat on our next visit. Jean said, "Tripe!" Mama glowed, and the rest of us nearly passed out. All of us, except Mama and Papa hated tripe. We could not stomach the purchasing, cleaning, cooking, and eating it. It was forbidden food for us. But it was a joy for Mama to cook it and offer it to anyone who liked it. She found her match in Jean and so began a more-than-imagined relationship. Jean found a gold mine of tripe in this new friendship. Mama smiled happily as she prepared and delivered tripe to Jean, and you could almost hear her sigh, "Losing a husband. Who cares? You have my tripe to keep you warm." About a year later, Jean was on steadier ground, had bought some land close by, and started building her dream house—a studio to paint in, an enameled wood stove with an exposed pipe to go through the roof, and an oversized gilded Chippendale mirror to be hung on a high wall in the living room. The roof rafters were in place with the sun shining through on the day we planned a foodie event for her. We set up two card tables under the rafters and their shadows cut across the tables—a perfect al fresco setting. Jean had vodka and an assortment of wines, and we brought food for us and food for Jean—including a quart of tripe Mama made secretly in New York, put up in an empty plastic container that once held ricotta. Jean was deliriously happy—she hadn't asked for the tripe, but Mama knew what would please her. Mama, in an unaccustomed shy way, said the tripe was a welcome-to-your-new-home present. We drank and ate, ate, and ate until the sun began its trip over the horizon—truly, a gorgeous summer day in the country, in an unfinished house. Later, Jean told us she had leukemia. She had a few chemo sessions and decided not to have any more. She declined any further medical help. Jean was a natural-born gambler. There was usually a copy of the *Daily Racing Form* sticking out of her purse or coat pocket. Often, when some of us joined her to go to Saratoga for a few days, we inevitably (thanks to Jean) ended up in a putrid motel or hotel room filled with awful smells of stale smoke—probably cigar smoke that penetrated the draperies, the bed covers, the pillows. These rooms had old-fashioned transoms, and they were always open. For some strange reason, the foul-smoked air would linger below the transom and never pass through to the other room, which was already infested with more stale cigarette and cigar smoke. The air seemed so thick and smelly. Like a pulmonary infection, it never broke up and moved on.

Jean knew how to bet on horses. When we wanted to bet, we would ask Jean to place them for us. Whatever we gave her, two-, five-, or ten-dollar bills, she always came back with more. So went the betting, race after race. She was lucky at the track but unlucky with the leukemia. A few weeks before she passed away, she took Mama's hand and said, "Angela, will you be so kind and make me some of your delicious tripe?" Mama made her three quarts. We dared not kid Mama that her tripe killed Jean, but the thought ran through our minds. You either like tripe or you don't! You either become a tripe-aholic, or a tripe-aphobic. We kids could not take the soaking of it in orange juice (Mama's method) and the continual cleaning of it. Tony the butcher said it was "steam-clean" and didn't need to be cleaned. Mama did not trust this advice; she employed her old-fashioned way of dealing with all this. We had only one stove, one kitchen, and we kids pined and thought if only it could be cooked outdoors. If it made Jean happy, and it did, wasn't tripe an easy answer to happiness. You know what Mama would say.

Mushroom Stew

Zuppa di funghi
Serves 4 to 6

4 tablespoons (½ stick) butter
2 tablespoons olive oil

2 large onions, finely chopped
2 large garlic cloves, finely chopped
2 tablespoons chopped fresh tarragon, or 2 teaspoons dried
1 bay leaf
2 tablespoons all-purpose flour
2 cups chicken or vegetable broth
2 cups fresh or canned tomatoes, peeled, seeded, drained, and chopped
½ cup dry white wine
2 pounds mushrooms, sliced ¼ inch thick
½ ounce dried mushrooms, cut into small pieces
Salt and freshly ground pepper
¼ cup chopped fresh parsley

1. In a saucepan, heat two tablespoons butter and one tablespoon olive oil. Sauté onions until they begin to color, about five minutes. Add garlic, tarragon, and bay leaf and cook two more minutes.
2. Add flour and mix well. Cook until flour is blended, about two minutes. Add broth, tomatoes, and wine and cook until all comes to a rapid boil. Reduce heat and simmer ten minutes. Remove from heat and set aside.
3. In a flameproof casserole with cover, heat remaining two tablespoons butter and one tablespoon oil. Add fresh and dried mushrooms and sauté over high heat for three minutes. Add tomato mixture, salt, and pepper, cover, and cook five minutes. Stir in chopped parsley; taste and adjust seasoning. Serve hot.

Zia Zeppe's Beef Roll with Vegetable Stuffing

Rollatini di manzo imbottito di legumi alla Zia Zeppe
Serves 6 to 8

To make the filling:

2 tablespoons olive oil
2 tablespoons butter
1 ½ cups onion, chopped

1 ½ large carrots, in thin curls, 1 inch long and less than inch thick (use a potato or vegetable peeler)
¾ cup celery, including leaves, sliced very thin
2 garlic cloves, chopped fine
4 slices white bread, crusts removed, soaked in ½ cup milk
¼ cup fresh parsley, chopped fine (or 1 teaspoon dried)
½ cup grated Parmesan cheese
1 teaspoon dried oregano
1 egg, lightly beaten
Salt and pepper, ground fresh

1. In a skillet, heat oil and butter. Add onions, carrots, and celery, and cook six to eight minutes, until the onions begin to turn yellow. Add garlic and cook one minute. Transfer mixture to a large bowl.
2. Squeeze bread to remove some of the milk but keep it fairly moist; break into small pieces and add to vegetable mixture. Mix in parsley, cheese, oregano, and egg. Add about one teaspoon salt and sprinkle liberally with freshly ground pepper. Mix well and set aside.

To prepare and cook the beef roll:

1 ½ to 2 pounds round steak, cut in one large piece approximately ½ inch thick
Salt and freshly ground pepper
1 tablespoon olive oil
1 tablespoon butter
⅓ cup brandy or Cognac
½ cup dry red wine
1 cup beef or mixed broth
¼ cup tomato paste (or ½ cup tomato puree)
1 teaspoon dried oregano

1. Spread the steak on a flat surface. Pound it with a mallet if necessary to achieve desired thinness. Salt and pepper liberally and

spread stuffing as evenly as you can. Beginning with the smaller or narrower end, roll the steak, jellyroll fashion: secure it with string, toothpicks, or small skewers.

2. In a large, covered saucepan (a casserole or Dutch oven), heat oil and butter and brown beef roll on all sides. Remove pan from the heat and quickly add brandy or Cognac. Ignite it and let it burn off. Then return pan to the heat. Add wine, broth, tomato paste or puree, and oregano. Allow liquid to come to a boil and simmer, uncovered, five minutes. Cover pan and cook fifty to sixty minutes, or until the rollatini di manzo is done. During the cooking, baste the beef roll every ten or fifteen minutes.
3. To serve, place the beef roll on a large serving platter; remove the string, toothpicks, or skewers; and slice carefully.

Vegetables in an Eggplant Mold

Vegetale in uno stampo di melanzane

Serves 6 to 8

1 eggplant (about 1 pound)
Salt
Vegetable oil for deep-frying
1 ½ tomato sauce
2 red bell peppers, cored, seeded, and cut into 1-inch squares (about 2 cups)
4 eggs, hard-cooked, peeled, and coarsely chopped
8 ounces Fontina cheese, cut into ¼-inch cubes
Freshly ground pepper
3 tablespoons freshly grated Parmesan cheese
2 tablespoons unsalted butter

1. Cut off top and bottom ends of the eggplant; it should be able to sit upright. Do not peel. Slice lengthwise into very thin slices. Reserve the first thin slice (which is totally unpeeled on one side). Cut a two-inch circle (this will serve as a "button" on top of the completed mold) from this piece and prepare it as you do

all remaining slices. Freely salt each slice and lay in a colander to drain for one hour. Pat each slice dry and set aside.

2. Heat about three inches of the vegetable oil in a deep fryer until hot enough to fry eggplant slices, about 375°F. Deep-fry several at a time until golden brown, about one and a half minutes per side. When done, remove with tongs to paper toweling to drain.
3. Preheat oven to 375°F. In a large bowl, combine the tomato sauce, red peppers, eggs, Fontina cheese, and salt and pepper to taste. Set aside.
4. Liberally butter a two-quart ceramic soufflé dish and line it with about three-fourths of the eggplant slices (the slices will extend slightly above the edge of the soufflé dish and must overlap each other). With a large spoon, transfer the egg and cheese mixture to the soufflé dish. Fold over the ends of the eggplant slices to cover. Add the remaining slices, including the "button." Sprinkle the Parmesan over the top and dot overall with butter. Bake until heated through, thirty minutes. Let it cool for ten to fifteen minutes, then run a sharp knife around edge to loosen mold. This mold may be turned out, and it will be especially attractive if you do. If you do unmold it, move the "button" to the top of the turned-out mold. Sprinkle with additional Parmesan and run under broiler just for a minute or two. Slice carefully to serve.

Homemade Tripe

Trippa casalinga

Serves 6

1 medium to large onion, peeled and chopped
2 slices of pancetta, cut into small pieces. If pancetta is not available, use salt pork or bacon.
1 small clove garlic, minced
1 tablespoon finely chopped Italian parsley
2 tablespoons homemade tomato paste, preferably, or store bought
1 cup water

2 pounds tripe, cooked ahead, see below, and cut into batons ½ inch by 2 inches in size
Salt and freshly ground pepper
Red pepper flakes, optional
¾ cup freshly grated Pecorino cheese
⅓ cup finely chopped fresh mint

Note: Most butcher shops sell tripe that is cleaned and preboiled. You may have to ask the butcher in the special meats department for this; or better still, try to find an Italian butcher shop who will know all about tripe. If, by chance, the tripe is not preboiled, you should cook it in water for four hours before following this recipe.

1. In a large skillet, combine onion, pancetta pieces (or its substitute) with the parsley and garlic and brown slowly, stirring every once in a while, about ten to fifteen minutes.
2. Add tomato paste and water, cover slightly, bring to a simmer, and cook about ten minutes Add the sliced tripe and continue cooking by lowering heat to get a simmer, cover slightly, and simmer for about one hour. Add salt and pepper and red pepper flakes to taste. Taste as you go along, as you do not want to make the tripe too mushy or overcooked. If the sauce is too thick for your taste, thin with a little more water to get the consistency you prefer.
3. To serve, spoon some into individual dishes or into a large platter for all of it. Add Pecorino and mint, according to taste, and serve.

21

MAMA COOKS WITH COUSIN BEA

Over time, cousin Bea gained a greater identity with her aunt than with her own mother. After all, our mother was born in Italy too and did not come to this country until she was eight years old, just like her niece, Bea. Mama's stories of her eight children, her three miscarriages, her work in the textile district, and her eventual break or release from certain strict Italian ways of life, such as bobbing her hair or wearing some colorful clothing, were of interest to Beatrice. She began contrasting Aunt Angela with her mother Rose, and she began to feel more in step with Aunt Angela than her own mother.

One day, Mama said to Bea, "Do you think it is easy living with Uncle Joe?"

Bea was in quandary about an answer, but Mama did not wait.

"Look," she said, "he has a very steady job—he honestly has not lost a day's pay. When I worked, I came home late, but he was always home no later than four o'clock in the afternoon—he was always hungry and wanted a snack, and it was Mary, his favorite daughter, who helped."

"Oh really, Aunt, I didn't know that," whispered Bea.

"Ha, there's a lot more I can tell you. Everybody liked him, naturally, but he could be a pain in the *culo* (ass) when he had a few drinks. He is always good to others when he has a drink, promising them this and that. But at home, he can be a problem. And those nights he played cards with his bunch of friends—that's another story.

He says he'll be home at nine, and sometimes its midnight when he tries to tiptoe into the bedroom. But, Bea, he has never put a hand on any of the kids. I promise you that. Once, when I was angry with my Beatrice, my hand slipped, and it looked as if I was slapping her. I was not. 'Cristo, Cristo,' he yelled at me, and I thought he was going to strike me."

"Did he, Aunt Angela?"

"Oh no, Bea, he's like a barking dog that doesn't bite. Can che abbaia non morde" (Most people think he has no temper, but he has one). Mama changed the subject to "Bea, what about your Jack—what was he like?"

"He was not interested in the family—my family—Mama, Marie, and Filomena. Papa was no longer with us, but he was not nice to my sister's husbands. He didn't like the way they dressed or the way they talked. His favorite expression was 'What do they know? Nothing.' He spent a lot of time with his friends at the insurance company. They pretended to play golf. I don't think they were good at it, but they liked being on the golf course and in the club. And, Aunt, I'm sorry to say this, he did not like Italian food."

Mama gave a soft laugh as if to say, "Screw him, who cares?" but she never uttered those words.

Bea added, "He was not much help with Barbara, our daughter. He thought it didn't matter that she lied about her heritage. He said she was proud to be Irish, and as long as she felt good being part Irish, who cares if she wants the other half to be French."

Bea went on, "So to keep peace in the family, I gave in on everything, and sometimes I knew I shouldn't have. It's strange, Aunt, when you look back on things, they often appear clearer. I can now better see some things I should have opposed. In all, Jack was okay. In a way, I married him to get away from home. Most of the time, he was no trouble, so time passed, and things went on not too much changed. Certainly, our Barbara has not."

"Have you talked with her since I saw you last?"

Bea said, "Yes, several times. I asked her if she would like to take a trip with Genevieve and me to Rome. I was testing her. She surprised me by saying she would think about it. She said that some friends of her in-laws had just returned from a fantastic trip to Italy, seeing the major cities and eating in good restaurants, and they thought the food was excellent. They said they would go back for more. They came home with recipes they bought in shops that sell cookbooks in Italian with English translations. They want to cook a dinner for the in-laws. The in-laws seemed impressed, but when the company had left, her mother-in-law asked, 'What could possibly interest them in that dirty country?' Barbara said, for the first time, she talked back to her mother-in-law, 'How could it be such a great country for your friends and dirty at the same time? Look at the grandchildren and their schoolteacher—a private school with an Italian/American teacher. Maria Elisabetta Monte, they absolutely adore her.' 'Oh well,' said the mother-in-law, 'let's not go any further. I'm tired and am going to bed.'" (Mama could picture her dragging her broad WASP behind into the bedroom. Mama finally learned the word "WASP" and liked it. She wanted to use the word again, and when she did, she stumbled one time and said "WISP," and everyone missed her point).

Mama told Bea the terrible time she had had with Uncle Joe when she wanted to bob her hair. They fought for weeks over this.

"I will never let it happen," he would pledge. And Mama would give him her long list of reasons why she needed it: her family was grown, it would be easier for her to tend, and it would be more stylish; all her lady friends—most of them Italian/Americans—were bobbed; she didn't want to appear like she was a country girl just off the boat. And Papa would come back fiercely with "Well, you were born in Italy, and you did come off the boat. Me, I was born here. It makes a big difference, born in Italy or born in America. *Sta zita* (Be quiet)," he would threaten. "Anna, remember, Potenza is a college town—Accettura didn't have a high school when you were there."

"So what happened?" Bea said excitedly.

"Well, Bea, after months of 'I'm gonna bob'—'No, you're not gonna,' I finally announced that I was going to his barber Frank Cardone who had agreed to do it for me, as he had for many other women in the neighborhood." Papa replied most directly, "If you do-a this, I kill myself." Mama said she went off to the barber and had her hair bobbed, and it looked good. She came home, opened the kitchen door, and found Uncle Joe (Papa) on the floor with a lot of red stuff over his body. Mama took one sniff and knew it was ketchup. She poked him in the shins and said, "Get up and clean up the ketchup." Believe it or not, Papa got up and laughed. His only disappointment was not the haircut but the fact that Mama didn't find the joke as funny as he did.

Cousin Bea began cooking specific Italian dishes, thinking some Italian thoughts, and loving New York and the Italians in it. Then the day to make tomato sauce arrived.

Bea brought her own aprons, white and starchy. She brought some rubber gloves and the usual box of pastries—this time some cannolis and sfogliatelles. Mama thought, "Well, she must know sfogliatelles or why would she bring them?" Mama was so pleased over her interest in her, Mama's family, and the food they're about to cook. All the ingredients, unmeasured, were set on the kitchen table. Bea knew the routine and was perfecting it. She had her notebook out with two sharpened pencils and was ready to go at any minute. (Mama thought, "I can't believe what's happening here, and I just love it. Whoever would have thought this transformation was possible? Well, I did, didn't I?")

The phone rang, and it was Zia Zeppe, Papa's aunt who lived across the street. She and Mama always spoke to each other in Italian, and it was a bit embarrassing for Bea to sit through this. Mama sensed this and didn't talk too long. The discussion was simply that one of Zia's children, Rose, was coming to see her tomorrow and would it be okay for them to come over and visit Mama. Of course it was all right.

Mama explained to Bea that the meatballs they had made the other day had to come out of the refrigerator to get to room temperature. That once the sauce was made, the meatballs would be added to the sauce, and the sauce would be enriched beyond belief.

Mama had a jar of her homemade tomatoes—one jar held about two cups, Bea noted. Mama had her chrome food mill on the table, sitting over a bowl large enough to hold the mill comfortably. She asked Bea to put two cups through the mill, and Bea did a good job, and she herself said it was necessary to do this to rid the tomatoes of their seeds and skin to leave a nice tomato pulp. Then, Mama said they needed a large skillet, one already in Mama's hand, to melt half the butter, which Mama had put on the table, one-half stick. Bea said four tablespoons were needed; she measured, put two tablespoons of butter in the skillet, and melted it. She had already chopped two small onions in the same fashion she had done the parsley the other day, and that was ready to be added to the skillet. They need to be cooked until soft. In the meantime, she minced one large garlic clove and added that after the onions cooked three or four minutes. Mama had precooked four slices of finely chopped pancetta, now sitting there in a small bowl, waiting to be used. When all this and the pureed tomatoes and cooked pancetta bits were added to the skillet, they would add salt and pepper, and they did just that.

"Bea, this has to be brought to a boil and boiled hard for about three minutes." Bea stirred as Mama watched her and, once in a while, would take her hand and move it around. "Don't be bashful," she would say. "Don't be afraid to stir. I like a wooden spoon best. I have a lot of them here."

Now for the secret: Mama took a bottle of Marsala and poured some in a measuring cup. Bea measured too, and it was a neat one-half cup, and that was added to the skillet along with a shy teaspoon of dried oregano. Mama said they didn't have to hand-rub this oregano, because it would cook for a good while in the tomato sauce and release its flavor. They cooked the contents of the skillet five minutes and set it aside.

Mama explained to Bea that they would need six of the twelve meatballs for this amount of pasta and sauce, and that is why she returned the other six to the fridge. Bea made considerable notes and seemed to comprehend what was going on here. "Oh dear," she said, as she looked at her apron soiled by a bit of tomato. Mama said, "Bea, just leave the apron here, and I'll launder and iron it for you, and you'll have it here the next time you come."

And Bea with her "Oh, Aunt Angela—you are too wonderful. I can't believe you and my mother are sisters. You are so different."

They added the six meatballs to the sauce and cooked them about ten minutes, to heat them and to allow them to flavor the sauce. "We must taste, Bea, to see if it's what we want. Bea, take a sip with a tablespoon and let me know what you think."

Bea was careful as the spoon approached her lips; she blew on it a couple of times and tasted. "Mmmmm," she said to her aunt Angela. "This is really good—maybe just a wee bit more salt." Mama tasted it and agreed, and they added a sprinkle more overall and stirred gently.

"We don't want to break up the meatballs, Bea." Having said that, she went to her closet and pulled out a bright red apron that said in Italian, "Non mi rompere il caglione" (Don't break my balls). As she showed it to Bea, who did not understand it at all, Mama laughed and said Uncle Joe found it in a gift shop downtown, next to Ferrara's, and he brought it home. Mama, feeling a bit gay over the success of her tomato-sauce session, explained as demurely as she could the meaning of the apron. Again, a surprised Bea laughed out loud and said she wanted to get a couple for certain girlfriends, Genevieve and others, and would Uncle Joe do her the favor.

Before they were ready to cook the pasta, one-half pound of vermicelli (very thin spaghetti), Mama checked the supply of Parmesan cheese and told Bea it would be okay to use also a Pecorino, made from sheep's milk, instead of Parmesan, made from cow's milk. The doorbell rang, and in walked Phyllis Cardone, the barber's daughter who hadn't seen Mama in years. Phyllis had married and moved to Long Island. (Mama wondered why do all these newlyweds move to Long Island? When our Mary lived there, I was not so fond of it—I prefer Forty-Sixth Street. But these were only thoughts, not utterances.) Mama hugged Phyllis a long time. Phyllis was another potential girlfriend of Jerry's, and in that moment, Mama's mind went wild over the thought—if only Jerry had married Phyllis, he would be here with us making this pasta and sauce. "Disgrazia," she said in Italian (What a disgrace), and she meant it in her heart. Yet she knew

Jerry was happy, and that is what mattered most. Mama changed the subject to remind the "girls" that a link or two of sausage could also be added to the sauce. It anyone wanted to do that, they would slice the sausage in pieces, sauté them first, and then add to the sauce at the same time as the meatballs. "But tonight, we are not going to add the sausage," Mama said, "because we have accomplished a lot in a fairly short time." Bea sent up praises, and in time, the "golden girls" sat at the table and supped. Mama showed Bea how to fix individual plates. She asked them to help themselves to the grated cheese, and they did. The bread had been warmed, and both butter and oil were available as was salad. "I can't live without salad," said Mama all of her life. In fact, it kept her going for many years. During supper, Mama told the story about Papa, the bob cut, and Phyllis's father, the barber. They enjoyed a warm, wonderful time together, and Bea said she would never forget the evening.

Years went by; and cousin Bea, living in a retirement home in Connecticut, became ill. For about a year, she was in and out of nearby hospitals and nursing homes. We visited her half a dozen times, each visit taking the form of a confessional. Beatrice clearly understood the mistakes she and her daughter made in denying themselves the love and joy of being Italian/Americans.

We hadn't seen Bea for months, but on this particular visit, we were struck by her appearance. The change in her was great. We felt disturbed and anxious. She was propped up in bed as we entered; she probably realized our feelings, for we hesitated instead of rushing to her bedside to say, "How are you?"

That moment of hesitation filled my mind with images of Bette Davis who had starred with Claude Rains many years earlier in a film called *Mr. Skeffington*, a remarkable film. In the movie, Bette Davis attempts to keep herself young and younger to attract men and to keep up an image of herself that seems unreasonable and impossible to achieve. As she ages in the film, she goes sailing with a new suitor, and the seas become rough in more ways than one can imagine. Her body swirls and sways, fighting the wet winds, the kerchief on her head to protect her hair gets wet and becomes undone, and at full screen, the image of Bette Davis's face is grotesque, lines drawn through the Sahara during a storm, ripple after ripple after ripple. Her false eyelashes fly off into eternity. Cousin Bea had that look. She must be quite sick.

We recovered and went quickly to her bedside. I took her hand into mine and asked how things are going. She had arranged for a chair to be placed next to her bed so one of us could sit down. There was an opened box of cookies on her night table, and she offered us some. We said thanks, but no. We had just eaten lunch.

In a weak voice, with little strength, she told us that Phyllis Cardone had moved into a beautiful apartment in Manhattan Plaza, a city-sponsored housing project on Ninth Avenue and Forty-Second Street. It was a block long and an impressive building. (We knew about this because Hartley House had assisted in the completion of her application to live there.) Bea was happy for Phyllis, but it also meant she had a new opportunity to come back to the old neighborhood. She mentioned a number of shops familiar to us and the names of several restaurants she and Phyllis used to go to.

"I miss your mother so much. I can never forget those splendid visits and cooking times with her. I miss her common sense about life and its problems," she said so softly. She took a deep breath and said, "Barbara and I have grown closer than we have ever been. She comes here to take good care of me. She pays my bills, answers letters, and I am so thankful for her. She is my main champion, and right now, life would be difficult without her. I think you know that when Genevieve, Phyllis, and I went back to Italy, she joined us for a week. We had such a grand time, and she liked the food so much, and I've taught her some of what Aunt Angela, your mother, I mean, taught me."

She went on and reviewed the steps in making pasta. She spoke at length about her ability to make ravioli and manicotti—her favorite. And meatballs too. "Like your mother said, I made a batch at a time, froze them, and then I could reach in and take two or four of them, whatever I needed, heat them in that fabulous tomato sauce with the sausage. You wouldn't believe your cousin Bea and the pots of soup I made, enough to last me a week: soups with pasta, rice, beans, fish, meats, and vegetables. Your mother showed me how to make pasta frolla. I'm sure you know what that is, and we used it to make cheesecakes and jam and fruit crostatas. I have a small appetite these days, but when I think or talk about Italian food, my stomach beckons, and I feel I could eat a full, full meal. But right now, I have no appetite at all." Her face cracked more as she talked, and we knew she was getting tired. So tired. I held her hand tightly, and as we started to leave, she whispered, "You know, I pray every night for your mother. I know she hears me up there, and she knows how much I love her."

The trip to see cousin Bea in Farmington, Connecticut, took two hours, and one or more of us visited every other month or whenever we could. We sympathized with the *Skeffington* look and paid no attention to it—she was our cousin Bea, young or old.

She told us Barbara, her daughter, was to become a grandmother; and if it is a girl, they would name her Beatrice. She repeated it again. She reported that Barbara's in-laws had passed on and that she and her daughter felt it was no longer necessary to deny their Italian connection. "We both felt like new people," she admitted in a pious tone. "And we have prayed together to ask forgiveness. When I was in Italy," she said, "with Phyllis, Genevieve, and Barbara, we had prayer beads and crosses blessed by a priest at St. Peters. If you look on my night table, you will see them. I cling to them every night with prayers for forgiveness and to thank God for my aunt Angela, who opened my eyes to many simple joys and happiness. And I thought of one of Papa's favorite sayings, 'Ogni tempe arrivete, ogne frutte ammatturete' (All seasons will come, all fruits will ripen), and Papa would add in English, 'You will know when you know.' During the last two visits, she slipped Mass cards into my hand. The reason for the Mass card was not as important as was the act of her giving it. This act was Italian. All our young lives, we witnessed Italian women giving and receiving Mass cards, for whatever reason. It was as if she were saying, 'I am so proud to be an Italian/American.' Thanks to you and your family, and especially your mom, for helping me."

As I left Farmington, I saw cousin Bea trying to get to Accettura. Another cousin, Nick Belmonte, retired from a firm in Connecticut and now living in Accettura, was leading cousin Bea over thousand-foot tall ridges with haphazardly spaced olive and fruit orchards. They climbed on foot for hours, with some relief through the cool oak forests of Bosco Montepiano, where cousin Bea had walked before as a little girl, to breathe the soft, velvety, woodsy, and "tiramisu" air. She could see between the openings in the trees, drama personified, and one look down the steepest slope into the valley was Accettura, like a princess of Basilicata with its bright white mosaic of buildings and small, curving alleys, as if all roads lead to Accettura and its steeple over its big church, shining silver beacons at high noon. Nick let go of cousin Bea's hand.

She had arrived.

Cousin Bea died in January. We shall miss her visit for lunch this spring.

Special Tomato Sauce

Salsa di tomate speciale

Serves 4

- 2 cups fresh or canned Italian tomatoes
- 4 tablespoons butter, divided
- 2 small onions, finely chopped
- 1 large clove garlic, minced
- 2 to 3 ounces (4 slices) finely chopped pancetta
- Salt and freshly ground pepper
- ½ cup Marsala
- 1 teaspoon dried oregano
- 6 baked meatballs at room temperature
- ½ pound vermicelli
- Parmesan or Pecorino cheese

1. Put tomatoes and their juice through a food mill. Set aside.

2. Melt two tablespoons butter in a large skillet. When it is foaming, add chopped onions. Cook four minutes. Add minced garlic, stir, and cook one minute more.
3. In another skillet, sauté chopped pancetta until crisp, about four minutes. Drain on paper towels and set aside.
4. Add tomatoes and fried pancetta pieces to skillet with onions. Bring to a boil; boil uncovered for three minutes. Add salt and pepper.
5. Add Marsala and remaining two tablespoons butter and oregano to skillet with onions. Bring to a boil and cook five minutes. Add meatballs, lower heat, and simmer, covered, five minutes.
6. Cook pasta according to manufacturer's directions. Drain well and add to the skillet. Toss well over heat one or two minutes and serve with either of the grated cheeses.

22

THE NEIGHBORHOOD

The Italians and the Irish dominated West Forty-Sixth Street and its environs. Aromas of *ragu* or corned beef and cabbage permeated the atmosphere. There was a sprinkling of German families, so add sauerkraut smells. The corner candy store was owned and run by Jewish Bernie and his wife Sara. He was always in the store; she always sat outside in charge of the newspaper and magazine stand as she avidly observed what was going on the avenue. Both of them had lunch in the store, and we could smell the pastrami sandwich they ordered from a nearby Jewish deli. Just the smell of it would make us kids hungry. The sandwich came with a small container, and when its lid was off, we saw delicious coleslaw.

Bernie sold loosies—a single Wings brand cigarette—for a penny and chocolate candies from an open box for one cent apiece. If your chocolate had a pink center, you'd win a prize of absolute nominal value. I tried to inspect the chocolate pieces to see if the bottoms had been nail-pierced to show color, and many had been so violated then returned to the box. Obviously, none of those raped had pink centers. Bernie would cuss me out, thinking I was the guilty one, and at times I was. He had a soft spot for me and would give me a prize after I spent three or four pennies and garnered only white centers. He knew us well, for we bought daily newspapers and lined composition books with gray and white marbleized cardboard covers and dead black cloth spines. He also sold Charlotte Russes—Bernie use to call them

"Charley Roose"—three cents apiece, and they were a favorite with us kids. They were also a favorite of Jewish Americans and popular not only in New York but also in other major cities in the northeastern part of the country.

The dessert was made of sponge cake topped with whipped cream with a cherry on top. The cake and cream were set in a frilled cardboard holder. You pushed up the center cardboard to get at more cake and cream. The name Charlotte Russe is French (*russe* in French means "Russian," and Charlotte was the name of the sister-in-law of Czar Alexander I)—imagine selling these in this shop on Ninth Avenue at Forty-Sixth Street.

Our shoe repair shop was across the street from Bernie's. Joe, its Italian owner, was thinly mustached, balding, and molesting. My sisters hated going into his shop. They said he commented on their bottoms and their bosoms and was crudely flirtatious. Our parents knew Joe and were tolerant of him, believing he was incapable of such behavior. Eventually, it was Mama and Papa who brought in and picked up our repaired shoes. In those days, it was not unusual to resole the same pair of shoes two or three times.

Joe, the shoemaker, always had a carton of food sitting on one of his shelves, food whose smell was obvious to his customers. We all thought he ate well—it was easy to identify the roasted lamb chops with rosemary one day and, on another, chicken cacciatore. If he had ravioli, they were made at home. He ate a lot but was quite thin, just like his mustache.

There was always the smell of cheese. At times, we would see a whole loaf of Italian bread sitting on top of a pair of shoes. He must have had bread-and-cheese snacks all during his workday.

Close by was Bruno's Ravioli company. Our ravioli were always homemade, so none of us did business there. Their customers came from local restaurants, bars, small hotels, and some non-Italian families. Also on Ninth Avenue was a Greek pastry shop, Poseidon, owned now by Lillian and Tony Fable, descendents of the original owners. If they knew you, it was a thrill to be invited to go to the back room to watch them spin their handmade phyllo dough so thin you could see through it. Only very good friends were offered a gratuitous cookie. When we had some extra pennies, we would buy a piece of baklava, phyllo dough layered with honey and nuts, baked and cut into diamond shapes. A diamond piece would be picked up and put on a small square of waxed paper, and we would eat it out of hand.

Other than Manuel's, the grocery in our building, the next best-known shop was in the middle of our block, across the street from Manuel's: Tony's Butcher Shop. The meat was prime and custom cut. The meat ground for meatballs and meat loaves was ground in front of the customer. The unique feature of Tony's operation was he opened Sunday mornings, and these may have been his busiest hours. Tony worked the shop alone—opening it very early in the morning and closing late at night except Sundays. Mama shopped at Tony's for seventy-five years, and that is a fact.

Meat and some other food were rationed during World War II, but Tony found a way to remain open on Sunday mornings to satisfy his demanding shoppers; although on Sundays, the front of his shop appeared closed.

One entered the main hallway of the tenement building, walked halfway down the hall to enter the shop. Tony did the butchering in the rear room. His nose was pink-red, and his fingers more so from handling the cold meats and going in and out of his large custom-built refrigerator. If you were at the right angle, you could see the carcasses hanging inside the large fridge. In the main shop, a shiny stainless steel rod with large hooks followed the contour of the wall on both sides of the counter. Sausages, salamis, and prosciuttos hung on the customer side; fresh killed rabbits, still in their skins, hung on the butcher's side. There was no problem in getting special meats from Tony's such as dressed pigs weighing twenty-five pounds and up (Esposito's, on Ninth Avenue and Thirty-Ninth Street, supplied them also), lamb heads (capuzelle), and large pieces of caul to wrap around other meats for braising, roasting, or grilling. Tony's veal cutlets were superb—a family favorite for many years. You wouldn't believe the many pounds of intestines we bought at sausage-making time (usually November). Tony would sell these salted and precleaned, but Mama always washed them again, adding some orange juice to the water in which she let them stand, to sweeten and perfume them. Calves' liver was another specialty, and Mama cooked it every other week. Mama's cooking often "went north," and she prepared liver *alla veneziana*, stuffed veal breast alla Piedmontese, and steak *alla Fiorentina*.

There was Tony behind his oversized wood block, with its depression in the center from years of butchering on it—an unforgettable picture. He appeared automated. His movements were quick, precise, and always on the mark. It was a treat to watch him prepare veal cutlets, dress a chicken, or grind meat. When grinding meat, he would always throw away the first handful of ground meat oozing forth from his commercial-size grinder. He weighed his ground meat after discarding that first handful. Tony was too busy to do much cooking, but he knew all about it and shared many suggestions with his customers. In addition to his fine meats, the neighborhood appreciated his interest in food. One of his special preparations made at home by his wife and daughter was flank steak stuffed with eggplant that was cut in cubes and sautéed in butter and oil and combined with onions, garlic, celery, oregano, parley, and seasonings. All this was later mixed with a cup of homemade bread crumbs and two eggs. This "stuffing" was then placed in the pocket of the flank steak (most butchers will make a pocket for you; Tony did so obligingly). Then came the fun of securing the packet. Mama used to sew it "like you baste a hem," she would say, but it could be secured with small skewers or even toothpicks. It was browned in a large covered casserole on top of the stove; carrots, more onions, and tomatoes were added, along with herbs and seasonings and some red wine. It cooked about one and a half hours. To serve it, it was cut into wedges like pie. People just seem to love this dish. A number of families in the neighborhood had this recipe and cooked it after purchasing the flank steak from Tony's.

His business was profitable. He bought the building and, in time, acquired most of the buildings on the west side of Ninth Avenue between Forty-Sixth and Forty-Seventh Streets. He turned over the main butcher's job to his son-in-law Bob, who, for many years, carried on in Tony's fashion. The ending of Tony's life is sad. When Papa died,

Tony arrived to pay his respects on the last evening of Papa's wake. He stayed until the funeral parlor, Berkeley's, on West Fifty-First Street, closed at 10:00 p.m. Tony lived in a house on Long Island (the only overt sign of his wealth), and that night, he took the subway home and was badly mugged. He died two weeks later. He could have afforded a taxi or a limousine ride home, but Tony opted for the subway—to save money perhaps; creature of habit, probably. What a loss to the community.

In the spring, summer, and fall, neighbors sat on their stoops or on chairs brought down to the street, leaning over windowsills or against the building itself. Kids were in the streets, except when they were in school, playing stickball, the favorite street game. It was not unusual to see one or more family members eating slices of homemade pizzas or taking huge bites out of sandwiches made of Italian bread filled with sausage and peppers or cold cuts from Manganaro's. You knew what was being eaten because you could see it and *smell* it. It always seemed like a small picnic on West Forty-Sixth Street.

Every family knew other families. One mother or father on the street cared for her children and for all the other children. It was a built-in security system. When one kid misbehaved, the message was sent down the street, and the offender was corrected either by one of your his parents or one of the neighbors. Kids were rough, tough, bellicose, and pugilistic. But as soon as a fight started, it ended. If you tried to light a cigarette, it was quickly snuffed out. Any parent took care of that.

We didn't hear the word "mafia" until we went off to college. However, we were suspicious of one family with three grown sons and a daughter. The sons were always parading up and down the block in their movie-star clothes—neatly dressed with sparkling shoes, brand-new fedoras, and expensive-looking topcoats. They were replicas of the movie stars James Cagney or George Raft.

One of them once asked me to bring a full brown bag to their flat on the second floor, several buildings away from our own. The door was open, and I called, "Tessie" (I think that was her name). Tessie was plump, not pretty like her brothers, bleached her hair a shocking orange-red, and in every way imaginable not ready to receive a visitor or errand boy. The place was cluttered with pizza boxes—everywhere you looked was something that brought pizza. I guess that was all they ate.

"Come in here, Joey," Tessie called in hoarse voice. She took the bag into the first bedroom, as she pleaded, "Stay there a minute."

She didn't realize I could see what she was doing from where I stood. She emptied the brown bag onto of the bed, stacked the bills in six or seven piles, and placed them under the mattress. I think she knew I had caught a glimpse of what she was doing. As she came out to the kitchen, her face was flushed and said quickly, "Here's a dime, Joey—you can go down now." Years later, we found out they were part of the numbers racket.

A most horrific neighborhood tragedy happened on St. Patrick's night in the 1930s. It was and still is family tradition to remain home on important holidays. Our biggest celebration was New Year's Eve. To bid farewell to the old year and ring in the new, we played games at home and ate lots of food the way we did on Christmas Eve. Mama and Papa, with help from most of us, were able to provide a beautiful New Year's Eve dinner. We always had to have lentils in one form or another, as they mean good fortune in the New Year. Mama would stew lentils with small pieces of duck and follow that with *tagliatelle*, homemade pasta, in a delicious Parma ham (prosciutto) and saffron sauce.

The main course was usually pork roasted with Marsala wine. If artichokes were in the markets, we'd have them. There was always an important vegetable preparation such as slices of fennel roasted in *besciamella* sauce, topped with Pecorino cheese. The green salads were simple, dressed in good olive oil with either a red wine vinegar (often homemade) or fresh lemon juice. The fruit and cheeses followed, and because it was the last day of the year, Papa would have a variety of Ferrara pastries. If Mama had time, she would add a homemade cheesecake (made with ricotta and orange zest). Homemade bread was a fixture of the meal.

We were allowed to stay up as long as we were able to stay awake. But that St. Patrick's night at 2:00 a.m., Papa opened the front-room window and yelled to whoever was on the street.

"What is all that noise out there?" he demanded. "What is going on down there?" "Extra! Extra! Extra!" he heard them cry in the streets.

"I have to go down," he said as he raced through the flat and down the stairs. Newsboys were selling the *New York Daily News* and *New York Daily Mirror*. Papa bought several newspapers, hurried upstairs, and read the headline: "Five People Killed in Automobile Accident." The article reported that our neighbors and friends (the Salles), two sisters, their husbands, and one brother-in-law, had died in a head-on collision with another car. They were paisanos and close family friends. Mama wept, tears fell from Papa's eyes, and shock set in for weeks. When we think of that evening, we all tremble. One of the couples had three daughters, the eldest my age. We played together every day. Eventually, the girls moved in with their mother's parents and grew up there. From that time forward, Papa, to his dying day, swore that no child of his could celebrate holidays outside our home. This restriction held for many years, and it still echoes in our hearts and minds as we plan holiday events.

Most families in the neighborhood were self-sufficient when it came to money. The several families who were getting assistance were considered a lower class of people. Mrs. Simmons, one of the self-sufficient ones, would say to Mama, "Angela, can you believe the McCarthys getting help? For Pete's sake, they've got three bicycles and two radios." Most immigrant families were proud, and if they were offered help, they would refuse it. But they were not turned off by several bargain offerings during these hard times. The city set up "milk stations" where families could buy up to six quarts of fresh milk daily (depending on the size of the family noted on a card, which had to be shown at the milk station). We all made many early morning trips before school to pick up our allotment of milk. The milk was not free, but it was three or four cents a bottle cheaper than you could buy it at Manuel's or any other grocer.

We were friendly with a Greek family on Forty-Eighth Street, between Eighth and Ninth Avenues; they lived in a building across from the Belvedere Hotel. I liked the middle daughter, Sophie, who was two years older than I. All my life, she was "Sophie, the Greek." Their flat was on the top floor, and Sophie and I would look out the window of their front room. She would describe the various whores who were entering the Belvedere Hotel across the street with their temporary (hourly) boyfriends. I think she was trying to excite me, and I found her descriptions of these Runyonesque characters impressive. One hot summer afternoon, when both of us were at the window, she suddenly asked why I didn't grab her tightly and "plunder" her with hot kisses. At that time, my mind was on Anna, a young teenager from Birmingham, Alabama, who was related to the Sicilian barber on Tenth Avenue and Forty-Sixth Street. Anna's speech was deep southern, and she was an outrageous flirt. On those summer days, she would appear in the doorway of the tenement opposite ours. As I was usually reading at the front-room window, intoxicated by the smell of the drying tomato conserve, I would look down at her and catch her eye. For about a month, I went down and met her in the entryway. In time, we would work our way to the inner entry hall. She smelled of fresh peaches, the fragrance of the soap I imagined she brought up from Alabama and used for bathing just before our meetings. Her hair was short and showed off her svelte neck. Her simple cotton dress showed her young breasts and nipples—she seemed to know every movement to make inside the dress. Her brown hair, brown eyes, and light, smooth olive complexion rendered her the Sicilian Scarlett. The other Scarlett was in the opened book I left on the chair by the front window. When I held Anna's tiny waist close to my body, I felt something happening to me below. Almost always when this happened, we would hear someone approaching either to exit or enter the building, and we would instinctively break apart and move to the front entry. The kissing and petting went on for a number of weeks. I thought of screwing her, but it never came off. I simply didn't know what to do. At the end of the summer, after she returned to Alabama, I learned I had only been warming her up. An older guy, with lots of experience, had muscled his way into the picture and entered her often, without my knowing it. "Oh well," I thought, "I did enjoy the several meals at her aunt's and uncle's home—they usually served macaroni with eggplant. It seemed that they cooked that all the time."

As for Sophie the Greek, she eventually accepted the idea that she was a friend, not a lover. She continued to insist on every dance at those wonderful Friday summer night dances, sponsored by the city's Department of Recreation. Every Friday night, a different block was cordoned off, music was broadcast over loud speakers, and we teenagers went wild. The area was filled with outdoor vendors selling pizzas, grilled sausages, salami, meatballs and mortadella sandwiches with optional cheese and sliced tomatoes. The food stalls were as crowded as the dance floor.

Sophie wanted us to dance at Roseland, the top dance palace at the time. I didn't wear a tie the first time I met her there and couldn't gain admittance because of a "tie" rule. She looked in her purse and pulled out a worn black shoelace, put it under my shirt collar, and tied a bow. They let us in, and we danced for hours. During the war, she married a sailor and lived the rest of her life in Texas, her husband's home state. Some years later, I met her in New York for lunch. I asked her about her marriage. She looked at me as she had in our teen days with those piercing dark eyes of hers and said, "Oh, Joey, I get so bored I sometimes eat an apple while we're doing it."

Sophie's mother, Eva Calogridis, born in Cyprus, made known to everyone her utter dislike for the Turks. She was one of the most peaceful personalities you would ever meet until the subject of Turks came up. She said she married her husband to get out of Cyprus and get away from "the Toorkish people, I do not like" was her inimitable phrase. She had a large family and was a great cook. She always offered—time of day didn't matter. We loved the way she made vegetable casserole. She would first oil an oval baking dish, its size about fourteen by nine by two inches. Then she would finely slice two onions and put half of them in the casserole, spreading them to cover the bottom. She peeled a pound of potatoes, washed and dried them and sliced them one-fourth inch. She removed the ends of six small zucchini and made one-half-inch slices. In the summer, when tomatoes were fully ripe, she cored two of them and put them in boiling water—"Count one, two, three, all the way to ten," she would advise, then pull them out with a large fork through the center, run them under cool running water, and start to peel with a small knife. All the peel came off with two simple gestures. She rid them of their seeds by squeezing them and chopped them into half-inch cubes. She grabbed two large red bell peppers and cored, seeded, removed the membranes, then sliced them thinly into long strips. She put these veggies in a large bowl and added some minced garlic (about one tablespoon), along with a tablespoon of sugar and salt and freshly grated black pepper. She tossed that and then added about one-half cup of chopped Italian parsley and some dried fennel seeds (a good tablespoon). Another toss, and the entire mixture was poured into the oval baking dish. She added the remaining onions on top, poured about one-half cup of olive oil overall, and baked it, covered, in a 350-degree oven for at least one and a half hours. Ten minutes or so, before the bake time was over, she would remove the cover and test the doneness of the vegetable s with a fork. "Just put the fork in a few vegetables, and you'll know if they are tender," she added.

A dish made for the Greek gods. Thank you, Eva Calogridis.

In the neighborhood, Christmas Eve was the high point of the holiday season, for nothing else could compare to picking out and carrying home a fresh-cut Christmas tree, live from Paddy's Market. The market stretched from Thirty-Sixth to Forty-Second. Both sides of the streets were lined with pushcarts, each overflowing with fresh chestnuts and cauliflower, fennel and fish, turnips and Christmas trees. Selecting a tree was serious business, a family decision made by Papa. Trees cost one dollar. Then one dollar twenty-five. Each year they cost more. Full, fresh trees, six, eight, and ten feet tall. Short needle pines. The selection ritual was terribly cold. A shivering team, we stood before each tree stand and viewed the full offering. Papa would reach in, pull out a tree, bounce it four or five times on the sidewalk until the tree branches were in full sway, and ask, "Whaddaya think?" We'd go past each tree stand on the east and the west side of Paddy's Market.

Often, we'd return to two or three stands for a second look. When we agreed that Mama would like "that one," Papa's bargaining over price would begin. On average, the deal was consummated in a few minutes. Sometimes we'd walk away downhearted and disappointed, only to go back after Papa agreed to pay twenty-five cents more.

Those evenings were filled with instructions and counsel about food, because Grandma or Grandpa would be with us too. Food then in the market was unpackaged, unprocessed, and unfrozen as well, although sometimes naturally frozen by the cold weather.

The landmark shops in addition to Tony's Prime Meats were Piccinini Brothers, another butcher shop at 633 Ninth Avenue, both over sixty years old; Manganaro's at Thirty-Seventh Street, famous for its hero loaves, there for almost ninety years; and Molinari's, another Italian deli at Fifty-First (north of Paddy's area but considered part of it) for fifty years; along with Central Fish, 527 Ninth Avenue; and Sea Breeze, 541 Ninth Avenue, both fish markets, where squid and octopuses overflowed counters or sat in barrels filled with ice. International Spices at Thirty-Ninth Street, then and now, on the sidewalk and in the shop, displayed one-hundred-pound sacks of herbs and spices and barrels full of olives. We learned to reach in and sample one or two before buying. If a grandparent whispered "Sono amare" (They're bitter), that meant the olives hadn't been in brine long enough.

As we grew up, we thought green olives were American and black ones Italian. The fact is that green olives are those that are picked unripe; the black ones are those that are left to ripen on the tree. In this market, they sold both.

One of the greatest delicacies in the shops was the fresh greenish purplish figs. We were taught that figs predate the Bible, were loved by the Romans and all other Europeans, and were brought to America by the Spaniards, the French, and our grandfather.

One of Grandma's market tests was the fingernail pea-pod press. She would hold a pea pod in her hand and press a cut into the pod with the fingernail of her thumb or index finger. If she didn't buy a pound or two of them, it was because no moisture appeared in the cut. But if the cut was moist, the peas were fresh, and the sale was consummated. She would also pick up a pea pod, open it, and eat the peas to test for freshness.

There was fresh fennel and dried fennel seed, both a vegetable and a flavoring agent, a source of anise flavoring, sometimes called Roman fennel. The Florentine *finocchiona* is salami flavored with fennel. We tasted fennel before we tasted celery. For us, great food was slices of fresh fennel dipped in olive oil, heavily seasoned with salt and freshly ground pepper. (Today, it's good crudités with cocktails—don't fret over the olive oil; it's a reliable stomach liner.)

The *mala insane*, or the raging apple, was eggplant soaked in salt and cold water to remove its "insanity." We salted and drained it, not because we feared its poison, but because we wanted it less bitter. We bought smaller-sized eggplants, and we looked for those with lovely green, capelike bracts with stems firmly attached. If the bracts were loose, we knew it had started to spoil. Eggplant has to be firm, and we wanted seeds that were snow white.

The street vendors in Paddy's Market knew Grandma would not buy oranges unless they would allow her to dig into the orange rind with her thumbnail. If the skin was a bright orange color, that usually meant the orange was ripe and flavorful. It wasn't always that she would utter "Ha sapore" (It has flavor). We remember the vendor saying often, "Per favore, signora Beatrice, non toccate gli aranci (Please, Signora Beatrice, don't touch the oranges). When you buy oranges, pay attention to the skins. They should be unblemished," she would say.

We fought over who was to carry the tree home. The trip was only a half-dozen blocks away, but it was always later than we thought, and we were hungry, so we hurried and took turns carrying the tree. Mama's food, except for the last-minute pasta, was always on the table. On Christmas Eves, it never occurred to us that anyone else in the world, Italian or not, was not warm, enjoying home-cooked food, and anxious to dress the tree on Christmas Eve. "Depression days" was not one of our household expressions, and in retrospect, that may have been the best Christmas gift of all.

One year, leaving Papa home, the "golden girls" (Mama and two of her friends) took a four-month trip starting at Paris, France, to Alessandria in northern Italy to the very south of Italy so Mama could visit Accettura and see her relatives and how they had grown. Mama had in mind giving Grandpa's house and property to her niece Beatrice who has been living in it for years. This was the home of Mama's older sister who never came to the United States. When Grandma left to cross the Atlantic, she had her eldest daughter in Italy continue to live in that house. And Mama accomplished that with the help of two lawyers, one in the United States and the other in Italy.

After Mama's trip with her friends, they talked about what they ate, what they liked and didn't, where they ate, and how to make it. Elvira and Rose, who went to Italy with Mama, developed a special liking for the chicken *ferragosto*. (Ferragosto is the Feast of the Assumption and is celebrated on August 15, but this dish can be made any time of the year.)

Chicken with Tomatoes and Roasted Peppers

Pollo Ferragosto
Serves 6 to 8

To prepare the peppers:

1 pound sweet red peppers roasted, seeds removed, peeled and cut into 1-inch squares.

To roast peppers:

1. Preheat the broiler. Wipe the peppers clean with a dampened paper towel then place them on a rack in a broiler pan and broil, turning every so often, until the skins are charred on all sides, fifteen to twenty minutes. Place the charred peppers in a plastic or brown paper bag, close the bag, and let the peppers sit for ten minutes. Shake the bag. This will help loosen the skins.
2. When the peppers are cool enough to handle, peel off and discard the skins. Remove and discard the cores, ribs, and seeds, and cut

the peppers into squares. Roasting can be done a day or even a week ahead of time. Roasted peppers should be stored in the refrigerator in a plastic or other covered container. They may also be frozen without mixing with oil.

To prepare the chicken:

6 whole chicken breasts, boned, skinned, and halved to make 12 pieces
Juice of ½ lemon
3 tablespoons olive oil
1 tablespoon butter
2 large garlic cloves, halved
1 chili pepper, seeded and diced
1 large onion, chopped fine
4 cups fresh plum tomatoes, peeled and skinned
(or canned plum tomatoes)
Salt

1. Wash the chicken-breast halves in cool water. Trim off all fat with a poultry scissors or a sharp paring knife. Without drying the chicken pieces, put them into a bowl. Add lemon juice, stir chicken in it, and set aside ten minutes.
2. In a skillet, heat olive oil and butter and sauté garlic pieces until they are light brown. Discard garlic. Dry chicken-breast halves with paper towels or a tea towel and add as many as will fit into the skillet, leaving about one inch of space between pieces, and cook on both sides until they are light brown. Transfer them to a flameproof casserole.
3. Pour off oil from skillet, leaving just enough to coat bottom. Add chili pepper and onion and cook five minutes, stirring frequently. Add tomatoes and salt to taste and cook fifteen minutes. Pour the vegetable mixture over the chicken pieces in the casserole and cook slowly until the chicken is done, about fifteen minutes. Do not overcook the chicken.
4. Just before serving, add roasted pepper squares to the casserole. Serve as soon as the peppers are heated through.

Flank Steak Stuffed with Eggplant

Bistecca di fianco, farcito con melanzane
Serves 6

To make stuffing:

3 tablespoons butter
3 tablespoon olive oil
¾ pound eggplant, peeled and cut into ½-inch cubes
1 cup onion, chopped fine
1 garlic clove, chopped fine
½ cup celery, including leaves, sliced thin
½ teaspoon dried oregano
1 tablespoon fresh parsley, chopped fine (or 1 teaspoon dried)
1 teaspoon salt and freshly ground pepper
1 cup bread crumbs
2 eggs

1. In a large skillet, heat butter and oil and sauté eggplant cubes ten minutes. The eggplant will absorb the oil and butter; in fact, the skillet will be quite dry by the time you add the next ingredients. However, do not add more oil or butter. If you keep stirring the ingredients, you'll have no problem sautéing them for the required cooking time.
2. Add onion, garlic, celery, oregano, parsley, salt, and pepper, and cook five minutes. Remove skillet from the heat and transfer its contents to a large bowl. Add bread crumbs and mix in well. Beat eggs lightly and add. Mix well and set aside.

To prepare the flank steak:

2 ½ to 3 pounds flank steak
1 recipe eggplant stuffing above
3 tablespoons butter
3 tablespoons olive oil
2 carrots, sliced fine
1 large onion, chopped fine

1 cup fresh tomatoes, cored, blanched, peeled, and chopped fine (or 1 cup canned Italian plum tomatoes; use as much pulp without liquid as you can)
1 ½ cups dry red wine
¼ teaspoon dried oregano
Salt and freshly ground pepper
Few sprigs fresh parsley

1. Ask your butcher to trim excess fat from the flank steak and make a pocket. Lay flank steak on a flat surface and fill the pocket with eggplant stuffing. Secure pocket with a six-inch steel skewer or toothpicks, tie it with string, or sew up the opening.
2. Heat butter and oil in a large, covered casserole. Cook flank steak until it is browned all over. Add carrots, onions, and tomatoes, and cook ten minutes on low heat. Add wine, oregano, salt, pepper, and cover the casserole. Simmer for one and one-fourth to one and a half hours. When stuffed steak is done, put it on a warm serving platter.
3. You may use the sauce as it is, with carrot slices and so on. Or you may strain it or puree it and pour it over the steak. Add a touch of fresh parsley before serving. Cut the steak into wedges, just as you would slice a pie. The stuffing is puffed and attractive; it is somewhat firm and will adhere to the meat if you cut and serve it carefully. You can, of course, simply slice the steak, but it seems unfair for two of the servings (the two end cuts) to get far less stuffing.

Calf's Liver with Fennel and Bread Crumbs

Fegato di vitello con finocchi e pane grattugiato
Serves 6

Mama forced us to eat liver because it was rich in vitamins A, B, and C and had lots of iron. At the beginning, we would eat it if it was well done—only later did we learn to appreciate it served with a pinkish center.

1 to 1 ½ pound calf's liver, sliced ¼ inch
Juice of 1 lemon
⅓ cup flour
Salt and freshly ground pepper
1 to 1 ½ cups fresh bread crumbs
1 scant teaspoon anise or fennel seed
Egg preparation, see below
2 cloves garlic, each peeled and cut in half
½ stick butter
¼ cup olive oil
12 lemon wedges, seeds removed

Egg mixture:

Combine one egg with some salt and pepper. Add one teaspoon water and olive oil and whip until well combined.

1. Pour lemon juice over liver slices, turning each slice. Leave twenty minutes or so.
2. Salt and pepper each slice.
3. Combine bread crumbs and fennel or anise seeds and put in blender to chop fennel seeds. Do not overprocess. Add parsley and blend for several seconds.
4. Brush each slice with egg mixture and coat with crumbs
5. Heat oil and butter in a large skillet. When butter is dissolved, sauté the garlic until it turns golden and discard. Add liver slices, as many as you can fit into the skillet, and cook until golden. Repeat with remaining slices.
6. Plate the slices, add some of the olive oil and butter sauce, and add one or two lemon wedges. Serve hot.

23

HOLLY HOUSE

Hartley House, a settlement house now called a community center, was on our street—up the block near Ninth Avenue. It has been there since 1898—it started with one building, then another, and in a few years more, a third and a fourth building. These were gifts from Marcellus Hartley, a man who made money in munitions manufacturing. The four buildings are made of red brick with appointments and decorations of brownstone. At the beginning, they each had a stoop to the parlor floor, but all were removed except one, which became the main entrance. This was done to create an inside large meeting hall, two stories high with a balcony, that spread across the interior of the three remodeled buildings. A floor was added on top to provide a large gymnasium. At the rear of the four buildings is a large courtyard, a playground, if you will, with a "studio" building in the rear used for various activities. This building began as a manufacturing outlet for civil war uniforms, until it was converted when Mr. Hartley bought the buildings. The studio had a secret door that opened into the rear yard of Hawley Truax, one of the founders of the *New Yorker* magazine. When I was a youngster, I was led through this door into the amazing rear garden of the Truax home on Forty-Seventh Street to talk with Hawley and his lovely wife, Althea. I didn't say much, as I was under the spell of the secret garden gate. The Truax family were ardent board members who gave considerable financial support to the House. Their daughter-in-law Betty Truax Kramer and her daughter Alice Truax are currently on the board, and Hartley looks like a large private home on Forty-Sixth Street. There is nothing institutional in its appearance or the way it conducts its activities.

Papa could never pronounce Hartley House. He said "Holly House," but everyone knew what he meant. We spent hours trying to teach him to pronounce "heart-lee," but he never could. He didn't care about the pronunciation, for he knew we knew what he meant. I can't explain why Mama was able to pronounce it perfectly.

Cooking classes were held at Hartley for many years. In 1901, "Holly" House published a cookbook, *The Hartley House Cook Book* by Ella A. Pierce, published by Lentilhon and Company. The copy in my library is a fifth edition of the book. It includes macaroni Milanesi, lentil soup, stuffed flank steak, meat balls, and salt codfish chowder.

If a parent couldn't find a child, he or she would first search Hartley House, which was always full of activity, largely because of the Works Progress Administration, a federal government program that touched Hartley because it paid the salaries, however small, of an extended staff of writers, artists, and musicians there. They all helped mold our lives.

I fell in love with Ms. Poirier. She worked in the lower floor of the civil war uniform building where we made handicrafts. My first project was a papier-mâché mask, finished in silver paper with jet-black accents. Perhaps it looked like Fu Manchu, but to me and Ms. Poirier, it was a work of art. It hung on a wall in my room for a long time.

Ms. Poirier was a little woman with a definite French bearing. Her hair was blond and short and cut in a mannish style. She wore a blue smock and rarely changed it. It was marked all over with the colors of the rainbow, sort of like a modern painting. In addition to art instruction, she encouraged us to participate in peace parades and union meetings. In today's language, she would be considered extremely left wing. Left wing/right wing mattered little to us. We liked her, and I did especially; and even today, I try to figure out why I remember her as well as I do. She often appears in my dreams.

There was another art teacher I remember as well, perhaps better—Ms. Jerald, an English lady who was the opposite of Ms. Poirier.

Ms. Jerald was very feminine and taught us watercolor painting. We liked her because she would take six or seven of us by bus or train, sometimes by car, to the rural areas of northern New Jersey to paint watercolor outdoor scenes, many of which included old red barns, trees, and blue skies. Each of us carried an easel, and we shared large jars of watercolors. Their contents were put in little containers for us to dip our brushes into. I thought there was nothing more beautiful and satisfying than some of those summer days just a few miles away from the city, finding a place in the grass near an old barn and pretending we were famous French painters. Ms. Jerald, not as small a person as Ms. Poirier, usually wore a hat with a brim and a small feather on the side, the kind you might see in the English countryside. She was gentle and moved among us to hold a hand with brush, guiding it this way or that, or to give us a new sheet of paper to start afresh. Some of the paintings executed under her direction still hang in Holly House.

Mr. Rasch, gym teacher at PS 17 on Forty-Seventh Street, worked extra hours at Hartley as gym instructor in the afternoons and early evenings. His kingdom was the gymnasium, high above the four buildings. He was no-nonsense, tough, and demanding. We had basketball and softball teams, and he wanted us to win the intracommunity center basketball competitions. And we did. We, the Kings, were one of the best teams on the west side of New York City.

Hartley's executive director, Ms. Matthews, lived at the House over sixty years. She started to work there in the early 1900s. She was a Mt. Holyoke graduate and came from a fine Paterson, New Jersey family. She wore her hair high, in large braids kept together with a large pin, and devoted her life to social service. She was stately, conservative, soft spoken, and wore tiny eyeglasses. Her speech had a touch of Boston, and this alone set her apart from others in the House. She never wasted words. Her carriage was upright; some would call it finishing school demeanor. We all loved going to the House and usually were there before the doors opened at 3:00 p.m., except on the days Grandma baked bread. At times, some of us were a bit too anxious to get inside and would keep knocking on the outside door. One time, Ms.

Matthews opened the door, came out on the street, and grabbed Joey by the ear, asking, "Joseph, why do you think you have to spend every available minute of your time at Hartley?" This was not typical of her behavior, and she recognized it quickly, for she let Joey through after he said, "Ms. Matthews, I like it here a lot."

She was kind, gentle, and thoughtful, and she gave me summer jobs to help me get through graduate school. One summer, I was asked to work with three young boys who had become problems because they stole typewriters from PS 17 and had messed up in other ways. Ms. Matthews wanted me to take them to ball games, to the parks, museums, and generally hang out with them perhaps to show them a better side to life. Well, I did, and near the end of the summer, I met with her to discuss our progress. I reported that I felt I had wasted my time, that I had had no influence on these boys, and that their actions were as bad at the end of the summer as they were at the beginning. I told her to think of what I might have accomplished had I worked with three promising youngsters, lads who needed to find a way to get into college or solve job problems or whatever. Ms. Matthews listened to me. Yes, these "bad" kids needed attention, probably on a professional level beyond my capability, but should it be at the expense of some better youngsters who needed a boost? Instead of spending all my time with the troubled kids, why not spend time with those who showed some promise, e.g., college potential? I felt I learned more than anyone that summer, for it gave me a perspective I hadn't had before. From then on, I seemed to pay more attention to potential achievers than those who might have ended up in jails. The accent on the positive seems to suit me better. I think I was the one who learned about growing up that summer.

Gladys McPeek was assistant director, and I spent time with her, especially after Ms. Matthews passed away. With a degree in social work from Ann Arbor, Michigan, Gladys was a truly keen observer of people. She encouraged me in several pursuits: getting a graduate degree, writing my war memories, and spending time in Europe. She loved our home, our food. For years, Hartley sponsored Friday night dinners for its neighbors, and Italian dishes predominated.

Mama's Friday night food was popular, and because her kids were doing something at Hartley House on Friday nights, Mama found it easy and truly enjoyable to offer her time and food (the cost of which Gladys subsidized) to the group that came to these dinners. One favorite was Mama's Swiss chard and ricotta tart with an uncooked tomato sauce. Mama, the expediter, cooked the tarts at home, sometimes as many as six of them, after Gladys gave her a head count. We all helped carry them to Hartley for reheating in their kitchen. Mama was able to prepare the uncooked tomato sauce as early as a day before, and it gained flavor merely sitting around. She cooked this dish in the summertime because she was fascinated by the bushels of fresh tomatoes that one could buy at almost any vegetable stand in Paddy's Market. The tomatoes were so large, so utterly red and ripe, you could smell them before entering the market. Mama loved peeling them, cutting, and squeezing juice and seeds out of their insides, combining them with garlic and onions and fresh basil, and sprinkling them with oregano and rosemary. She was happy having a large bowl of these mixed ingredients standing to one side in her kitchen, often overnight, looking at them, breathing their exciting, God-given perfumed aromas, and carrying the sauce to Hartley House for others to enjoy.

Mama also cooked many of her other dishes for dinners at the community center. She made spaghetti with meatballs, and if the group wasn't too large, the sauce would be her Sunday's best, but the uncooked tomato sauce with the Swiss chard and ricotta tarts were easiest and most satisfying for her.

Gladys liked Mama and visited her often and left our home with spaghetti sauce spots on her clothing. One of her favorite dishes was veal cubes with saffron and wine, included here. We all were happy to have Gladys at our kitchen table.

At Hartley, we also worked with George Fleming, a Renaissance man, who was good looking, nattily dressed, and had an Ivy League style and an Irish sense of humor. He was a good writer, gave ideas to cartoonists at the *New Yorker*, a theater buff, a fan of Billie Holliday. I was seventeen or eighteen when he took a small group of us to the Onyx Club on West Fifty-Second Street to see Billie Holiday perform.

I don't know how we got in. With him, I saw my first Broadway show, *Amphitryon 38.* Thank you, Mr. Fleming! What I remember most of all is the play a group of us wrote, *Only the Cows Are Contented.* We wrote and acted in it under Mr. Fleming's guidance and entered it in a citywide drama contest. At the time, an economic issue in New York State had to do with the plight of the upstate dairy farmer, who, at the time, was getting only two or three cents for a quart of milk that sold for fifteen cents, the big difference going to the so-called middle man. Our play was to show the plight of the poor dairy farmers and what might be done to help them. It took our group about a year to develop this project, and Mr. Fleming was with us all the way. We performed it for Hartley House audiences several evenings and then mounted it at the Waverly Street Theater as part of the citywide competition, losing first prize to the performance by the blind group from the Lighthouse. The famous actress Maria Ouspenskaya was one of the judges.

I edited a weekly "magazine," six to ten mimeographed pages, called *PEACE* at Hartley House. It covered the problems of Japan's imperialism and the beginnings of Hitler. There was fire in some of our bellies to set the world right. I thought at that time that if I protested as I did, I would rid the world of wars, hate, and crime. Where did I go wrong?

Other activities were of a lighter nature. I remember lovely Jane Farwell, from northern Michigan, and her dirndl skirt, which flared like Marilyn Monroe's in *The Seven Year Itch.* Jane taught us to square dance and how to call it. A coincidence: my great-niece now lives in Farwell, Michigan, the small town named after Jane's family.

There was also Hartley Farm, a summer camp for inner city boys and girls. All of us went there for a minimum of two weeks each summer. Some, such as sister Bea, were luckier. She was there all summer, first as a junior counselor and then as a senior. Boys' camp was away from the girls' cottages. There was a main building known as the "White House" in which we had meals three times a day. We had good food—lots of vegetables from our own garden and nearby Jersey truck farms. There was delicious creamy butter to slather over fresh ears of corn, lots of tomatoes for spaghetti sauce with fresh basil, and fresh yummy strawberries and rhubarb for the cook, Mrs. Steiner's, pie. Before camp season started, selected families were sent to the White House for family vacations. What a nice idea. In the fall, older teenagers were allowed to go for weekends, usually without much supervision. When I was eighteen years old, I was at the Farm with Jean, a junior at one of the Ivy League women's colleges. I was alone with Jean, and the building we were in had no heat other than from a wood fire. It was a cold end-of-October weekend. The seduction began with lots more wood on the fire and the addition of a heavier blanket to the bed. Jean knew exactly what and how to have sex with a virtual virgin. I was willing and knew it was time for this to happen. When I think back, I remember the entire sexual encounter but also smile at the hot and cold side of the affair. It was not easy to keep the covers in place, and a bare ass could freeze within seconds.

Doing graduate work at Columbia University, I had a part-time job at Hartley House. One of my tasks was to supervise the Saturday morning children's art class held in the Studio Building. The kids were rough sometimes and threw paint at each other, but mostly they seemed dedicated and smeared watercolors on large sheets of white paper, which I then hung on the walls. One morning, I was told that Ludwig Bemelmans wanted to visit. At that moment, I did not make the name connection and thought it was just another neighborhood youngster who wanted to get into the class. In walked a distinguished-looking gentleman with his wife. He surveyed the paintings on the wall and asked if he could borrow some. He was willing to purchase them, but I said he could simply borrow them. During the next few months, he visited several times—picked up new paintings and returned the ones he had borrowed on previous visits. I realized who he was and was happy to share this work with him. Several years later, when Ed Murrow interviewed him on *Person-to-Person*, he was asked where the inspiration for his paintings came from. He said one source was the children's paintings at Hartley House. The staff were thrilled, but the kids took this nationwide recognition of their work in stride. They went on painting as they did before, pushing and sometimes throwing jars of water color paints as they had done all season.

One of my coworkers, a man with deep-set eyes and a kindly manner, Tony Smith, a few years older than I, had become friendly. He was married, and his wife Jane, making a name for herself in the opera world, had to travel to other cities to perform. Tony loved coming home for dinner with our family. He loved sitting at our kitchen table, enjoying Mama's food and Papa's descriptions of the clergy, Aunt Margaret, and her churchgoing passion, and any other subject Papa discussed. Tony loved the food. That alone made us happy to have him. One evening, after a triumph of vegetable lasagna, Tony saw the sealed opening under the front room's marble mantle. He asked if it was a working fireplace. It was, but Mama had closed it years ago for fear we would set fire to the flat. At Tony's suggestion, we asked Mama and Papa if he could check it out and perhaps make it workable again. The next day, Tony went to the roof after he opened the fireplace in the front room and ran a wire with a lightbulb at the end of it down the chimney. He said the flue looked okay. He removed the dated mantle and built a square brick mantle that one could call "modern." We planned and built some bookshelves on either side of the new brick installation, and Tony's idea was to paint everything white, brick fireplace and shelves.

Soon Jane was back in town, and he asked me to join them for cocktails in their Greenwich Village apartment. It was my first Bohemian scene, and I felt very suave. Of course, they served cocktails, and I had one. What I remember however were the pieces of fried Italian sausages, each piece on a toothpick, passed around for munching. They also served toasted pieces of bread with sautéed eggplant slices on them, sprinkled with grated Italian cheese and run under the broiler. It reminded me of our home, and I thought perhaps Tony was influenced by the food he had enjoyed with our family on many visits.

On that special evening, he walked me to the other apartment on his floor and introduced me to a young man who was bent over, skimming paint from a stick in a pail of paint onto a canvas that was smack on the floor—a large canvas, almost the size of the room. He was introduced as Jackson Pollock, but not once did he look up or utter a word—he was so intent on the task before him. At the time,

Tony was not known for his sculpture or artwork, but he now is world famous. The Museum of Modern Art did a retrospective of his work a couple of years ago. Jane was becoming famous sooner than he and she had opportunities to sing at European opera houses. Tony left the States for five or six years, perhaps longer, to be with her, and we lost touch. When he returned, his work began to be recognized.

That was the joy of being part of Hartley House—a place with outstretched arms, welcoming and helpful to anyone in need.

We know that without "Holly House," we would have missed out on a lot that has meant so much to each family member over the years. Holly House was one of the most important experiences in our lives.

Gladys McPeek loved veal cubes in saffron, tomato, and wine sauce. George Fleming wanted risotto primavera. What a beautiful dish. It is Italian rice cooked with vegetables: zucchini, green beans, carrots, snow peas, and mushrooms with some cream and freshly grated Parmesan cheese.

Tony Smith loved lasagna of fresh fennel with eggplant and zucchini. This is lasagna without pasta; instead, it uses slices of sautéed eggplant and zucchini. Also in the dish are onions, fresh fennel, Italian green peppers, and tomatoes, and the result is a delicious lasagna.

Swiss Chard and Ricotta Tart with Uncooked Fresh Tomato Sauce

Bietole e crostata di ricotta con salsa di pomodoro crudo
Serves 6 to 8

- 1 pound 6 ounces fresh Swiss chard or two 10-ounce packages frozen (to make 2 cups), leaves and stems squeezed dry and finely chopped
- 2 tablespoons vegetable or olive oil
- 2 tablespoons butter
- 1 cup finely chopped onion
- 1 garlic clove, finely chopped

4 large or 5 small eggs
1 cup whole or skim milk, ricotta
¼ cup finely chopped fresh parsley
1 cup freshly grated Parmesan or Pecorino cheese
½ cup light cream
Salt and freshly ground pepper
Pinch of freshly grated nutmeg
1 baked 8 x 11-inch tart shell, plus pastry for lattice strips
Uncooked fresh tomato sauce, see below

1. If using fresh Swiss chard, wash and cook in boiling salted water. Drain and squeeze dry. If using frozen, cook, drain, and squeeze dry.
2. In a skillet, heat oil and butter and cook onion slowly until it colors. Add cooked Swiss chard and garlic and cook several minutes to further dry out chard and to combine with onion. Transfer to a bowl and allow to cool.
3. Whisk eggs in large bowl. Add ricotta, parsley, three-fourths cup cheese, cream, salt, pepper, and nutmeg and mix well. Add cooled Swiss chard mixture and pour into baked shell. Bake in preheated 350°F oven for about forty minutes, or until set.
4. When tart has baked twenty minutes, remove from oven and arrange lattice pastry on top of tart. Distribute remaining Parmesan cheese on top. Return to oven to complete baking. Allow to rest for ten minutes or so before cutting.
5. If top of tart has not browned properly, run under broiler for a minute or two.
6. Serve with fresh tomato sauce, see below.

Fresh Tomato Sauce (uncooked)

Salsa di pomodoro crudo

3 large ripe tomatoes, peeled, seeded, and cut into ½-inch pieces
1 clove garlic, peeled and chopped fine

1 small onion peeled and chopped fine
8 large basil leaves, washed, dried, and chopped fine
(or 1 teaspoon dried basil)
1 tablespoon finely chopped fresh oregano, or ½ teaspoon dried
1 teaspoon finely chopped fresh rosemary, or ½ teaspoon dried
(chopped fine or rubbed between palms of hands)
1 ½ teaspoons salt and freshly ground black pepper
½ cup olive oil
Juice from 1 lemon, strained

Place tomatoes in a bowl. Add all other ingredients and mix well.

Note: This sauce can be prepared ahead of time and held at room temperature for as long as half a day. If made the day before, refrigerate the sauce but bring it to room temperature before adding to the tart.

Veal Cubes in Saffron, Tomato, and Wine Sauce

Cubetti di vitello in salsa di vino, pomodoro e zafferano
Serves 4

2 pounds boneless veal shoulder (or breast), cut into 1 ½-inch cubes
2 tablespoons all-purpose flour
1 teaspoon salt and freshly ground pepper
2 tablespoons olive or vegetable oil
2 tablespoons butter
1 herb packet: 2 celery stalk pieces, 3 inches long, tied with string to form a cylinder, filled with sprigs of parsley, thyme, and rosemary, and 1 bay leaf
1 cup shallots (or onions), chopped
1 large clove garlic, chopped fine
2 cups fresh tomatoes, cored, blanched, peeled, and chopped
(or canned plum tomatoes)
½ cup dry white wine (or ¼ cup dry vermouth and ¼ cup water)
1 cup beef broth
1 teaspoon saffron strands

1. Put veal cubes, flour, salt, and pepper to taste in an eleven-by-fourteen-inch plastic bag. Hold the bag closed with one hand, hold the bottom of the bag with the other, and shake it vigorously to coat the veal.
2. Heat oil and butter in a large skillet, add veal cubes in batches, and sauté until they are light brown. As pieces brown, remove them to a covered, ovenproof baking dish. Add herb packet to the casserole.
3. In the same skillet, combine shallots, garlic, and tomatoes, and cook ten minutes. Add tomato mixture to the veal.
4. Still using the same skillet, combine the wine, broth, and saffron. Mix these ingredients well over high heat and scrape the sides of the skillet clean. Pour this liquid over the contents of the casserole, cover, and bake in a preheated 350°F oven one and a half hours. Remove and discard herb packet.

Rice with Vegetables

Risotto Primavera

Serves 6

2 ½ quarts chicken or vegetable broth
8 ounces small zucchini (1 x 5 inches)
8 ounces green beans
8 ounces carrots
8 ounces snow peas
6 medium mushrooms
12 tablespoons (1 ½ sticks) butter
3 cups Arborio rice
½ cup whipping cream
1 cup freshly grated Parmesan cheese
¼ cup finely chopped flat-leaf parsley
Salt and freshly ground pepper

1. Bring broth to boil in a large saucepan. Lower heat and keep at lowest possible simmer.

2. Trim ends from zucchini, green beans, carrots, and snow peas. Wash and dry vegetables. Slice zucchini and carrots diagonally into one-half-inch pieces. Slice green beans and snow peas diagonally into one-inch pieces. Clean and slice the mushrooms.
3. Melt eight tablespoons (one stick) butter in another saucepan and sauté zucchini, carrots, and green beans four minutes, tossing frequently. Add snow peas and mushrooms and sauté one minute. Add rice and cook two minutes, stirring to coat all the rice with butter.
4. Add one cup hot broth to the rice and vegetable mixture. Cook and stir gently for several minutes until the liquid is absorbed. Repeat with five more cups of stock, one cup at a time, stirring gently all the while until each cup of liquid is absorbed. When all the stock has been absorbed, add the remaining four tablespoons butter, cut into pieces, and the cream. Remove from heat and add two-thirds of the Parmesan and parsley. Season with pepper and toss lightly. Add salt if needed. Sprinkle remaining Parmesan and parsley on top and serve.

Lasagna of Fresh Fennel with Eggplant and Zucchini

Lasagna di finocchi, melanzane e zucchine

2 small eggplants
Salt
4 small zucchini
¼ to ⅓ cup olive oil
2 medium onions, thinly sliced
3 garlic cloves, finely chopped
4 green frying peppers, cored, seeded, and cut into thin strips
1 large fennel bulb with leaves, thinly sliced
2 cups cored, blanched, peeled, and seeded fresh tomatoes cut into ½-inch cubes, or canned plum tomatoes put through a food mill
2 tablespoons chopped fresh dill, or 1 teaspoon dried dill weed
Leaves from 6 fresh parsley sprigs, finely chopped
Salt and freshly ground pepper

1. Wash and dry eggplants. Discard ends. Do not peel. Cut into thin slices, salt lightly, and place in a colander. Wash and dry zucchini. Discard the ends. Cut into thin slices, salt lightly, and add to the eggplant slices. Allow vegetables to drain about thirty minutes.
2. Dry vegetable slices with a paper towel. Heat a small amount of the oil in a large skillet and sauté eggplant slices in small batches; don't worry if they are lightly scorched. Transfer to paper toweling to drain. Add zucchini slices and sauté, adding a little more oil as necessary during (don't overdo). Set zucchini on paper toweling to drain. Add a little more oil to same skillet and sauté onions and garlic about five minutes; do not let garlic burn. Add peppers, fennel, tomatoes, dill, and parsley. Cook two minutes and remove from heat.
3. Arrange a layer of eggplant slices and then a layer of zucchini slices in a covered 2 two-and-a-half-quart casserole. Spoon some of the tomato mixture over the slices. Add salt and pepper. Repeat the layers of eggplant and zucchini. Top with remaining tomato mixture. Season with salt and pepper. Cover and bake in preheated 350°F oven about one hour.

24

THE FIRST TRIP TO ITALY: CHOCOLATE, COFFEE, CIGARETTES, AND OVERRIPE APPLES

During my teens, I dreamed in English, French, and Italian. Getting to Europe, Italy especially, was a declared goal. At that time in my life, in fact since high school, I was a Francophile—thanks to my high-school French teacher. Because of World War II, this goal was put on hold, but the year after the war was over, a friend I met at Columbia University decided to join me on a trip that would last almost a year. We headed for Genoa, Italy, on a converted troop ship—the fare was about one hundred dollars, and to earn money for this extended trip, we had worked the summer before as "bar boys" at an exclusive Jewish resort on the water in Long Beach, Long Island. As the clientele of this posh place dripped in minks in July and August, we served them drinks at lunch, dinner, and worked the cabaret on Wednesday, Friday, and Saturday nights. We were tipped handsomely, as word got around that we were college kids. In fact, the cabaret manager allowed the two of us to organize a barbershop quartet with two other college students. Wearing bowlers, mustaches, and vests, we performed on a couple of Saturday cabaret nights along with Joey Adams, Milton Berle, and other stars on the circuit. I kept a "black book" of monies earned that summer, as did my friend, Bernie Kinzer. We each made over four thousand dollars, a lot of money for that time—almost enough for us to survive nine months in the war-torn areas we were to visit. Sister Mary, ever generous, sent me five dollars a week, and that helped too. We learned to hitchhike and lunch or sup on bread, cheese, and wine. At times, we added grapes or figs or whatever was cheap and easy to get. For seeing everything we had dreamed of, the sacrifice seemed minimal.

We didn't pack a lot of clothes; instead, we loaded a steamer trunk with chocolates, cigarettes, and coffee, the things relatives in Italy begged Mama and Papa to send them after the war. Bernie and I referred to this cache as "the three Cs."

We decided our home base would be in Geneva, Switzerland—a country untouched by the war and therefore physically intact. We rented a room in an apartment owned by a Finnish/French widow, Madame de Pilverman, later known by us as Madame de Pilule (pill). She looked like the female equivalent of Charles Laughton. She was so dedicated to languages, she arranged for us to be tutored in Italian and French at little cost. We may have called her "pilule," but she actually was quite the opposite. Our plan was to spend December in Italy, Easter in France, and late spring in England—each visit to last about a month. In between, we planned other trips back into these countries, but the trips were of shorter duration. Christmas Eve had to be spent at St. Peter's in Rome.

The beginning of my love affair with Rome was taking place, an affair that has lasted over fifty years, and the passion continues. The city is like a movie star past her prime—still alluring because she exudes all the confidence and personality of someone who knows she has nothing left to prove. Neither age nor years of decadent excess can wither her.

On that first trip to Rome, we found an inexpensive pensione, damp because of its old stone walls but well located near the Vatican. We did everything in Rome one is supposed to do. A tragic happening almost took place Christmas Eve in our pensione room as we were waiting for a friend to take us to Mass. It was chilly, really cold, and we complained to the concierge. A chambermaid brought up a pot of charcoal and set it in front of me. I was sitting at a table drinking coffee to keep warm. The next thing I remember was being slapped on both cheeks by a doctor summoned by the rooming house as he revived me. I had inhaled fumes from the charcoal pot still giving off poisonous gases. The chambermaid was in a hurry to get to her own Christmas Eve Mass and hadn't waited for the coals to burn down before bringing them to our room—an absolute cardinal sin. The doctor said how lucky I was to be alive.

All roads lead to Rome, and one of the first we experienced was the famous Via dei Fori Imperiale, one of the most impressive walks in the ancient city. As we walked straight down the middle of this legendary street in a direct line from the Piazza Veneziana, where Mussolini once gave speeches from his residence there, to the Coliseum, our eyes opened to Rome's grandeur and history. We learned quickly that Romans are robust eaters and hearty drinkers. Romans breathe deep and approach life with gusto. Everyone seems to have the flair of an Anna Magnani, and the *appetito* of Uncle Patsy.

Food was limited after the war, as was train service, but we made it to Florence to ring in the New Year. Art and architecture, rolling countryside, soft pastures, olive trees and cypresses, bread and oil, beans and *bistecca*, the winding Arno and its bridges with palaces looking onto its banks, and the seat of masterpieces of every kind all make this city one of the most beautiful in the world—a joy to visit.

At the suggestion of a friend living in Florence, we got a room at the Villa Constantin, which must have been a beautiful private mansion at one time. We never found out why the *E* or *O* was left off the name but felt lucky to have a room there with delicious breakfasts and dinners for a small price. There was a vast marble foyer with a curved, graceful marble staircase, and everything was beautifully appointed. We had a large bedroom—its best feature was the bathroom with a full tub and frescoed walls and ceiling. When sitting in the tub, you met the eyes of a cherub, clad in swaths of soft-colored silks hiding his or her private parts, and blowing a horn. All cherubs, or *putti* as they are called, were painted with curly locks; and unless private parts were exposed, their gender was anyone's guess. The delicious, modest suppers were offered in the marble foyer—eight or ten small round tables set with lovely damask linen, fine china, silverware, and sparkling glasses, remarkable for any Italian home after the war! It is now rare to find a pensione of this quality anywhere in Italy. During our first dinner there, we were distracted by the reflections from a large diamond ring worn by an older white-haired lady, obviously American. We thought, imagine the gall of showing off such riches immediately after the war in Europe. After two meals or so, we discovered she was from Cleveland, Ohio, a widow, with an Italian lover who had been killed during the war. She had returned to place a headstone on his grave. Because she was American, and we were touched by the reason for her sentimental journey to Italy, we became friends with Molly Rouse—although at times, we thought she was a model for a Helen Hokinson *New Yorker* character, when during a conversation, she remarked, "Oh, those Russians, what do they know about war?" We loved being part of the villa with one exception: the owner's ten-year-old son played his violin in the most discordant way.

The Constantin offered us breakfast and supper. Sometimes we skipped lunch, and when we didn't, we frequented some small *trattoria* still struggling to get a semblance of an Italian meal on the table. There didn't seem to be a shortage of pizza or calzone—a food of folded pizzalike dough filled with almost anything—but meats were missing, as was anything exotic to serve as toppings or fillings, such as Parma ham, the more expensive cheeses, or sausages. At the villa, they served spaghetti with a nonmeat Italian sauce sprinkled with measured amounts of grated cheese. We didn't expect Parmigiano-Reggiano, and we didn't get it. It seemed to us that every other night was pasta e fagioli (beans), and that was quite tasty. It's difficult to ruin this dish in Italy, even if all you are using for flavor is the tiniest piece of a prosciutto end or a small piece of sausage. There were one or two Florentine dishes we liked: eggs over spinach and beef liver. The first was made by cooking spinach with butter, salt, and pepper and spreading it over thick pieces of toasted Italian bread; then an egg was poached and put over the spinach with a touch of tubed anchovy paste and a sprinkle of cheese. This was baked for about ten minutes.

In the second dish, slices of beef liver were dredged in flour and fried with olive oil, minced garlic, and five or six sage leaves. Salt and pepper were added, and the liver was removed after five minutes of cooking and set aside. A post–war-torn type sauce was made then by adding a little oil to the skillet in which the liver was fried plus two tablespoons each tomato paste and water and stirring in the skillet over heat until well blended and heated. The sauce, of course, was poured over the liver. For dessert, there was almost always a "cake" made with chestnut flour, salt, olive oil, water, raisins, pine nuts, and chopped rosemary and cooked in a pie plate. Another one was called *stiacciata* pie—a yeast dough to which eggs, salt, sugar, and orange zest were added after its first rising. When all ingredients are in the dough, it is worked again with a good bit of lard. It has to rise again after being spread on a cookie sheet. After it has risen, it is baked, cooled, and sprinkled with confectioners' sugar, before slices of it are served.

In one week, we saw the highlights—you know what they are. Years later, I decided to go back to the Constantin. No one was at the front desk, so I took the liberty of entering. I was appalled to see an elevator had been installed by cutting through the marble stair, and to make it worse, the elevator was plastered with contact paper. I took the horrible elevator and went to my old room. I had no difficulty whatever finding it, and it was just as I had left it, with my little cherub still there on the bathroom ceiling. As I left the villa, I ran into a man who acted like the owner. I apologized for my indiscretion of entering unannounced. After a brief conversation, I discovered he was the son of the owner, the little boy with the cacophonic violin. The pieces fell into place, and I understood why he would cut through that gorgeous stairwell. I turned around to leave and thought, "How could he possibly be Italian?"

The challenge of Florence on that first visit was how to get to Naples and then further eastward to Potenza, a town near Mama's and Papa's hometowns. Getting from the north of Italy to Rome by train was easy by comparison. Arrangements were made for us to leave this Florentine villa by horse and carriage at 4:00 a.m. to catch the only train going south. Everyone was complaining about the lack of train service. Although Florence had more than one track operating, Naples had only one. The morning ride was as bitter cold as it will ever get for me. We were wrapped in a horse blanket, and our puffs of breath turned into virtual cotton candy—tiny clouds, frozen midair. Of course, we made it. The three Cs had been transferred to four large suitcases, and each of us was carrying two. The weight of the suitcases was formidable. The little bit of clothing we were carrying was tightly packed in knapsacks over our shoulders.

Getting from Rome to Naples was like traveling with Barnum & Bailey Circus. The trains were filled with Italians, many of them peasants carrying livestock. Chickens were everywhere on that train. Yet during our time in Italy, we were told again and again about the shortage of poultry. Naples was like the Black Hole of Calcutta. It had been bombed and people were living in put-together stone caves along the track beds. They held out their hands, begging for food, money, or both, and you could touch them. We parted with some of our candy bars and some cigarette packs, which not only helped the needy but also lightened our load. It was difficult for me to go through this area, bombed by Americans, though I knew it had been to free the country.

In Naples, some serious problems set in. Trains were not running to Potenza. Our only solution was to find someone who would drive us by car. We were given some leads, but none worked out. Finally, one cagey and shrewd Neapolitan recognized an opportunity—"Americani con molti baggali" (Americans with lots of baggage). To make a long story short, we agreed to pay him one hundred dollars and give him lots of chocolate, cigarettes, and coffee. He was more interested in getting the three Cs than the money. The big tips at Long Beach and how easily we had earned them softened the blow; a matter of easy come, easy go. We thought we would never get there. Winters, even in Southern Italy, can be weird. We had to make detour after detour, not all caused by war damage. At times, we wondered if the driver had ever made this trip before—he kept asking for directions every few miles and always the answer was the same: "Diretto, diretto," meaning "straight ahead." How could he go straight ahead when he came to a fork in the road? This old car puttered and creaked, squealed and choked. The cold air made us hungry. We stopped at snack bars for simple calzone and cheap wine that kept our juices flowing. The trip took all day, and by early evening, when we did find a trattoria open, we decided a rest from the road (and the driver) was needed. We made the mistake of including him in the meal—it seemed the only decent thing to do. The first food we saw was a big bowl of Neapolitan salad, the one with pieces of cauliflower and some others vegetables (whatever one has on hand) with oil and vinegar dressing, and it was very similar to the salads I used to enjoy in Staten Island at Marie and Rocky's sweet home in the summer ten years earlier.

The cook and owner came over to us and apologized for the lack of menu, which was never presented. We went along with the omelet he proposed and were quite happy with it. He asked us to watch him do it, as there was no one else in the place.

He used leftover spaghetti and sauce, about three cups of it, and added four beaten eggs, salt, pepper, parsley, and some grated cheese and mixed it well. He gave us glasses of wine and refilled them with haste when he saw empties in our hands. He put a bit of oil in a skillet and cooked the omelet fifteen minutes or so on each side. He gave us good bread, and we ate it, the omelet, and the salad, and more wine.

And believe it or not, the food tasted better. We saw a plateful of something that looked like zeppole, but we passed on that, as it looked soggy and stale. This meal was very inexpensive.

We were half frozen when we got to Potenza. Once there, we started the bargaining all over again with another driver. More money, more giving away of the three Cs. Almost half our loot was gone and a good bit of our money.

We were trying to get to Ruoti, a suburb of Potenza, the town where Papa spent eight or nine years of his youth. It was a town he chose to forget because of the priests. He never wanted to return to Italy and, in fact, never did. We were impressed by the village as we entered it. All the streets were paved with cobblestones, and the long, long row of small shops looked picturesque and familiar, for they bore names known to me: there were Scavone's Shoe Repair Shop and Bochichio's Butcher Shop. Every storefront bore the names of people belonging to my father's Italian Society. We found a coffee shop in the center of town, and I looked through the phone book and found half a dozen entries with my name, spelled exactly as I do mine. I telephoned each, and they all kindly asked us into their homes. The homemade cordial or wine was tasty, as were the salami and calzoni, but we could never make a family connection. There was one house and family I was sure were relatives. When I entered the downstairs courtyard, there were five or six ladies putting raffia seats on antique chairs—they worked so gracefully, slowly, and surely, and one lady in particular reminded me of the Zias in New York, both my father's aunt and the Zia in the next building who used to cure my ills with olive oil, a prayer, and some cash. But no luck. Since the driver was in a hurry to get back to Potenza, we left in several hours. I was hoping to find a distant relative, but that was not going to happen until years later in New York, when we were trying to establish my father's date of birth.

We had to spend the night in Potenza; we were dragged out and couldn't go another step. Bernie blamed the wine, and he was correct of course. The next morning, again a new driver with an old beat-up machine—again, too much money and more of the Cs, but we couldn't back out of this now. We had to get to Grassano, where I was to meet Nick, an old family friend who had worked in the States for about twenty-five years and returned immediately after the war to his hometown in Italy: Accettura, Mama's hometown. In addition to the bad roads, delays were encountered along the way by people traveling on donkeys known as the *mulattiera*. They too were going long distances. This was a long, difficult trip. Our main diet was cheap wine and calzoni. This journey, from the north to the south of Italy, came too soon after the war.

Back in the States, we'd have calzoni parties, serving better wine and calzoni with imaginative fillings. "Calzoni" in Italian means "trouser leg," an apt description for this piece of dough that is filled with all sorts of things. The dough is made with yeast, like most pizza, then is shaped into a circle and folded over the filling to make a "turnover." If the dough is kept in tubular form, it becomes a calzone. They are really the same thing, but when it comes to food, the Italians can be quite exacting.

Here are some of our favorite calzoni recipes. Perduto, certamento!

Vegetable and Sausage Turnover (Calzoni)

Calzoni di verdure e salsiccia

Serves 6 to 8

To prepare dough:

1 envelope dry yeast or 1 cake fresh yeast
¼ cup warm water
3 ¼ cup all-purpose flour
1 teaspoon salt
1 teaspoon sugar
1 egg
1 tablespoon vegetable oil
⅔ to ¾ cup warm water
Olive oil

1. To make dough, dissolve yeast in one-fourth cup warm water and set aside for ten minutes.
2. Place two cups flour in a large bowl. Make a well in the center and add salt, sugar, egg, and yeast mixture. Add oil and warm water a little at a time, stirring with a wooden spoon until dough leaves the sides of the bowl. Turn the dough onto a lightly floured surface and knead, adding flour as necessary for fifteen minutes or until smooth and elastic. Transfer to a large buttered bowl and turn to coat all sides. Cover and let dough rise away from drafts, until doubled in bulk, about one to one and a half hours.
3. When the dough has risen, punch it down and let it rise again until doubled in bulk, about one hour. Turn onto a lightly floured surface and cut in half for two large turnovers. Cover and let rest fifteen minutes before filling.

2 sweet Italian sausages
2 tablespoons oil
1 large carrot, coarsely chopped
1 cup coarsely chopped leeks
1 cup ricotta

¼ cup finely chopped fresh parsley
¼ cup freshly grated Parmesan cheese
Salt and freshly ground pepper

1 recipe calzone dough
Egg wash made of 1 egg beaten with 1 tablespoon water

1. Remove casing from the sausage. In a large saucepan, heat one tablespoon oil over medium-high heat and brown the meat. Transfer sausage to a medium bowl.
2. Pour off all but one tablespoon fat from saucepan and add one tablespoon oil. Cook carrot over moderate heat three minutes, stirring constantly. Add leeks and cook an additional two minutes. Add vegetable mixture to sausage along with the ricotta, parsley, Parmesan, and salt and pepper to taste. Mix well.
3. Preheat oven to 475°F. Shape each portion of dough into a ball; press down to flatten slightly. Roll out one portion of dough into eleven-inch circle. Brush with olive oil. Spread half of the vegetarian mixture over half of the circle, leaving three-fourth-inch margin at edge. Lift up the unfilled half and fold it over the filling; press edges together to seal and flute with fork. Lift the calzone carefully with a wide spatula and place on a cornmeal-sprinkled baking sheet. Repeat with other half of dough. Prick tops with a fork and brush entire top and edges of each calzone with egg wash. Bake twenty to twenty-five minutes, or until nicely browned. Let the calzone sit for ten minutes before serving.

Variation number 1

Leeks, Peppers, Mushrooms, and Herbs in Calzoni

Calzoni con porri, peperoni e funghi
Serves 6 to 8

2 slices bacon
1 tablespoon olive oil

3 medium leeks, washed, dried, and coarsely chopped
1 medium-size red bell pepper, cored, seeded, and coarsely chopped
1 medium-size green bell pepper, cored, seeded, and coarsely chopped
8 ounces mushrooms, thinly sliced
1 large tomato, cored, blanched, peeled, seeded, and cut into ½-inch cubes
1 garlic clove, minced
½ teaspoon fennel seed
8 large pitted black olives, sliced
2 tablespoons finely chopped fresh basil, or 1 teaspoon dried
Salt and freshly ground pepper
2 cups shredded Fontina cheese

1. To make filling, cook bacon slices in a large saucepan until crisp. Remove and drain on paper towels, then crumble.
2. Add one tablespoon olive oil to the bacon grease. Add the leeks and red and green peppers and sauté over medium-high heat for two minutes. Add the mushrooms and sauté for two minutes. Add the tomato, garlic, fennel seed, olives, and crumbled bacon and sauté for one minute. Let the mixture cool for five minutes then add the shredded cheese. Season with salt and pepper and mix well. Set aside and use to fill calzoni.

Variation number 2

Green Onion and Swiss Chard Calzoni

Calzoni con cipolle verde e bietole
Serves 6 to 8

1 pound fresh Swiss chard, leaves separated and rinsed in cold water
3 tablespoons olive oil
8 green onions (including tender green parts), coarsely chopped
3 garlic cloves, minced
Salt and freshly ground pepper
⅓ cup freshly grated Parmesan cheese

¼ teaspoon red pepper flakes
Egg wash made of 1 egg and 1 tablespoon water
1 tablespoon sugar
6 to 8 pats butter (1 stick), optional

1. Peel Swiss chard stems with a vegetable peeler and cut into two-inch lengths. In a large saucepan, cook the leaves and stems in boiling salted water for ten minutes; drain. When cool enough to handle, squeeze all the moisture from the chard. Set aside.
2. In a large saucepan, heat olive oil over medium-high heat. Add the green onions and sauté two minutes; add garlic and sauté one minute. Remove from heat and add Swiss chard, salt, pepper, Parmesan, and red pepper; toss well. Taste and adjust seasoning; set aside and use to fill calzoni.

25

ACCETTURA: TO SEE IT IS TO BELIEVE IT

The province of Basilicata, called Lucania by the Greeks, is the setting of Carlo Levi's book, *Christ Stopped at Eboli.* The area also was described years earlier by Norman Douglas when he wrote *Old Calabria*, by George Gissing, in *By the Ionian Sea,* and more recently by David Yeadon in 2004 in his brilliant *Seasons in Basilicata.* While these books capture conditions in *Basilicata*, the famous Italian writer, Italo Calvino, summarized it best for me.

> And there was Gagliano, perched on a sort of jagged saddle rising among ravines. It wound its way like a worm on either side of a single street sloped abruptly down the narrow ridge between two ravines . . . steep slopes of white clay with houses hanging from them . . . the peasants' houses were all alike consisting of only one room . . . At night the empty blackness of the sky hung over the darkened village. Eventually, I came to understand the hidden virtues of this bare land and to love it.

Basilicata sits atop the arch or instep of Italy's boot, a mountainous region with a relatively short coastline. It includes a broad part of the southern Apennines, and numerous streams and rivers flow through the province on their way to the Ionian Sea.

We had previously arranged that Nick, who had lived in America for twenty years before returning to Italy, would be our guide. He and Mama, both from Accettura, had become friends in the United States. He met us about twenty miles from town to guide us to its center, the place of Mama's birth. When we spotted him drive up in a bright, new, red American-made pickup truck, we felt we had found a long-lost friend with a new car. The truck clearly was new, but Nick told us its first task had been to carry a load of manure to Grassano from Accettura. We sat in the front seat with Nick, our baggage in the rear protected from the truck's bed by some rags.

To reach Accettura, we drove through more *tonanti* (U-turns) than I cared to count—one was more than enough—and viewed eroded canyons and buttes reminiscent of certain long, desolate stretches of New Mexico. We traveled through the light-streaked oak forest of Bosco Montepiano, which, despite the recent war, seemed to have been well cared for. (We later learned that one of Mussolini's projects had been to ready the forest to be a site for a national park.) Along the way, it was easy to determine which pieces of land were olive groves and fruit orchards; they were always on the edge of a cliff. How did the farmers ever get to them? And then we spotted Accettura, sitting on top of a steep slope of white clay, its houses following crooked, narrow paths with some appearing ready to fall off the edge of the cliff described so precisely by Mr. Calvino. Typical of Italian villages, in the center of town stood the large church with its roof glistening in the brilliant noonday sun.

Before we plunged into the carefully orchestrated meeting with never-seen cousins and paisani, Nick drove us to his own old, old house. The main room had a dirt floor and an open fire with an iron grill nestled in the rear for cooking. A suckling pig was tied to a bedpost in the same room.

Two of Nick's daughters, who had remained in Italy while he was in the States, prepared fried eggs with prosciutto. As they cooked, they moved carefully around the hearth with its open flame. They served a side dish of macaroni cooked with garlic, olive oil, salt, and black pepper, also cooked over the wood fire, and offered us homemade red wine to wash down the meal. We ate little, as we knew that eggs and other foods were difficult to get in postwar Italy.

After this light yet fortifying meal, it was time to meet my family. In some ways, it was only natural that after many years of reading her letters, fulfilling her many requests for clothing, chocolates, and cash, I was to meet Mama's blood niece, Beatrice. I felt intoxicated with the anticipation of meeting a woman about whom I had heard so much.

Beatrice was the daughter of Mama's older sister who had remained in Italy. By this time, Beatrice had had seven children; the youngest, named after my mother, was six years old. Her first husband had fathered five of her children before he passed on. She then had two more children with a tall, good-looking man named Gianni, who wore well-tailored Italian clothes and shiny caramel-colored leather boots, and whom she never married.

Nick walked with us to my grandmother's home, where my mother and her sisters had been born. This was where my grandmother had waited for eight long years before joining her husband in New York City. Beatrice, Gianni, and their family had lived there for many years after Grandma left, and the house looked basically as Mama had described it, with one major change: there was now a private toilet in the kitchen in place of an outhouse.

Grandma's bedroom was on the main floor of the ancient stone house, with a large bed covered with the whitest linen I had ever seen. A small canopy of the same material shielded the head of the bed, a bed so high you had to climb two small, crude-looking steps to reach it. There were several statues of saints on the sill of the single window, which commanded a sweeping view of the countryside. When I entered the room, the sunlight came through the window, lighting the statues with a shimmering beam that seemed to come from the heavens. When I looked at the bed, all I could think of was Mama's comment, "The bed was as white as a pillow case."

Also on the ground floor was another room with a fireplace for heating, cooking, and gathering. There were more bedrooms upstairs in which lived two of Beatrice's married children as well as a few unmarried ones. I discovered early on that it was a waste of time to figure out who slept where. I was given Grandma's room for the duration of my short visit.

It was cold outside when we arrived, and we were shown the shed across the road. It was called the cantina and was filled with salamis, capocollo, and prosciutto, as well as scores of jars of tomatoes, tomato paste, vinegar peppers, mushrooms, and eggplant. The homemade wine was stored there too. I was reminded of the well-stocked cellar on West Forty-Sixth Street when I was a boy.

Bernie's and my first view of Beatrice was dramatic. She framed herself in a doorway, and even after seven children, she showed off a ballerina figure. Her body was wrapped in a full black skirt that nearly reached the floor and was topped by a black blouse. Her tiny waist rivaled that of Scarlett O'Hara, and jet-black hair, pulled back on each side of her face and tied in a chignon, framed high cheekbones and almond-shaped black eyes. She pointed out something special about her clothing: on her shoulders was a knitted shawl that Mama had sent from America. She was a stunning woman who was not yet forty years old—an Italian beauty who reminded me of Mama. Every bodily movement was measured, and every word she spoke was short, clearly stated, and convincing. You knew instantly she was a prominent figure in the small town of Accettura.

Beatrice had one remaining sibling, a sister with the beautiful name of Annunziata. The two had not spoken for years, probably because Beatrice was living in Grandma's house. I was not supposed to visit Annunziata, but because Nick understood that I could not return home without news of her, the two of us slipped around corners and ducked into the shade of nearby houses one day when Beatrice went to market and made our way to Annunziata's house. When I was face-to-face with Mama's other niece, who looked remarkably like her sister, I quickly realized they were in fact polar opposites. It did not take long to recall Aunt Rose, one of my mother's older sisters who lived near us in New York. Sadly, Rose had let life slip past her, breathing heavily with exaggerated pain as a way of putting off any show of friendliness. We knew her as "No-Touch Aunt Rose."

Beatrice had strong feelings about one of my grandmother's nieces too and did not want me to visit her. Again, Nick came to our assistance, and I was very happy he did. As it turned out, spending a little time with Maria Martello (Grandma's maiden name) was especially memorable. I felt as though I was actually with my grandmother—down to her preference for freshly baked bread slathered with butter and eaten with hot milk spiked with a little coffee.

When Beatrice, our hostess, found out about our secret visits, she nearly spoiled the overall stay, but I was determined to ignore her incessant criticisms in the hopes she would accept my state of neutrality. Finally, she realized she was getting nowhere with me, and because we both wanted to cement an alliance that was to last a lifetime, she wisely acquiesced. After all, more clothing, more chocolates, and more cash from America were hanging in balance before her dark eyes. Italy was suffering in the years following the war, and Beatrice was not about to jeopardize the well-being of her family.

Upon our arrival, Beatrice beamed at the treasures I extracted from our large suitcases, and she immediately took charge of the gifts. (I had known beforehand that Annunziata would get nothing, so I had saved some goodies in a small bag, which I was able to give her when I visited with Nick.)

During the two days I spent in Accettura, I was rarely far from Beatrice's side. I saw one familiar face after another, although I was meeting new cousins. Every paisano I had seen at family feasts on Long Island, who had visited our family from Connecticut or New Jersey or who played cards with Papa, seemed to have a doppelganger in this small, hillside village. The friendly faces I encountered there reminded me of a parent, aunt, uncle, cousin, brother, or sister back home. The faces I didn't immediately recognize could have been related to people I had met at Italian feasts and religious parades in New York. No one looked like a stranger.

In those days, everyone went to church daily, an old habit that took on new life during the war and that had not yet faded with modern times. As Beatrice and I and our constant entourage of various family members traveled through the village after church, we made frequent stops for espresso on our way to visit the *cugini* and paisani chosen by Beatrice. Bernie and I were young and very American, and we were embraced everywhere we went. Some people were just happy to touch us, and we heard frequent chants of "Gli Americani!" (The Americans!) Many of the townspeople waved American flags, and in the distance, we heard refrains of our national anthem.

Beatrice planned a big, celebratory dinner during our brief visit. She rented a hall, probably used for local community meetings, and arranged tables, draped with pure white cloths, in a horseshoe. The main part of the meal was served after antipasti of sliced salami, capocollo, hot and sweet vinegar peppers, and large loaves of Italian bread. It was clear Beatrice and her daughters had been cooking for days, and the meal included familiar family dishes, including one of Mama's famous soups.

The soup is a family holiday soup in the United States and Italy, made for New Year's Day, Easter Sunday, Christmas Day, birthdays, and all other important and festive occasions. Some family members didn't add pasta, but others did because this course was followed by a separate course of homemade pasta or ravioli. The soup was special because we knew Mama, Grandma, and that part of her family that remained in Italy had been making it for years. The beef meatballs cooking in the homemade chicken broth created wonderful aromas. Beatrice was cunning to bridge the United States of America and Italy in serving this common denominator concoction.

She had learned both these dishes from her mother who was taught by our mutual grandma. The pasta she served surprised me greatly, because it was not a typical Accetturese preparation, except for the handmade pasta, cut as tagliatelle. It was the sauce that goosed my curiosity. She didn't include meat in it, and she lavished it with butter and only onions and carrots for flavor. It was shocking not to use garlic and tomato paste and no olive oil. The more we thought about it, we concluded she was showing off, and that that was perfectly okay.

Most of us in the family liked that quality about her, as it indicated an independent spirit of "I wanna be me" (and the hell with tradition for everything I cook and everything they taught me—surely I can depart with at least one different pasta dish). I asked her about this dish later, and she said Gianni had met a lot of soldiers during the war, many of them from the North, and they passed on this idea to him. They had decided it would be a different thing for all of us. Her lamb dish was very traditional, another one of those foods that were passed down from Grandma to her daughters and then to their daughters: roasted lamb chops heavily doused with oregano, basil, parsley, and garlic. Potatoes were added to the side and tomatoes, salted and sugared, were added overall, as was some olive oil and peas.

Everyone crazy for Italian food has a version. When Papa made it, he doubled or tripled the recipe and packed it for our picnics on Long Island. It is as delicious at room temperature as it is just out of the oven.

For a vegetable dish, Beatrice roasted broccoli and cauliflower. Since that trip, we have cooked it as Beatrice did in Italy. It's healthful, tasty, and so Italian. To us, the beauty of the dish is its simplicity.

For a sweet, she made Grandpa's panettone bread pudding. Panettone is the classic Italian holiday bread. It may be sliced and toasted and served with butter and a special jam, but for special occasions, Italian food crazies like to layer it and bake it as a bread pudding with special ingredients—in this case, figs, honey, and rum. If you prefer something other than figs, try pieces of dark chocolate. This is best if made with fresh figs, but if they are not in season, use diced, dried figs after they have been steamed in some water and white wine.

Mama would have said, "*Brava*, Beatrice!"

At the end of the meal, Beatrice brought out two bottles of *limonce* (elsewhere called *limoncello*), which she had been saving for a special occasion. She waved the bottles around, telling us how long it took her to make the liqueur. We had drunk four or five glasses of wine, and adding homemade limoncello was surely gilding the lily, but we did with little or no hesitation. After all, why had we crossed that big, wide, sometimes turbulent ocean? Besides, this was surely not the time to refuse Beatrice—in her mind, she made it just for us. Madonna, did it give us a jolt.

Beatrice served this meal at a special place, a special time. And with the food, she served hearty helpings of folklore, philosophy, old Italian sayings, and wit.

We danced the tarantella in the center of the horseshoe, accompanied by accordions. Bernie and I sat for hours answering questions about America and listening to long, wonderful descriptions of major celebrations in this corner of Italy. The guests playacted some of the pageantry of the San Giuliano Festival that takes place in January, the Carnevale in February, and San Rocco di Spagna in September, a festival that honors a family whose descendents still occupy a palazzo in Accettura. Most attention was given to the description of the Festa del Maggio—Feast in May—which everyone agreed was the best event in Basilicata, if not in the entirety of Italy. Although Bernie and I had never participated in this feast of fertility, everyone's enthusiasm was at such a high pitch; we nodded happily at the joy they obviously felt describing it. I realized this feast was similar to one I used to attend in Long Island, although ours was not as elaborate. In Italy, young men drive white oxen carrying one large pole of oak and another from a holly tree. The two are lashed together and anchored firmly in the ground so that they soar a hundred or so feet in the air. Before the poles are raised, many prizes are attached to the tops, and the young men clamor up the poles to claim them, much to the delight of the unmarried girls in the crowd.

During all this conversation and gaiety, someone passed around a large box of Perugina Baci, the chocolates still popular today in Italy as well as here. To great hilarity, different paisani read the sayings on the sheer paper ribbons, often with sarcastic comments.

Before I went to bed that night, I read the words of Ann Cornelisen, author of *Torregreca* and *Women in the Shadows*. In the latter, she wrote of southern Italy: "The south is not for the easily discouraged. It is for those who can imagine living in another time—in a mirage world, created by light so piercing that it sears the eye."

As I lay my head on my grandmother's high, old bed, with its pure white sheets and pillows cases and the sky outside the window dead black, I thought the physical description of this part of Italy was spot-on accurate. I also thought about the group of people I had spent time with who, after the horrible war, were filled with more spirit and songs in their hearts than some writers may want us to believe.

When it was time for us to leave Accettura, Beatrice arranged for an automobile to transport us to the train station miles away. The car was a relic that I estimated wouldn't get us even two miles out of town and was to pick us up in the center of the main piazza, about two hundred yards from the house. We now had four large, empty suitcases and a small one with our few clothes. As we approached the piazza, we saw it was filled with townspeople. The women held bulging aprons away from their waists, all of them filled with apples. I knew they had little else to offer; the war years had deprived them of so much, but they were ready to offer fruit from their root cellars to bid us farewell. There were so many apples in so many aprons, it was impossible to take them all, which I asked Beatrice to explain as she helped us fill each suitcase to capacity. Much of the fruit smelled ripe (many apples had rotten spots), and there was no way the apples could survive the long journey to Switzerland. Beatrice made apologies for us, and most people understood our problem, although an emotional discussion ensued over whose apples we would take; everyone wanted to give to "gli Americani." There were hugs, kisses, fond pats, the national anthem, and many cries of "Buon Fortuna Americani!" Everyone pleaded for us to carry regards to family members in the United States, from California to Maine. We were deeply touched and wondered if either of us would return.

As the beat-up car made it to Grassano and then on to Potenza, the aroma of the apples was stifling. Once aboard the train to Naples, we knew we had to discard the fruit. After a bit of sorting, we selected a dozen or so worthy of eating during our return trip. We then lugged the bags to the last car on the train and, bag by bag, unloaded them along the tracks as the train rattled over them. We hoped hungry people from the countryside would come to claim them.

We went back to our seats, and I told Bernie what one of the old Italian women said to me as she took me in her arms in a farewell embrace. "Where are you going, young fellow?" she asked. "To America," I answered. She looked into my eyes and said, "America, A-mer-i-ca, *A-mer-i-ca*—what a beautiful Italian word."

Escarole Soup with Beef Meatballs

Zuppa di cicoria e polpette di carne di manzo
Serves 6 to 8

1 thick slice Italian bread, crust removed
⅓ cup whole milk
¾ pound lean ground beef
¾ cup grated Parmesan cheese
1 large egg, well beaten
½ cup finely chopped flat-leaf parsley
Kosher salt and freshly ground black pepper
1 head escarole, about 1 pound
2 ½ quarts homemade chicken broth, or 5 cups canned, with 5 cups water

1. In a small bowl, soak bread in milk until bread is thoroughly moist, about five minutes. Squeeze dry and crumble bread into a larger bowl.
2. Add beef, one-fourth cup cheese, egg, parsley, salt, and pepper. Mix well and form into marble-sized balls, about sixty in number, and put them on waxed paper or on a plate.
3. Trim and separate the escarole leaves. Rinse well and cook in boiling salted water until tender, five minutes. Drain and put leaves in cold water, drain again, and squeeze dry. Thinly slice the leaves.
4. Bring broth to boil over medium heat, add meatballs, and simmer, covered, five minutes. Add escarole and, partially covered, cook ten minutes longer. Serve in large bowls and pass remaining cheese.

Tagliatelle with a Buttery Tomato Sauce

Tagliatelle in salsa di pomodoro burrosa
Serves 4 to 6

Tagliatelle pasta:

1 ½ cups all purpose flour
2 large eggs, beaten

Sauce:

2 pounds ripe plum tomatoes, or 2 cups canned Italian plum tomatoes
¼ pound butter, cut into 8 pieces
1 medium onion, peeled and quartered
1 medium carrot, peeled and quartered
½ teaspoon sugar
1 ½ teaspoons kosher salt
2 egg recipe for tagliatelle, see above
½ cup freshly grated Parmesan cheese
¼ cup finely chopped flat-leaf parsley

To make the pasta:

1. Put flour on a flat surface or in a bowl and form a well deep enough to hold the eggs. Put eggs in the well. With a fork or with your fingers, begin to pick up a little of the flour from inside the well. Incorporate the flour until the mixture is no longer runny. A good technique for mixing, if the flour is on a flat surface, is to incorporate with one hand, and with the other, hold or support the outside wall of flour. By gently pushing the outer edge of the flour wall with your hand, some of the flour will fall into the well. If the dough ends up sticky, add a little more flour.
2. With both hands, bring all the flour from the outside of the well toward the center and make a ball with the dough, including the crumbs of flour caked on the working surface (use a pastry scraper). Put ball of dough on a flat surface and push down firmly in the center with the heel of your hand. Give dough a slight turn and push down again. Dust your hands with flour because the dough is likely to stick in the beginning. Knead six or seven minutes until the dough becomes smooth and satiny. Cover with a kitchen towel or a bowl and let it rest ten to fifteen minutes.
3. Roll out by hand or use a pasta machine. Pasta machines are fitted with smooth rollers that will produce several thicknesses of "sheet," which is what pasta is called when it has been rolled out by hand or machine. A knob can be turned to widen or narrow the opening between the rollers. Most machines have six settings.

Cutting rollers that can be attached to the machine, slice the sheet to various pasta widths. Only one pasta width can be cut at a time. Tagliatelle are one-fourth-inch wide, so use the appropriate cutter.

4. Before using the machine, cut dough into six equal pieces. Cover five of them and run the sixth two times through the widest opening. Then run it through a narrower opening. It is not necessary to run the pasta through every opening. For example, on a 6-notch machine, roll the dough through setting 6 (the thickest), 4, 2, and 1 (the thinnest). Lightly, very lightly, flour each strip of dough after it is rolled. After sprinkling the dough with flour, rub the palm of your hand up and down the dough strip to cover it lightly with flour. Lay pasta strips on cloth toweling while completing the task. Repeat procedure with five other pieces of dough .Cut into tagliatelle size, loosen the pasta strands with your hands, as if unraveling them, and place carefully on towel to dry, for about one-half hour before cooking.

To make the sauce:

1. If using fresh tomatoes, wash them well, cut each in half, and cook over low heat in a covered pan for fifteen minutes. Put them through a food mill to have a fine purée. If using canned tomatoes, measure two cups into a food mill along with about one-half cup liquid from the can and process for a fine purée.
2. In a medium saucepan, put butter, onion, carrot, sugar, salt, and tomato purée. Over low heat, simmer about forty minutes, partially covered. Stir frequently and be sure the simmer does not turn to a boil.
3. While sauce is cooking, cook the pasta and drain.
4. To serve, pick out onion and carrot pieces from the sauce and adjust salt seasoning. Add cooked pasta to sauce, toss well, and divide among individual plates. Add pieces of cooked vegetable, if you wish, and sprinkle some chopped parsley overall. Pass the Parmigiano-Reggiano.

Herbed-Roasted Lamb Chops with Peas, Potatoes, and Tomatoes

Costolette di agnello arrosto alle erbe con piselli, patate e pomodori

Serves 4

8 shoulder lamb chops, 1 ½ inches thick
3 tablespoons olive oil
1 teaspoon oregano
1 teaspoon fresh or frozen basil, finely chopped (or ½ teaspoon dried)
1 teaspoon flat-leaf parsley, finely chopped (or ½ teaspoon dried)
1 garlic clove, finely chopped
5 potatoes, peeled and cut into ¼-inch-thick slices
1 teaspoon kosher salt
½ teaspoon sugar
¾ cup fresh or canned tomatoes, peeled, seeded, and chopped
1 cup canned peas
2 tablespoons grated Parmesan cheese

1. Preheat the oven to 350°F.
2. Cut away most of the fat from chops. Oil a roasting pan with one tablespoon olive oil. Put chops in the pan and top each one with oregano, basil, parsley, and garlic. Add potatoes to the pan alongside the chops. Add salt and sugar to the tomatoes and pour them over the chops and potatoes. Sprinkle two tablespoons olive oil on top of chops and potatoes.
3. Bake for twenty-five to forty minutes.
4. For the last five minutes, add peas mixed with cheese on top of potatoes.
5. Remove chops and vegetables with a slotted spoon onto a large platter and serve immediately.

Roasted Broccoli and Cauliflower

Cavolfiore e broccoli arrosto

Serves 6

4 cups broccoli florets including tender stems (1 bunch)
3 cups cauliflower florets (1 small to medium head)
½ cup extra-virgin olive oil
¼ to ½ cup freshly made bread crumbs
Kosher salt and freshly ground black pepper

1. Preheat oven to 425°F.
2. After cutting off the broccoli florets, take some of the heavy stems and cut away the bottom half of them and discard. Pare the remaining stems, using a small sharp knife, and cut in half-inch widths. Use about one cup of these plus three cups of the broccoli florets to make four cups.
3. Put broccoli and cauliflower pieces in a large bowl and pour olive oil over them. Toss well to be sure to coat all the vegetable pieces, as this helps seal in their moisture.
4. Arrange vegetables in one layer in a baking pan. Bake eight minutes, turn over the vegetables, and cook another eight minutes. Check for doneness by putting a wooden skewer into a vegetable—if it pierces easily, the vegetables are done; if not, cook several minutes longer.
5. When done, remove vegetables from oven and salt them; liberally add freshly ground pepper. Sprinkle a tablespoon or two more of olive oil. If ready to serve, sprinkle with bread crumbs. If you are going to serve right away, add the bread crumbs at time of serving. These may be served lukewarm.

Panettone Bread Pudding with Figs

Panettone budino di pane con fichi

Serves 10 to 12

16 slices panettone, 2 inches wide by ½ inch thick by 6 inches high
1 ½ sticks (6 ounces) butter, cut into 6 pieces

¾ cup honey
½ cup dark rum
12 fresh figs or 1 cup diced dried figs
6 large eggs
¾ cup sugar
1 ½ cups heavy cream
4 ½ cups milk
1 cup heavy cream, whipped (optional)

1. Preheat the oven to 375°F.
2. Butter a twelve-and-a-half-by-eleven-by-two-and-a-half-inch oval glass or ceramic baking dish. Cover the bottom the dish with slices of panettone, overlapping as necessary.
3. In a small saucepan, melt butter over low heat; add honey and rum. Increase heat and cook, stirring constantly, until mixture bubbles and thickens. Remove and pour over bread, spreading it as evenly as you can.
4. If using fresh figs, brush clean and remove stem. Cut each fig into four pieces. Put these over bread and butter mixture as evenly as you can. If using dried figs, put the pieces in a small saucepan adding one-half cup water and one-half cup white wine. Bring to a simmer, cover, and heat this way for fifteen or twenty minutes. Spoon figs and any liquid left in the pan over bread in the dish and distribute as evenly as you can.
5. Beat eggs and sugar in a large bowl until well combined. Slowly mix in cream and then the milk. Be sure the mixture is well mixed. Carefully pour over bread and figs.
6. Bake for twenty minutes. Reduce the heat to 325°F and bake twenty minutes longer, until bread has a golden color and pudding is set. Let rest for ten minutes before serving with a dollop of whipped cream, if you want to.

26

MAMA AND THE LADY IN RED

Mama came to this country when she was eight years old and was just shy of sixteen when she married Papa, who was ten years older. Their children were born every eighteen months until there were eight of us; six survived and two died at very young ages. My parents were happily and unhappily married for fifty-nine years at the time of Papa's death. Mama outlived him by eighteen years.

As the years rolled by, my brothers, sisters, and I would ask Mama at least once a year if she wanted to give up her apartment and move in with one of us. "Are you crazy?" she would say emphatically. "Don't think of it. When I need help, you'll know it."

On one such visit with Mama, long after we all had grown and moved away, we sat down for our customary midweek meal. She had baked bread and cooked a delicious pot of zucchini stew flavored with sausages, adorned on top with opaque egg whites, the glorious centers of their yolks golden bliss. We were at the dining table, sipping wine, when Mama dropped the pot as she was carrying it from the stove to the table. Zucchini splashed everywhere on her new rug, the eggs breaking like mixed white and yellow paint. Mama sat down, cupped her face in her hands, and as silently as possible, she wept. At first, we were terrified, but we also knew the time had come. She needed her family's help.

Mama spent the last four months of her life with family members in Key West, Florida. Her companion, Miriam, a native Jamaican who had helped Mama after her hip replacement the year before, was with us. We all loved tall, big-boned, ebony-faced Miriam, who had a ravenous appetite. If ever there was a person crazy in love with Italian food, she was it!

Miriam had a broad, delicate smile, and it seemed the corners of her mouth touched her earlobes as they stretched to show peacefulness, contentment, happiness, and her love of Mama. The only demand she ever made was for one of us to drive her in the big car to church each Sunday morning and retrieve her one hour later. She dressed to the nines for church and wore her favorite color, which was red. She always stood out in her red snug dress, purse, hat, and shoes. Each Sunday morning before leaving for church, Miriam moved close to Mama; and before she could ask "How do I look?" Mama pinched at her rear end, as if to pull the red fabric away from Miriam's body, and exclaimed, "It's too tight, it's just too tight! No pasta tonight!"

It was difficult to find the right church for Miriam. We tried seven or eight in Key West before she settled on a permanent one, a church with a good-looking minister who was always there to receive her as she arrived in the big car and always there one hour later to say *ciao* as she stepped into the big car to be driven home.

After caring for Mama for almost a year, Miriam returned to Jamaica for a visit, a needed three-week vacation. Several of us travelled with Mama to our country house in Pawling, New York. Mama never returned to Key West, and the way she died is memorable.

When Miriam returned from Jamaica, we met her at the Pawling train station. We were home in ten minutes and soon enjoying Miriam's "welcome back" supper at the kitchen table. Mama cooked some of Miriam's favorites: pizza with ricotta salata cheese and sweet peppers and penne with homemade pork sauce. (For the following day, we had planned manicotti for lunch and the family's favorite meat loaf for supper. These were dishes Miriam loved, and much of it was already prepared and in the refrigerator.) Mama got up on her walker, took a few steps, fell to the floor, and was sick to her stomach. The doctor was called, and he said immediately, "Call an ambulance."

In less than a half hour, we rushed into the emergency room at the New Milford, Connecticut, hospital, a ten-mile drive, door to door.

We arrived at the hospital at 10:00 p.m., and the tests began. Between tests, Mama took my hand and said, "You have to remember, I'm ninety-one. I can't live forever, and I don't want you or the others to worry about me. You have a lot to do, and you should do it." I saw the tears in her eyes, and I know she saw the same in mine.

Numerous tests and four hours later, the doctor on duty instructed us to take Mama home. Shocked, we couldn't understand why. He explained that there was no medical reason to keep her overnight in the hospital. All of her tests had proven normal; in fact, the results were extremely good. It was not easy for us to accept this, and the thought of anyone seeing us driving Mama and Miriam home at two thirty in the morning would think we were reckless and uncaring for older people. Tired and confused, we left the hospital and drove home anyway.

Early the next morning, about seven, Miriam called my name loudly, and I knew something was wrong. Mama and Miriam were set up temporarily in the downstairs library. I flew downstairs in my underwear. I took Mama's hand, and at first, I thought she was trying to regain some breath, but quickly realized "the rattle of death" was taking place. Within a short time, our family doctor, Dr. Morrison, came to the house and pronounced her dead.

Miriam later told us that Mama had awakened earlier and been sick to her stomach again. Miriam changed the linen on the bed and put a new nightgown on Mama. Dr. Morrison said she hadn't suffered and had felt no pain. This had been quite evident from the look on her face. What is a beautiful death? We have to believe that this was one.

Several years earlier, when Mama was eighty-five years old, she came with us to a rented house in France, seventy miles southwest of Paris in a village called Villeneuve-sur-Yonne. Mama was with us to visit museums, restaurants, and food markets. One day, she insisted on staying home. "Why?" we had asked her. She explained that she didn't like the way the housekeeper was doing our blouses and shirts, and she intended to spend the day doing laundry with the housekeeper. "But you don't speak French, and the housekeeper doesn't speak Italian or English," we had said. None of this mattered. Mama spent the day at home working, and when we returned from a day of sightseeing, the laundry was done and perfect. In fact, the owner had driven down from Paris with a new iron after the housekeeper had called to report that Mama was not happy with the old one. (What an ordeal this must have been for the house's owner, actress Leslie Caron, who rented the house under the name of M. Robert!)

Miriam had no idea, or perhaps she did, that changing Mama's bed linen and putting her in a fresh nightgown the morning she died was the perfect way for Mama to leave us.

Miriam was a foodie. She loved to eat and had an intense interest in its preparation. In one of my earlier books, I showcased her mango pie. She became intensely interested in Italian food, crazy like the rest of us, to be sure, about the spice and food of *la dolce vita*. She loved pizza and wanted to know all about it. I explained that pizza reached the height of its popularity during the Borboni (Bourbon) rule in the Kingdom of the Two Sicilies of which Naples was the capital. It was the food of the *lazzeroni* of the people. Miriam cheered that fact. I said pizza is a simple food in that it has no mystical or religious meaning as many other Italian foods do. For example, it does not represent money or power. It is the ultimate fast food, ancient to be sure, but with a huge appeal in modern times. Pizza has grown in popularity outside Naples and Italy for these reasons and also because anyone can add anything to it once the dough is made. No other food is so egalitarian. Miriam said that people loved pizza in Jamaica too. She asked if we could make a pizza and bring it to her minister.

Making and serving a pizza can seem like an easy task, and it is, but there are some preparation steps to pay close attention to. For example, if pizza dough fails, it is most likely because the water added was too hot. It is better to err by using cooler water. Kneading the dough will help it rise later. Also, kneading the dough should be thorough. You should knead the dough until it is smooth and satiny. The dough, while being kneaded, also needs to rest every once in a while. The process should be to knead and rest, knead and rest. (Miriam didn't quite grasp this concept at first, but finally accepted the idea after seeing the results.)

It would be impossible to count the number of times that Mama made pizza dough, not only in our home but also everywhere she went. She seemed never to tire of it. Many times, the request for pizza came from someone else. If our family was sitting outside on the lawn at Aunt Rose and Uncle Patsy's home in Connecticut, "Il Duce" (Uncle Patsy, affectionately) might say, "Sister-in-law, why don't you make a nice big pizza with cheese?" Mama would always say yes, and everyone who asked always seemed to have the necessary ingredients on hand. She enjoyed the kneading process and was not bothered by the waiting time for the dough to rise.

I remember so well a time when Mama went to see if the dough had risen enough for the next step of preparation. Observing her, I heard her sweet comments as she removed the moist towel and looked at the dough. First, she said, "Oh, Madonna, *che bella cosa*," which means "Oh, what a beautiful thing." The look in her eyes was like the look someone has waking up in the morning, looking at a sleeping child, and kissing the child who is still asleep. Studying the dough, she looked as though she was touching a baby's behind, bathing and caressing the child, looking into the baby's pure, loving eyes, and hugging her. "*Incantevole*," Mama said, "magnificent." She studied the dough and said she thought it had doubled in size. She looked at the clock on the wall, registering that an hour had passed. Then she said, "But the real test for rising is to put two fingers into the dough. If the indentations remain, the dough has properly risen. If the indentations disappear, the dough needs to rest more to rise properly." She poked two fingers, her index and middle fingers, into the dough. She waited a short minute and exclaimed, "The dough is ready for the next step. Can you see the marks of my fingers in the dough? Let's punch it down, form a ball, and put it back in the bowl to rise a second time." That's how I learned the proper way to prepare dough.

I continued my instructions to Miriam. To achieve a crisp cooked pizza, it is best to use a pizza stone and pizza paddle. They are available in shops that sell kitchen equipment. When adding toppings to the dough, be sure the liquids and juices have been strained out. If you are using ricotta or mozzarella cheese, put them in a colander with cheese cloth and let them drain for at least one-half to one hour before using them. Miriam nodded positively; she seemed to understand.

I went further and explained that she should always brush some oil on the top of the dough before adding anything else. If she applied tomato sauce, she should use just a thin coating. Pizza should be eaten as it comes out of the oven after just a few minutes rest, and the best way to cut it is with a pizza wheel. If pizza has to be reheated, put some slices on the stone, which has been preheated in the oven at a temperature of 400°F. Do not cover because that will make it mushy. Miriam was absolutely in awe of the pizza stone, and she learned this version of pizza making.

Miriam said that pizza was the one food she would ask for upon entering the Pearly Gates. To say she loved pork and tomato sauce is to say it all. Miriam, our beautiful, lovely Miriam, is out-of-sight "perdutamente." This recipe is for her. This sauce should be made ahead, and the fat should be removed. The pork shoulder can be served separately with a vegetable and salad. Enjoy!

A Favorite Pizza with Ricotta Salata and Sweet Pepper

Pizza con peperoni e ricotta salata

Serves 6 to 8

To make pizza dough:

- 3 cups unbleached all-purpose flour
- 1 scant tablespoon salt
- 1 tablespoon sugar
- 1 packet rapid-rise yeast (¼ ounce)
- 1 ¼ cups lukewarm water, no warmer than 105°F
- 2 tablespoons garlic-flavored oil, see below

To make the dough in the processor:

1. Put the flour, salt, sugar, and yeast granules in the bowl of the processor. Pulse to a count of four.

2. Combine the water and the oil and feed it into the bowl through the feed tube. Stop as soon as a ball of dough is formed. Let this dough rest two minutes.
3. Process dough for one minute but stop the machine every fifteen seconds for a few seconds. (This one minute of processing takes the place of manually kneading the dough.)
4. Turn the dough out on a lightly floured surface and form a ball. Put it into a bowl that has been lightly oiled. Turn the dough over to coat it, cover with a moist cloth kitchen towel, and let it rise in a warm, draft-free place. Let it rise to two times its size, about forty to sixty minutes. To test for rising, put two fingers into the dough—if the indentations remain, the dough is properly risen; if the indentations disappear, the dough needs to rise longer.
5. Turn out the dough, form it quickly into a ball, and return it to the bowl for a second rise (this is important—do not short cut this step). When properly risen the second time, turn it out into the pizza pan (with some cornmeal to loosely cover the bottom, and use your hands and fingers to fit the dough into the pan). If properly risen, it will stretch into place easily. If the dough resists, give it a rest for a minute or two and continue fitting it into the pan. Preheat oven to 450°F. Add the topping, let the pizza sit uncooked for a couple of minutes, and then bake fifteen minutes.

To make dough manually:

1. Combine the dry ingredients, add the water and the oil and mix with a wooden spoon. When it becomes difficult to move the spoon, start kneading with floured hands on a lightly floured surface. Knead for five minutes, rest for two, knead five minutes and rest for two until smooth, satiny dough is achieved.
2. Place in an oiled bowl, cover with a damp towel, and allow dough to rise in a warm place until twice its size. Punch down the dough and put it back in the bowl for another rise. To test for proper rising, put two fingers into dough—if the indentations remain, the dough is ready for the next step; if the indentations disappear, the dough is not ready and should be left to rise longer.

3. Fit the dough in a pizza pan with a little cornmeal strewn over the bottom of the pan. Do this with your hands—do not use a rolling pin. (If the dough has risen properly, it will stretch easily to the rim of the pan—if there is any resistance, let the dough rest a minute or two and then proceed. Preheat oven to 450°F. Let the dough rest again five minutes before adding any topping. Add topping and bake until golden and crispy, about fifteen minutes.

2 tablespoons extra-virgin olive oil for sautéing peppers
2 bell peppers, one red, one yellow or orange, cored, ribs and seeds removed, and cut into thinnest slivers possible
¼ pound grated ricotta salata
1 tablespoon each finely chopped fresh oregano (or 1 teaspoon dried, crushed), fresh parsley, and fresh chives
One 14- to 15-inch pizza dough (see above) ready to receive a topping
1 tablespoon garlic-flavored oil, see below

Minced garlic, or even thinly sliced garlic, put on top of the pizza before baking will usually darken or burn and become bitter. Some pizza makers like to add finely minced fresh garlic to the topping of a pizza after it has come out of the oven, but raw garlic dominates the other flavors in the topping and will burn the inside of one's mouth. The best way to get a good garlic flavor is by adding some drops of garlic-flavored oil to the topping. Here is a pizza built on this principle that is totally delicious, easy to make, and provide a fabulous one-dish meal. Just add a fresh green salad with your favorite salad dressing.

Garlic-flavored Oil

Olio all'Aglio
Makes 1 cup

Any amount you don't use will keep for a month or so if you put it in a clean jar with a cover and store in or out of the refrigerator. If refrigerated, bring to room temperature before using.

15 large cloves garlic, peeled and crushed
1 cup extra-virgin olive oil

1. Combine garlic and oil in a small saucepan and place over low heat. Cook until garlic browns, about fifteen minutes. Remove and discard garlic. Oil is ready to use or store.
2. Heat the olive oil in a large skillet over low heat and add the peppers. Toss lightly but well. Cover and gently sauté until the peppers become soft, about fifteen minutes.
3. In a small bowl, combine the grated cheese and the herbs and toss lightly but well.
4. Preheat oven to 450°F. Brush some of the garlic-flavored oil over the pizza. Arrange the peppers on top, covering the pizza, and sprinkle the herb-flavored cheese overall. Spoon one tablespoon of the garlic-flavored oil over the pizza. Liberally add freshly ground pepper overall. Put in the oven and bake until golden and crisp, about fifteen minutes.

Penne with Pork Tomato Sauce

Penne al ragu di maiale
Makes about 6 cups sauce.

3 ½ pounds boned pork shoulder (may be in 1 or 2 pieces)
2 medium cloves garlic, minced
1 cup finely chopped Italian parsley
6 tablespoons olive oil
1 large onion, finely chopped
½ teaspoon red pepper flakes
7 cups plum tomatoes (after putting them through a food mill)
1 pound penne pasta

1. Lay the meat flat on a work surface and add the garlic and parsley. Roll it and tie it with string. If two pieces of meat are used, do this for both, dividing the amount of garlic and parsley.

2. Heat oil in a large heavy pot and sauté the rolled pork over medium heat, uncovered, until it is browned all over, about ten minutes. Add the onion and sauté two or three minutes, stirring several times. Add tomatoes and pepper flakes and cook, covered, over low heat, about two hours. Taste for salt and add some if needed.
3. Remove the pork and set aside for later serving. If sauce appears thin, keep over heat and cook down to desired thickness, up to twenty minutes.
4. Cook the pasta according to package directions, drain well, and add one to one and a half cups of tomato sauce.
5. Serve the penne with the sauce first. Then slice the pork to serve as a separate course.

Manicotti

Manicotti

Serves 3 to 4

To make the crespelle:

- 3 eggs
- 1 cup water
- 1 cup all-purpose flour
- Salt to taste
- Melted butter

1. Break the eggs into a bowl and beat with a whisk. Stir in the water. Add the flour gradually, stirring with the whisk. Add the salt, stir, and let stand for minimum thirty minutes to one hour.
2. Heat a seven- or eight-inch crepe pan or small Teflon skillet over moderate heat and brush lightly with melted butter. Add about three tablespoons of batter and tilt the pan until the batter covers the bottom. (The shells should be quite thin but substantial enough to handle.) Cook about thirty-five seconds on one side; then turn, using a spatula or your hands, and cook on the other side briefly, two or three seconds. Slide crepe out of the pan onto a dish.

3. Repeat this process until all the batter is used, brushing the skillet lightly with butter if necessary before each shell is made.
4. Shells can be made one or two days in advance and refrigerated, or weeks in advance and frozen. Stack them on foil or freeze paper and wrap them well.

To make filling:

1 pound fresh spinach, washed several times
3 tablespoons butter, plus more for baking pan
1 tablespoons extra-virgin olive oil
1 cup ricotta cheese
4 tablespoons Parmesan cheese
1 egg
Pinch of nutmeg
Salt and freshly ground pepper

1. In a skillet, cook drained spinach with water still clinging to leaves for five minutes. Drain squeeze dry and chop finely. Clean skillet.
2. Add two tablespoons butter to skillet, melt, and add spinach. Cook three or four minutes over low heat. Stir frequently.
3. Transfer spinach to a bowl. Add ricotta, two tablespoons Parmesan cheese, egg, nutmeg, salt, and pepper.
4. Divide this mixture among twelve shells then roll each and place in buttered baking pan. Sprinkle remaining Parmesan cheese and butter over the shells. Bake twenty minutes in 350°F oven.
5. Serve as is, or add a simple tomato sauce

Our Family's Favorite Mozzarella Meat Loaf

Polpettone di mozzarella

Serves 6 to 8

2 pounds ground chuck
2 links Italian sausage out of casing

2 eggs, beaten lightly
2 small onions, peeled, finely chopped
2 tablespoons finely chopped Italian parsley
1 clove garlic, minced
½ cup grated Pecorino cheese
2 cups ¼-inch cubes fresh mozzarella
5 slices Italian bread, soaked in ¾ cup milk, squeezed dry
¼ cup chopped canned tomatoes

1. Preheat oven to 350°F. Combine ground chuck with sausage in a large bowl. Add eggs, onions, parsley, garlic, Pecorino and mozzarella cheeses, bread, and tomatoes. Also add a generous sprinkle of salt and freshly ground pepper. With splayed fingers, toss mixture lightly to blend well.
2. Transfer mixture to a flat surface and, with your hands, shape it into a loaf (like a long loaf of Italian bread) and put it on an oiled baking sheet with a rim (a jelly roll pan will do—this is to keep the meat juices from overflowing).
3. Bake one and a half hours. Remove from oven and allow to cool about ten minutes before slicing, or allow it to cool completely and serve it cold.

EPILOGUE

AFTER THE WAR

What a difference the war made. There were sweeping changes from old immigrant customs to more modern American living. The differences between Mary's and Bea's wedding celebrations (the latter held at the Great Northern Hotel on Fifty-Seventh Street) were huge, although they occurred only eight years apart but with a war in between.

Gone were the Palm Garden fetes of Mary's wedding day and homemade kaiser roll sandwiches for wedding guests. Who would dare serve pitchers of beer drawn from a hidden keg now? The big white satin bag for "ma-low-pas," or envelopes for cards and money, was no longer part of the wedding routine. Tarantella dances quickly became passé, and the Italian ladies, some with handkerchiefs to taunt their men, others with rising skirts for Italian folk dances, seemed quaint.

Change swept across New York's west side. Old flats turned into new apartments, and rents began to skyrocket. Where the two "Zias," like Aunt Margaret and others had been, a new type of person was moving into the neighborhood and snatching up the apartments. Many of these newcomers were independent workers, people who worked at home or easily walked to the avenues where huge corporations were building skyscrapers fifty stories and higher, named for themselves, such as Exxon, CBS, McGraw-Hill, the Bank of New York, Equitable, and countless others.

Tony the butcher moved his store to the corner of Ninth Avenue and Forty-Sixth Street, taking with him his *lucanica* sausage—also called *luganega* by some, and *lunganiga* by others—the famous and delicious sausage he carried,. The sausage was the pride and joy of Basilicata, Mama's home in Italy, and had once been prized by the Romans for its smack-in-the-mouth taste of fennel seeds. The sausage was so adored that it was imitated in Milan and Venice. Customers from outside the neighborhood saw Tony's new sign in the window: "SALSICCIA SOLD HERE." They flocked to his new store for that sausage and for veal cutlets. Tony's move brought more business and eventually a new Ninth Avenue building for him and his enterprising family.

It was sad for those original immigrants, the natives of the neighborhood, to see the disappearance of Manuel's Grocery Store, and with it the disappearance of the bushels of fresh greens, the layers of eggplants, the pyramids of lemons and tomatoes, and tied bunches of Italian parsley their stems in freshwater, all neatly arranged by Manual's wife Lucy and tended by their daughters. Gone were the fresh breads, the bins of macaroni, and all the wonderful smelling salamis and cheeses that filled Italian bread sandwiches for inspectors, policemen, and everyone else in our neighborhood. The St. Francis French Laundry vanished as well. One of our neighbors said it had moved to Astoria. We didn't know, but we missed the horse-drawn wagon deliveries with Brother Charlie holding the reins.

The Cohen's Laundry on Forty-Seventh Street, right across from the elementary school, closed as well, as did the synagogue across from Cohen's and to the west of the school. Two eighteen-year-olds from the Marquardt family, one who owned the deli on Tenth Avenue and one who owned a bakery on the same street, both died in the war, and their shops closed. Gone were the oversized dill pickles, the pickled pigs' feet, the barrels of sauerkraut, the head cheeses, the liverwursts, and their divine German potato salads. The Marquardt children left the neighborhood to seek better lives, better jobs, and better living conditions.

The changes on Ninth Avenue were also major. Although some shops remained, such as Esposito's Meats, the Fable's Greek Pastry Shop, called Poseidon, Manganaro's, and the International Spice and Herb Store, still showing off its spice and herb imports in large one-hundred-pound sacks outside their entry door, gone now were the individually owned small vegetable and fruit stands. Once, there must have been over one hundred stands of oranges, bananas, eggplants, celery, onions, countless types of greens, all dripping with water from their hourly hosing to keep them fresh, but they were standing no longer. It was a sad day when we learned of the death of Bernie, the owner of our favorite candy store, which had the delightful pink-centered chocolates. His wife, Sara, tried to carry on the business but couldn't, and the candy store closed.

And what about the Christmas trees? There was no one and nowhere to sell them. Gone too were the big oil drums that contained wood fires during cold months to keep the merchants and their customers warm. We also said goodbye to the materassi sellers, those merchants selling mattresses from trucks or horse-drawn carriages, jewelers, the linen salesmen, and the life insurance sellers who came to the customers' homes. Once, one of these sales might mean committing to two dollars a week for life; now, none of these sellers came to anyone's home anymore. So many things from our old neighborhood were gone with the war.

More neighborhood kids were going to college, graduating, and leaving the neighborhood for White Plains and other Westchester locations. By the time veterans came home, four in our family had married and no longer lived at home. Gone were our three bedrooms; Mama and Papa convinced the landlord to combine three bedrooms into two. My, the bedrooms looked palatial with their fancy bedspreads! We also wondered what Papa was using now as a holding station for his freshly made ravioli. Little did we know that a move was in the cards.

As if to bolster our spirits, the Ferrara fancy pastry shop continued to thrive downtown, and Papa continued his trips there with stops at kosher fresh chicken shops. Arthur Avenue in the Bronx was growing, and more and more Italian food shops were opening all over New York, including Bleeker Street, which was a long way for Mama to go to shop. However, she managed with the remaining Italian food stores nearby and was spry enough to try some new supermarkets that opened on Ninth Avenue. We know she found an Italian roasted coffee in one of them, and that made part of her shopping easier.

The increase in Italian restaurants was also monumental. Once Barbetta's, which had been the lone mainstay on Restaurant Row, Forty-Sixth Street between Eighth and Ninth Avenues, now Italian eateries were opening by the dozens. Italian restaurants were everywhere in mid-Manhattan.

During the war, a man named Renato Ottolenghi came from Turin, Italy, to New York City. His mother was Jewish and had suffered in Italy because of the ill-fated and terrible policies of Mussolini. Renato was able to come to the United States as a dentist, and he opened a practice in one of the buildings owned by Tony the butcher on the corner of Ninth Avenue and Forty-Sixth Street. It was up one flight, and the shingle on the first floor was easy to read. Toward the end of the war, my sister Bea worked for Dr. Ottolenghi as a receptionist and dental assistant. Renato was married to an overambitious woman who spent most of her time working on a PhD from Columbia University.

Renato closed his dentist's office at 1:00 p.m. every day and reopened it at 4:00 p.m., just as they do in Italy. He loved food, well, that is putting it mildly. In fact, he was totally "perdu" about it. Bea would invite Renato for lunch at Mama's, and he loved it and went back time and time again. All of us enjoyed his company. In addition to great food stories, he told us interesting stories of the war, recited in his bright, humorous style. He wanted more food exploration every day, which meant visiting restaurants throughout the city as long as the restaurant was Italian. Since he had the longest lunch period of any working person we knew, it was no problem getting to and from a restaurant in the village or one way over on the east side. He asked Bea and me to join him for lunch almost every day, but we couldn't accept that many invitations.

I too was at Columbia working on a graduate degree, so often I had the time to join Renato. Bea and I usually went once or twice a week with him. He was so ingratiating in his invitations that it was difficult to say no. Besides, what a perfect chance to eat good Italian restaurant food, learn about it, and come home to tell our folks about the experience. That's all Renato spoke about and all he wanted to talk about. He was a bizarre, interesting, and highly entertaining dentist who, we believe, cared little about teeth except when used for gnawing Italian food. We stopped making those treks with him when Bea got married and I took off for Europe.

It was during this time that surveys showed Italian food as the most popular in the city, state, and country. In addition to the explosion of Italian restaurants, lots of new Italian specialty food shops opened, such as Balducci's in Greenwich Village and in many of the suburbs. Ninth Avenue shops, such as Esposito's, Manganaro's, International Spices, and Poseidon, grew more famous as newspapers and magazines began writing about and photographing the shops and the people who ran them. Magazines about Italian food appeared, and more books were published on the subject. The newer restaurants specialized in Roman, Tuscan, Piedmontese, Venetian, and, yes, Neapolitan food.

In 1950, Ada Boni's famous Italian book on cookery, *The Talisman Italian Cookbook,* was published by Crown Publishers in New York and became a best seller; it was considered the equivalent in Italy of *The Joy of Cooking* in America. It was Mama's first legitimate cookbook, but still she clung to cooking her way. Mama once admitted liking Ada Boni's "Rustic Minestrone" because both sausage and spareribs were in it, and it was the way Mama cooked minestrone.

It was during this time, a few years after the renovation of the place where three bedrooms were made into two, that Mama and Papa left their old abode at 453 West Forty-Sixth Street to move to 417, on the same block and the same side of the street but much closer to Ninth Avenue. Their friends, Elvira and her daughter Rose, owned the beautiful brownstone at the 417 address, which had once been a private home with fireplaces in the front and rear rooms on every floor. Sometime before our parents moved, the building had undergone some major renovations. Each floor was turned into a separate apartment, so there were now basement, parlor, second-, and third-floor apartments. The third-floor apartment was available, and Elvira and Rose wanted Mama and Papa to live there. Once they made the move, they stayed almost forty years. The apartment was ideal for them.

When you entered the apartment, you came into a hallway; to the right was a full bath, a dining room with two windows and a fireplace, and a kitchen with a full-size window facing the back garden. To the left, was a small room that we turned into a dressing room for Mama. It too had a window between the newly created closets that we faced with shutter doors. Beyond the dressing room was the main bedroom that led into the living room, facing the street, with two beautiful windows and a fireplace. Through a door in the living room was a small bedroom we turned into a sewing and sitting room. The afternoon sun shone brightly through the window in that room. Mama would sit there and see what was happening on the block. After the kitchen, this room was her next favorite place in the new apartment. The fire escape was in the rear of the brownstone.

We asked Elvira and Rose, the owners, if we could update the kitchen and bath and make other changes. They kept the rent reasonable in view of these improvements. Almost all of our friends played a role in redoing this apartment. We all painted, hung beautiful wallpaper, found several special and appropriate pieces of furniture, and planned a kitchen to make Mama and Papa happy. Their four-foot pasta board seemed too large to use in the new kitchen, but Mama said she could use it on top of the dining table. "All I have to do is put an old blanket under the board," she said reassuringly. During this renovation period, Mama made her wonderful food and served it to all those working on the project. These meals surely encouraged them to return and do more work so they could eat more great food. Papa made his Savoy cabbage with spareribs to everyone's delight. Mama's lasagnas were huge hits too and so easy to serve to these hungry volunteers. They found it harder to work after consuming homemade cheesecake and coffee. This was a period of true Italian celebration for all.

Other adjustments also had to be made to the apartment, but Mama and Papa were completely happy cooking and living there. They invited Elvira and Rose and one or two other people to join them for supper almost every night. Mama still made her bread and cooked all the time. This was her life. With all of their kids grown and moved away, Mama and Papa made a new life again with food as its basis. It was the food that brought them and their friends together and united them—the unselfish act of preparing food, sharing it, and expecting little or nothing in return. Mama was a natural-born teacher who loved to show others how to make ravioli, knead bread, prepare artichokes, and cook broccoli rabe.

Years later in Pawling, when Dr. Morrison told us Mama was dead, it seemed as though within minutes the local undertaker, Mr. Thomes, was at the kitchen door. His visit took the family by surprise and annoyed us. He was told the family had not made plans on where Mama's wake was to be held. During telephone calls between siblings, the decision was made to keep Mama in Pawling. Most of the family would have to travel, and all of us worried about the inconveniences of New York City, such as hotel reservations and cost, parking availability and fees, private limousine expenses, and so forth.

Mama's burial place had already been determined—next to Papa in their vault at Ferncliff Cemetery, in Hartsdale, New York, about halfway between New York City and Pawling. One of the most serious moments at an Italian Catholic funeral is the closing of the coffin. Only immediate family members are there with a priest for the last prayer. Cousin Bea, who had been so helpful during the entire time at the funeral parlor, was asked to join Mama's children. It was a most appropriate thing for us to do. Mama was saying goodbye to us and her "seventh" child. Cousin Bea cried the whole time. We all wept. We are a weeping family. In the funeral home, on the morning of the last goodbyes to Mama, the family wept together.

The family decided that before Mama was put in her final resting place, the funeral entourage, encompassing some thirty or more cars including the limousines for the family and cousin Bea, were to go to New York City to pay last respects to the Clinton neighborhood where Mama and Papa lived and raised their family. The cars took a turn off West Side Drive directly onto Forty-Sixth Street, driving as slowly as possible, so we all could view their old place at 453 West Forty-Sixth Street. We drove down the street that no longer had

Manuel's Grocery Store, past what had been Grandma and Grandpa's flat now without the fig tree or the cat, past where Tony's Butcher Shop used to be in the middle of the street, past the French Laundry, by the flats of the two Zias, past Hartley House, by the storefront that was once Joe's shoe repair, and onto Restaurant Row, so we could go past Barbetta's Restaurant one more time.

At Eighth Avenue, the entourage turned left and went uptown to Forty-Seventh Street, turned to view the still-standing elementary school building and the synagogue next door, then we drove further down and across the avenue past Fr. Rosen's parish of St. Albert's, where all of us had been confirmed. We drove around more corners at a slow crawl through Paddy's Market and to view the building that housed Mama's piecework shop. Mama said goodbye to her neighborhood. The family wept together. We drove back to Ferncliff on that beautiful day in June, where peonies were in bloom everywhere, and we all threw roses onto Mama's coffin before it was put in the vault next to our father's.

On this long drive, we reminisced about the daily lives of Mama and Papa. They did not pursue pleasure. In fact, their lives contained their share of grief. There was the loss of two young children, Mama's ill father-in-law, the ups and downs of feeding, clothing, and educating six children and keeping them healthy, plus all the ensuing difficulties, not to mention the bad seed grandson and the difficult son-in-law. Naturally, there were plenty of happy times, and they certainly welcomed the achievements of those they loved. But overall, they did not seek pleasure for pleasure's sake.

Did Mama and Papa take real vacations? No. Did they eat out? No. They never spent a dime more than they had to. They spent time and money on family events, Christmas Eves, Christmas Days, and Communion and Confirmation lunches. When they celebrated such occasions, they brought joy to themselves, their kids, their relatives, and friends, and neighbors, and they enjoyed themselves as much as their kids did.

When Mama was buried that June day, we arranged a luncheon at Tony's Stazione, a local Italian family restaurant on Main Street, just a mile from Ferncliff Cemetery. We preordered a bountiful meal that Mama herself might have cooked, including artichokes and asparagus, a pasta with her Sunday meat and tomato sauce, several roasted meats with various vegetables freely crowned with oregano, a delicious fresh green salad with her oil and vinegar dressing, bowls of fresh fruit and cheeses, and a festive tray of specially baked cookies she would have liked for the younger ones. Cousin Bea sat at the head table with Mama's children, and we saw to it that everyone received one or more Mass cards.

Mama was the quintessence of immigrant America's ingenuity, hard work, and fighting spirit. Mama always seemed a bit more definite, a bit more decisive, than some of her relatives and peers. That day, we all began to feel one of the most common emotions mourners experience: a longing, a nostalgia for a past life that is forever gone. Losing a loved one vividly reveals the transience of our own existence. We all understand that Mama cannot be reinvented, she cannot be substituted, and she cannot be revived. And what we fully understand is that we are never entirely separated from those who help define us, even when they are gone.

– END –

LIST OF RECIPES

INDEX

D

E

F

G

H

Q

R

S

JOE FAMULARO (in knickers with his two brothers, 1933) is a cookbook author who has written eleven books and won two James Beard awards and an IACP book award. His books have sold more than 950,000 copies, with his most successful two, The Joy of Grilling and The Joy of Pasta, selling more than 525,000 copies together. Both had 26 printings. Other books are Italian Soup Cookbook (Workman), Celebrations (Barrons), Vegetables (Barrons), The Festive Famularo Kitchen (Atheneum), Healthy Grilling (Barrons), Healthy Pasta (Barrons), Supermeals For Supermarkets (Barrons), and Cook's Tour of Italy (Berkeley). Both Celebrations and The Joy of Grilling won James Beard awards; Vegetables won an IACP book award, and his most recent book, Viva La Cucina Italiana, co-authored with Cristopher Laus, won the cookbook award from Indie Readers Discovery Award. The Maria Luigia-Duchessa de Parma, Italy, award for *Il premio internazionale di giornalismo award was also granted to him.*

Joe has written for the New York Times, the New York Times Magazine, the Los Angeles Times, Bon Appetit Maagazine, House and Garden magazine, Coastal Living magazine, and Grilling Magazine. He is a contributor to Tastes of Italia for seven years and wrote more than 40 articles for the publication. Joe was a Senior Vice President at Mc Graw-Hill, Inc. He is retired and divides his time between Key West and Pawling New York.